B(

Palgrave Studies in Pragmatics, Language and Cognition

Series Editors: Noël **Burton-Roberts** and Robyn **Carston**

Series Advisors: **Kent Bach, Anne Bezuidenhout, Richard Breheny, Sam Glucksberg, Francesca Happé, François Recanati, Deirdre Wilson**

Palgrave Studies in Pragmatics, Language and Cognition is a new series of high quality research monographs and edited collections of essays focusing on the human pragmatic capacity and its interaction with natural language semantics and other faculties of mind. A central interest is the interface of pragmatics with the linguistic system(s), with the 'theory of mind' capacity and with other mental reasoning and general problem-solving capacities. Work of a social or cultural anthropological kind will be included if firmly embedded in a cognitive framework. Given the interdisciplinarity of the focal issues, relevant research will come from linguistics, philosophy of language, theoretical and experimental pragmatics, psychology and child development. The series will aim to reflect all kinds of research in the relevant fields – conceptual, analytical and experimental.

Titles include:

Anton Benz, Gerhard Jäger and Robert van Rooij (*editors*)
GAME THEORY AND PRAGMATICS

Reinhard Blutner and Henk Zeevat (*editors*)
OPTIMALITY THEORY AND PRAGMATICS

María J. Frápolli (*editor*)
SAYING, MEANING AND REFERRING
Essays on François Recanati's Philosophy of Language

Corinne Iten
LINGUISTIC MEANING, TRUTH CONDITIONS AND RELEVANCE
The Case of Concessives

Ira Noveck and Dan Sperber (*editors*)
EXPERIMENTAL PRAGMATICS

Palgrave Studies in Pragmatics, Language and Cognition Series
Series Standing Order ISBN 0–333–99010–2 Hardback   0–333–98584–2 Paperback
(*outside North America only*)

You can receive future titles in this series as they are published by placing a standing order. Please contact your bookseller or, in case of difficulty, write to us at the address below with your name and address, the title of the series and the ISBN quoted above.

Customer Services Department, Macmillan Distribution Ltd, Houndmills, Basingstoke, Hampshire RG21 6XS, England

Also by María J. Frápolli

F.P. RAMSEY: CRITICAL REASSESSMENTS (*editor*)

FRANK PLUMTON RAMSEY: OBRAS FILOSÓFICA COMPLETA (*editor and translator*)

MEANING, BASIC-SELF-KNOWLEDGE AND MIND: ESSAYS ON TYLER BURGE (*co-editor*)

EVALUANDO LA MODERNIDAD: EL LEGADO CARTESIANO EN EL PENSAMIENTO ACTUAL (*co-editor*)

EL VALOR DE LA VERDAD: SEMÁNTICA, HERMENÉUTICA, POLÍTICA (*co-editor*)

VERDAD Y EXPERIENCIA (*co-editor*)

UNA APROXIMACIÓN A LA FILOSOFÍA DEL LENGUAJE (*co-author*)

TEORÍAS DE LA VERDAD EN EL SIGLO XX (*co-editor*)

Saying, Meaning and Referring

Essays on François Recanati's Philosophy of Language

Edited by

María J. Frápolli

First published 2007 by
PALGRAVE MACMILLAN
Houndmills, Basingstoke, Hampshire RG21 6XS and
175 Fifth Avenue, New York, N.Y. 10010
Companies and representatives throughout the world

PALGRAVE MACMILLAN is the global academic imprint of the Palgrave
Macmillan division of St. Martin's Press, LLC and of Palgrave Macmillan Ltd.
Macmillan® is a registered trademark in the United States, United Kingdom
and other countries. Palgrave is a registered trademark in the European
Union and other countries.

ISBN-13: 978–1–4039–3328–7 hardback
ISBN-10: 1–4039–3328–6 hardback

This book is printed on paper suitable for recycling and made from fully
managed and sustained forest sources.

A catalogue record for this book is available from the British Library.

Library of Congress Cataloging-in-Publication Data
Saying, meaning and referring: essays on François Recanati's philosophy of
    language/edited by María J. Frápolli.
        p.   cm. — (Palgrave studies in pragmatics, language, and cognition)
    Includes bibliographical references and index.
    ISBN 1–4039–3328–6 (cloth)
    1. Récanati, François, 1952–   2. Language and languages—Philosophy.
    I. Frápolli, María José. II. Series.
    P85.R35S29 2007
    401—dc22   2006045559

10   9   8   7   6   5   4   3   2   1
16   15   14   13   12   11   10   09   08   07

Printed and bound in Great Britain by
Antony Rowe Ltd, Chippenham and Eastbourne

Contents

Acknowledgements

The origin of this book was the XIII Interuniversity Workshop on Philosophy and Cognitive Science that took place at the University of Granada (Spain), in February 2003. Most of the chapters included in this volume were developed from papers presented at this forum.

The workshop was devoted to discussing François Recanati's new proposals on philosophy of language. Esther Romero and Belén Soria were co-organizers of the Workshop with myself. It would not be the slightest exaggeration to say that without their philosophical, social and practical skills the meeting would not have possessed the theoretical depth it did and participants would not have enjoyed such a friendly atmosphere. To both of them I am extremely grateful.

My main debt of gratitude is to Professor Recanati, who not only accepted the invitation to attend the workshop and actively participated in the discussions, but was also willing to write comments on the chapters that appear below.

My thanks also go to Juan J. Acero, who at that time was chairman of the Philosophy Department at the University of Granada and president of the Spanish Society for Analytic Philosophy (SEFA), for his continuos support. Francesc Camós and Neftalí Villanueva were always ready to answer my calls for help during the workshop itself and the process of compiling and designing the book. The contributors have shown great generosity in allowing me to bring together their work in this volume. All of them have been most cooperative and understanding. I am fortunate to have met them in Granada and to have had the opportunity of remaining in contact with them through our work on this book.

Robyn Carston suggested Palgrave Macmillan for the publication of this volume. I am grateful to her for the suggestion and to these publishers for having accepted it. Jill Lake and Noel Burton-Roberts made insightful comments on a former version of the volume. To all of them, my gratitude. I also want to express my thanks to the Consejería de Educación of the Junta de Andalucía for financially supporting the publication of this volume.

A volume like *Saying, Meaning, and Referring* requires the effort, cooperation, and goodwill of many people. To all who, directly or indirectly, have helped to make it possible, my heartfelt thanks.

MARÍA J. FRÁPOLLI

Notes on Contributors

Robyn Carston is Professor of Linguistics at the University College, London (UK). She is the author of *Thoughts and Utterances: The Pragmatics of Explicit Communication* (2002).

Philippe De Brabanter is Lecturer in English Linguistics at the University of Paris 4 – Sorbonne and is also a member of Institut Jean Nicod. He has edited a volume on *Hybrid Quotations*, which was published as no. 17 of the *Belgian Journal of Linguistics* (2005).

Jérôme Dokic is Directeur d'Études à l'École des Hautes Études Sociales and member of the Membre Institut Jean Nicod, Paris (France). He is the co-author, with Pascal Engel, of *Ramsey: Truth and Success* (2002), and of *Qu'est-ce que la perception?* (2004).

Paul Egré is Researcher at the Institut Jean-Nicod, CNRS, Paris (France). He has recently defended his Dissertation on *Propositional Attitudes and Epistemic Paradoxes* (2004). His most recent publication is 'The Knower Paradox in the Light of Provability Interpretations of Modal Logic', *Journal of Logic, Language and Information* (2005).

Luis Fernández Moreno is Reader of Philosophy at the Department of Logic and Philosophy of Science at the Complutense University of Madrid. Among his publications there are several articles and two books, *Wahrheit und Korrespondenz bei Tarski* (1992) and *La referencia de los nombres propios* (2006).

María J. Frápolli is Reader of Logic and Philosophy of Science at the Department of Philosophy, University of Granada (Spain). She has recently edited *F.P. Ramsey: Critical Reassessments* (2005), and translated Ramsey's works into Spanish, *Frank Plumpton Ramsey. Obra Filosófica Completa* (2005).

Manuel Hernández Iglesias is Professor of Philosophy at the University of Murcia, Spain. He is the author of *La semántica de Davidson. Una introducción crítica* (*Davidson's Semantics. A Critical Introduction*) (1990) and *El tercer dogma. Interpretación, metáfora e inconmensurabilidad* (*The Third Dogma: Interpretation, Metaphor and Incommensurability*) (2003).

Jérôme Pelletier lectures in the philosophy of language and aesthetics at the University of Brest in France. He is a member of the Institut Jean-Nicod in Paris. His most recent publication is 'Analogical Uses of the First Person

Pronoun: a Difficulty in Philosophical Semantics' in the *Journal of Cognitive Science*.

Stefano Predelli is Associate Professor and Reader in Philosophy at the Department of Philosophy, University of Nottingham. He is the author of *Contexts: Meaning, Truth, and the Use of Language* (2005).

François Recanati is a Research Director at the Centre National de la Recherche Scientifique (CNRS, Paris). He has published many papers and several books on the philosophy of language and mind, including *Meaning and Force* (1988), *Direct Reference* (1993), *Oratio Obliqua, Oratio Recta* (2000), and *Literal Meaning* (2003). He is a co-founder and past president of the European Society for Analytic Philosophy.

Esther Romero is Reader in Logic and Philosophy of Science in the Department of Philosophy, University of Granada (Spain). She is co-author (with María J. Frápolli) of *Una Aproximación a la Filosofía del Lenguaje* (1998) and co-editor, also with María J. Frápolli, of *Meaning, Basic Self-Knowledge, and Mind: Essays on Tyler Burge* (2003).

Belén Soria is Reader in English in the Department of English and German Philology University of Granada (Spain). She is the co-author (with E. Romero) of 'Metaphoric Concepts and Language' (2005) and, with E. Romero, of 'Cognitive Metaphor Theory Revisited', *Journal of Literary Semantics* (2005).

Alberto Voltolini is Associate Professor of Philosophy and the Theory of Languages in the Department of Social, Quantitative and Cognitive Sciences, University of Modena and Reggio Emilia (Italy). He is the author of *Riferimento e intenzionalità. Per un'ontologia del discorso* (1992) and *How Ficta Follow Fiction. A Syncretistic Account of Fictional Entities* (2006).

Introduction: Representation and Metarepresentation[1]

María J. Frápolli and Robyn Carston

'Utterances and thoughts have content: They represent (actual or imaginary) states of affairs.' This is the opening statement of François Recanati's most sustained work on kinds of representation, *Oratio Obliqua, Oratio Recta* (2000), and it presents the core phenomenon which it is the task of the philosophy of language to explain. A primary function of language and thought, though not their only function, is to represent how things are or might be. As well as descriptively representing entities, properties, and states of affairs in the world, our thoughts and utterances may *meta*represent other linguistic or mental representations and several levels of representational embedding.

For a full understanding of how language represents (and metarepresents) we need to understand how each of the different kinds of expression in the language contributes to the proposition or thought expressed by a particular utterance. Over the last century, the philosophy of language has swung between two poles in addressing the representational properties of natural human language. Broadly speaking, at the one pole are those whose main focus is on the language system itself, rather than its users, and who emphasize the semantic power of the system, while at the other pole are those for whom it is speakers, specifically their mental states, and what they do with words that are fundamental. The two different orientations naturally lead to different ways of conceiving of the roles of semantics and pragmatics in language use.

One manifestation of the division is the opposition between the 'literalist' view, according to which the proposition expressed by an utterance of a sentence is entirely mandated by components of the sentence, and the 'contextualist' view according to which what is said often goes beyond what is linguistically anchored. From his earliest work on pragmatics, specifically on speech acts and explicit performatives (1979, 1981, 1987), Recanati has taken a nonliteralist position, which he has developed over the past 20 or so years, culminating in the publication of his most recent book, *Literal Meaning* (2004a). Here he lays out the detailed landscape of the literalist/contextualist debate and mounts a strong defence of radical contextualism, including the possibility of 'meaning eliminativism', according to which linguistic expression types do not have fixed meanings, so every tokening of an expression type is context-dependent, hence requires some element of pragmatic processing on the part of the hearer.

Looked at as a whole, an outstanding feature of Recanati's work is his bid for a comprehensive theory of linguistic meaning, thoughts, utterance content and the relations between them. This includes detailed accounts of specific linguistic expressions (indexicals, proper names, definite descriptions, adjectives, belief reports) and kinds of thought (descriptive, *de re*) and concepts. His view of linguistic communication, which he calls 'truth-conditional pragmatics' (TCP), combines a strong contextualist position (often thought of as Wittgensteinian) with the fundamental tenets of Grice's account of speaker meaning, including his insistence that conversational implicatures depend on a process of rational reasoning about the speaker's act of saying. Recanati's pragmatic (speaker-meant) view of 'what is said' (as distinct from more semantically-oriented or minimalist views) entails the controversial possibility of entirely pragmatically motivated components of the truth-conditional content of utterances. So while maintaining a distinction between semantics (the conventional linguistic meaning of words and phrases) and pragmatics (the use of linguistic expressions), Recanati's TCP rejects the claim that semantic interpretation can deliver anything as determinate as a truth-evaluable proposition (see Recanati 2004b).

The TCP framework engages with, and offers often novel solutions to, some major debates in the philosophy of language (and mind). These include the apparently opposed views of Frege and Russell on singular terms and of the neo-Russellian (Kaplan, Perry) and neo-Fregean (Evans, McDowell) positions that have descended from them, and the issue of whether or not linguistic expressions change their semantic value in metarepresentational or intensional contexts (i.e. semantic innocence or semantic deviance). The TCP approach respects the intuition that the crucial distinction between what is said and what is implicated is consciously available to ordinary speaker-hearers, and it challenges the long-standing theoretical assumption that the content of an utterance is either a semantic, hence truth-conditional, phenomenon or it is pragmatic, hence a conversational implicature. The essence of TCP is the third possibility, that the content involved is both pragmatic and truth-conditional. Crosscutting these debates is another distinction, that between externalist semantics (meaning is objective and environment-dependent) and the idea that thoughts and utterances have a narrow content (a subjective, internal component). Recanati (1993) addresses and defuses a range of objections to the notion of narrow content and, with qualifications, supports the two-component picture of content.

In order to give a little more of the flavour of his approach and its often-harmonizing effect on existing debates, we will address the following oppositions in turn:

   (i) Fregean *vs* Russellian accounts of singular terms
   (ii) Pragmatic contextualism *vs* literalism

(iii) Externalism *vs* internalism
(iv) Innocent *vs* non-innocent accounts of metarepresentational contexts

(i) Fregeans *vs* Russellians

It is fair to say that Frege initiated the modern philosophy of language with his idea that to understand a sentence is to grasp its truth-conditions, emphasizing the need to free semantics from matters of mental representations and processes. His distinction between the reference (semantic value) and the sense of expressions made it possible to explain both the objectivity of truth-conditions and the cognitively significant aspects of thoughts (Frege 1892). Russell rejected the notion of sense as a component of meaning additional to semantic value and differed from Frege on a number of other details to do with singular terms and definite descriptions. He distinguished between logically proper names and singular propositions, on the one hand, and definite descriptions (and ordinary names) and general propositions, on the other. For Russell, a logically proper name has as its meaning just the very object that it names. What it contributes to the proposition expressed is that object, so that singular propositions are hybrid entities composed of concepts and objects. Singular propositions are directly anchored to the world *via* the objects which are the meanings of logically proper names while general (or descriptive) propositions are object-independent. Much of the subsequent history of the philosophy of language can be seen as dialogue and argument between Fregeans and Russellians on the nature of meaning and content and the analysis of specific kinds of referrring expression.

In his account of direct reference, Recanati has endeavoured to accommodate the insights of both philosophical camps. He takes a Fregean perspective concerning the meaning of referential expressions in as much as he accepts that there is a distinction to be made between the semantic value that they contribute to the truth-conditions of an utterance and their cognitive significance or mode of presentation of that value. On this view, proper names and indexicals have what we can call a sense (linguistic meaning) as well as a reference. When we consider the meaning of sentences/utterances, then propositions, truth-conditions, and linguistic meanings are all to be distinguished. Propositions are truth-conditions considered through the particularities of the linguistic meaning (or sense) of the sentences at issue. Propositions as much as truth conditions are needed if we are to understand how language can be used to represent the world, and specifically how referential terms lok on to their referents.

However, the neo-Russellian aspect of Recanati's account lies in the way in which he treats the sense (or descriptive meaning, or mode of presentation) of singular terms as opposed to that of definite descriptions. With singular terms it is the referent alone that enters into the proposition expressed; with definite descriptions it is the property described and not the referent. This is perhaps best seen by first considering Kripke's notion of 'rigidity', then moving on to Kaplan's stronger notion of 'direct referentiality' and his important distinction between character and content. A linguistic expression (or designator) which has the property of rigidity is one that denotes the same object in all possible worlds (or situations) (Kripke 1972/80). Proper names are rigid designators but so, *de facto*, are some definite descriptions (e.g. 'the cube root of 27'), so the notion of rigidity is too weak to distinguish the semantic properties of names and definite descriptions. However, a directly referential term is one that is rigid *de jure* in that the term is directly attached to the object independent of its properties, so cannot fail to denote the same object in all possible worlds (Recanati 1993: 12). A rigid definite description is not directly referential, because it denotes the object that it does in virtue of that object having the property expressed by its descriptive content; it just so happens in such cases that this is the same object in all worlds. Direct referentiality implies rigidity but the reverse does not hold.

However, according to Kaplan (1977/89), indexicals such as 'I' and 'today', which clearly do have some descriptive meaning (e.g. 'the speaker of the current utterance', 'the day on which the utterance is produced') which plays a role in determining their referent, are one kind of directly referential expression. Here, he makes his important distinction between the *character* and the *content* of an expression, which appears to correspond with a distinction between linguistic expression-type meaning and the proposition expressed. For instance, when Tony Blair utters the sentence 'I am tired', the attribute or property of being the speaker of the current utterance is instrumental in taking us to the referent, namely Tony Blair, but this meaning (or mode of presentation) is not a component of the proposition expressed, which is: TONY BLAIR IS TIRED (a singular proposition). So indexicals have a *character* (linguistic expression-type meaning) and their particular tokenings have a *content* (or semantic value). This two-tiered account of meaning is similar but not identical to Frege's distinction between sense and reference. For Frege, the reference of a singular term (a name) is its bearer; its sense is some information about the bearer, information that could be expressed using a definite description; the sense of the expression determines its reference. For Kaplan, the content of a directly referential term is also the object it refers to in context, while character is generally associated with cognitive value and plays a role in determining content. As he says: 'a character may be likened to a manner of presentation of a content. This suggests that we identify objects of thoughts with contents and the cognitive significance of such objects with characters.' (Kaplan 1977/89: 530) and 'My aim was to argue that the cognitive significance of a word or phrase was to be identified with its character, the way the content is presented to us.' (ibid.: 531). However, Kaplan makes a further distinction, that between *content* and *denotation* or *reference*. Just as character and content are distinct for indexicals, so content and denotation are distinct in the case of definite descriptions for, as Russell maintained, what a description contributes to content is a property (or mode of presentation) of its denotation and not the denotatum (referent) itself.

Building on Kaplan's three-way character/content/reference distinction (and his use of the operator DTHAT to artificially enforce referentiality), Recanati makes an important addition to the account of the linguistic *type* meaning of genuine referential expressions (names, indexicals and demonstrative descriptions, e.g. 'this book'): as well as character they have a semantic feature, REF. It is REF that indicates that what they contribute to propositional content is just their referent, hence that the truth condition of the utterance in which they occur is singular. Definite descriptions, on the other hand, have no such feature as part of their linguistic type meaning, so their contribution to content is typically identical to their character (the property expressed by the descriptive meaning). As shown by Donnellan (1966), descriptions *can* be used referentially so as to express a singular proposition but, Recanati claims, that is a matter of speaker meaning, of context and pragmatic principles, rather than of expression-type meaning. Summing up, 'descriptions can only be *token-referential*, whereas proper names and demonstrative expressions are *type-referential'* (Recanati 1993: 31). In the case of referentially used definite descriptions, we see an important application of Recanati's TCP (truth-conditional pragmatics) in that the denotation of the definite description is a component of truth-conditional content rather than a conversational implicature of the utterance and it gets into that content, not through any specification in its linguistic meaning, but entirely through pragmatics.

(ii) Contextualism *vs* Literalism

TCP is intrinsically a contextualist position (pragmatics makes contributions to truth-conditional content that are not linguistically articulated). However, a major influence on Recanati's approach to pragmatics is Paul Grice who, in fact, tended to straddle the contextualist/literalist divide. Grice's main contribution to contextualist thinking is his notion of speaker meaning and his emphasis on its overtness (the speaker openly displays to the addressee her intention to, for example, give him a piece of information); his contribution to literalist thinking is his conception of 'what is said' as the minimal proposition expressed.

In his 1967 William James lectures, *Logic and Conversation*, Grice introduced the notion of conversational implicature with the aim, among others, of preserving the truth-functional semantics of natural language counterparts to logical operators ('not', 'and', 'or', 'if', etc), despite the apparent divergences (non-truth-functional elements of meaning) that arise in ordinary language use (see Grice 1975/89). The information that an addressee derives from a speech act is, on Grice's account, often richer than the propositional content that follows from the meaning of the components of the sentence uttered. Thus, one should distinguish between what is strictly and literally said and what is conveyed on pragmatic grounds. What is said is the minimal proposition, that is, that proposition which is in the closest possible correspondence with the linguistic expressions used and is also capable of being semantically evaluated (judged true or false). On the basis of what is said (or, at least, the act of saying it), a hearer might infer further propositional information, given his standing assumptions about rational communicative behaviour (i.e. the maxims of conversational logic). This further propositional meaning is a conversational implicature. Following Grice, advocates of what we may call Implicature Theory (IT) maintain that, apart from its role in determining the semantic value of referring expressions (a process of 'saturation') and the elimination of ambiguity, all other contextual contributions to speaker meaning fall on the side of what is conversationally implicated. What is implicated is separate from the truth-conditional content of the utterance, that is, it can be cancelled without having any effect on the truth value of the utterance. It simply sits alongside what is said as another component of speaker meaning.

Supporters of both IT and TCP acknowledge these two levels: what is said and what is implicated. The first level is responsible for the truth-conditions of the utterance, while the second one conveys some extra information with the peculiarity that the speaker may negate it without contradicting herself. The difference between IT and TCP lies with what is included in each of the levels or sides of the distinction. Characteristically, TCP places in the realm of the proposition expressed much of what IT treats as conversational implicature. Classic cases that fall under this generalization are the opacity of belief contexts and the non-truth-functional meanings of 'logical' connectives, although the debate applies much more widely. Since the different ways of dealing with expressions embedded in belief contexts is discussed below, we will focus here on examples that do not involve intensional operators. Consider utterances of the sentences in (1) and (2), where the elements of communicated meaning at issue are, respectively, the policeman's manner of stopping the car and the relevant temporal span of the breakfastlessness. Two questions arise here. Are these aspects of utterance meaning linguistically mandated? If not, are they components of 'what is said' or conversational implicatures?

(1) The policeman stopped the car
(2) I have not had breakfast

According to Recanati (1993: 240–2), there are three principles, which a defender of Minimalism might adhere to: the Linguistic Direction Principle, the Minimal Truth-evaluability Principle (these two borrowed from Carston (1988)), and a mixture of both, dubbed by him the Mixed Minimalist Principle. The Linguistic Direction Principle stipulates that the components of the proposition expressed by the use of a sentence must all be either supplied by the encoded linguistic meaning or at least licensed by it. The Minimal Truth-evaluability Principle says that, besides linguistically determined aspects of meaning, only those pragmatically determined aspects of meaning that are required to make it a semantically-evaluable entity belong to what is said by the utterance. TCP rejects the first principle because, it is claimed, there are always propositional elements that are not linguistically anchored (*unarticulated constituents*). And the second principle is rejected on the grounds that the minimal proposition expressed is often not the proposition intended by the speaker, and so is not a component of speaker meaning (Recanati 1993: 243).

According to TCP, in both (1) and (2) what is said incorporates information that is not expressed by or mandated by any linguistic element. In (2), the demarcation of the temporal span to the day of the utterance, and in (1) the contextual information that clarifies the meaning of 'stopped' contributes to the proposition expressed. Was the policeman the driver of the car and so stopped it by stepping on the brake, or was he directing traffic and so stopped the car by raising his hand, or some other possibility? In fact, there are two TCP analyses possible here: one involves composing an unarticulated constituent into what is said (e.g. BY RAISING HIS HAND) and the other involves an adjustment to the encoded expression-type meaning of 'stop' so that it is narrowed down to a particular manner of stopping. In other words, an *ad hoc* concept STOP* is constructed and occupies the position within what is said that is occupied by the verb 'stop' in the linguistic structure. The claimed essential occurrence of unarticulated constituents and/or meaning modulation is what makes Recanati's approach a contextualist one and distinguishes it from the minimalism of Grice and many others. Somewhat paradoxically, Recanati finds support for his contextualist view of what is said in Grice's insistence that what is said is an aspect of speaker meaning and, therefore, open to public view, from which it follows that ordinary speaker-hearers have quite reliable intuitions about what is said. According to such intuitions, what is said by (2) includes the restriction of the temporal span to the day of utterance and what is said by (1) includes the way in which the policeman stopped the car.

Recanati distinguishes two kinds of pragmatic processes: primary pragmatic processes and secondary pragmatic processes. Primary processes are those that contribute to the addressee's construal of what is said; they are local, sub-propositional, non-inferential and subpersonal (Recanati 1995, 2004a). Secondary processes, on the other hand, are responsible for conversational implicatures and indirect speech acts; they are properly inferential processes (global, propositional), taking as their input the act of saying what is said and the conversational maxims, as first outlined in Grice (1975/89).

Both IT and TCP acknowledge the existence of both kinds of pragmatic process, but, as one might expect, the repertoire of primary pragmatic processes embraced by TCP is greater than that accepted by IT. According to Minimalism and IT, the effect of context on what is said is complete once indexical expressions have been saturated and ambiguity has been removed. For TCP, context also contributes through processes of free enrichment, either syntactic or conceptual, and through transfer processes, either analogical or metonymical in nature. Since contextual effects on the proposition expressed are freed from any attachment to linguistic or grammatical elements of the utterance, the way is open for other possible kinds of primary pragmatic processes to come into play. Clearly, the more comprehensive the proposition expressed, the sparser the conversational implicature ground. Where the border between proposition expressed and proposition implicated falls is, according to Recanati's Principle of Availability, accessible to the intuitions of the participants in the speech act. We turn to this principle in the next section.

(iii) Externalism *vs* Internalism

Externalism can be expressed in a nutshell using Putnam's famous phrase: 'meanings just ain't in the head!' (Putnam 1973/77: 124). Many words, including names, natural kind terms and some adjectives, conceal an indexical component in their meaning. They stand for *this* object, *this* feature or *this* stuff out there, or as Putnam would put it, all the stuff that shares with *this* the relation of being 'the same *P*', *P* being a sortal term. Externalism has taken over as the mainstream theory of linguistic meaning since Kripke delivered his famous lectures at Princeton in 1971 (Kripke 1972/80) and Putnam published his seminal papers (1970/77, 1973/77, 1975). The basic tenet of an externalist stance is that a speaker uses her terms with the meanings that they acquired when they were introduced into the language for the first time, in an act of baptism, so to speak, or in any case with the meanings that the terms have in the speaker's community, meanings which in the normal circumstances (that is, dissociated from thought experiments) are bound up with her natural and social surroundings.

And once terms acquire their meanings, the metaphor continues, the meanings stick, and this connection is preserved from speaker to speaker in a causal chain. Thus, language does not accommodate to actual-but-not-normal contexts, it does not adapt itself, in a chameleon-like way, to serve every odd purpose to which the individual speaker might put it. On the contrary, words retain their fixed meaning when they are used to depict different possible worlds as much as when they are used to describe the actual world. Otherwise, and this is one of Kripke's insights, we could not understand counterfactual discourse. Externalism can thus be seen as preserving (pre-Fregean) Semantic Innocence (discussed in the next section). But externalism also has its Achilles' heel: if meanings (and so also concepts) are individuated by the natural and social environment, then the speaker no longer has privileged access to the meanings of the words she uses or to the concepts she entertains.

Recanati explicitly accepts an externalist view, and in Recanati (1993) he devotes a chapter to explaining the sophisticated version of it that he favours (in which he preserves a variety of 'narrow content' as well as the 'wide content' that comes with externalism). However, his contextualist view of the propositional content of utterances seems to present a threat to the externalist account. What is said in a speech act by a particular use of a sentence is, in part, determined by what the speaker intends to say. And the speaker (possibly together with her audience) has the last word about what the proposition expressed by her utterance is. This idea is what lies behind the Principle of Availability, a principle that gives great weight to the intuitions of ordinary speaker-hearers, hence to representations and processes internal to the individual. As mentioned earlier, Recanati acknowledges Grice as the source of this principle: 'That fact [the fact that what is said is consciously available] is easy to account for if one accepts what we may call the Pragmatic View: the view that "saying" is a variety of non-natural meaning in Grice's sense (Grice 1957, 1989). That view entails that what is said *must* be available – it must be open to public view. [. . .] Hence my Availability Principle . . . ' (Recanati 2001: 80). In fact, the principle has evolved in Recanati's writings, from a more rigid (1993) to a more flexible form (2004). First we have:

> *Availability Principle*: In deciding whether a pragmatically determined aspect of utterance meaning is part of what is said, that is, in making a decision concerning what is said, we should always try to preserve our pre-theoretic intuitions on the matter. (Recanati 1993: 248)

This version of the principle and Externalism might clash since Externalism frequently does not preserve our pre-theoretic intuitions. Rather, a community of experts must determine meanings, and in the worst case scenario, even they can go wrong. Externalism is a scientific approach to linguistic meaning, not an intuitive one. However, Recanati's position has softened somewhat:

> *Availability*
> What is said must be intuitively accessible to the conversational participants (unless something goes wrong and they do not count as 'normal interpreters'). (Recanati 2004a: 20)

But again, on an externalist view, there is no reason to suppose that 'normal interpreters' have direct access to the content of their speech acts. This conflict might be only apparent, depending on how the notion of content is construed and on the extent to which the various ingredients (such as lexical meanings) that go into 'what is said' are required to be 'intuitively accessible'. As the details of Recanati's big picture of linguistic meaning, thought content and utterance content emerge, we hope to see more clearly how his allegiance to the cause of Externalism and his Gricean Internalism are reconciled.

(iv) Semantic innocence *vs* semantic guilt

Recanati intends that his semantic/pragmatic analyses of natural language expressions should comply with the Principle of Semantic Innocence, which is a principle of theoretical economy, somewhat akin to Grice's modified Occam's razor. According to the Innocence principle, expressions (names, indexicals, definite descriptions, sentences) do not change their meanings from one linguistic environment to another; in particular, expressions embedded in intensional or metarepresentational contexts (such as belief reports) have the same semantic function and value as they have when they occur in simple sentences (Recanati 1993: 327; 2000: 119). On the other hand, non-innocent accounts of the Fregean kind, where certain expressions undergo a shift in their meaning in propositional attitude contexts, seem to be closer to ordinary speaker-hearer intuitions about belief reports when the person reported on does not possess complete information about the objects of her attitudes. Recanati manages to explain these Fregean intuitions without renouncing Innocence.

Both the IT and TCP approaches aim at analyses which respect the Innocence principle. Let's consider the familiar examples in (3),

> (3) a. Lois Lane believes that Superman can fly.
>   b. Lois Lane believes that Clark Kent can fly,

involving co-referential names in a belief context, and compare the ways in which the IT and TCP accounts manage to both maintain the principle and explain the apparently contrary intuitions. The intuition here is that (3b) does not follow from (3a), that is, that 'X believes that...' manifests the property of opacity (the failure of substitutivity of co-referring expressions). Frege's solution to this was to claim that in such contexts referential expressions do not have their ordinary reference (but refer rather to their sense); other Fregeans have suggested less radical but still non-innocent solutions. However, Implicature theorists (McKay 1981; Salmon 1986; among many others) maintain that, contrary to appearances, the inference from (3a) to (3b) *is* valid, and they explain the uneasiness that it produces in some speaker-hearers as a matter of pragmatics, specifically conversational implicature. According to IT, (3b) only *seems* to say something false and this is because pragmatically it implicates that Lois Lane would assent to the sentence 'Clark Kent can fly', which we all know she would not do. But since implicatures are external to the truth-conditional content of an utterance (what is said) this does not affect the truth value of (3b), which, after all, expresses the same proposition as (3a).

According to advocates of the alternative TCP analysis, specifically Recanati, this inference is not valid in every context, and, therefore, it is not valid on its own (in natural languages). The operator 'believes that' creates an unstable linguistic context, that is, a context in which an unarticulated component might appear that requires the verb to be understood as 'so-believe that' (believing something under a particular mode of presentation) and in which, therefore, the mode of presentation should be incorporated into the content of the embedded sentence (Recanati 2000: 148–50). If this is right, the above inference is an instance of the 'fallacy of equivocation' (ibid.: 141) because, despite the fact that 'Superman' and 'Clark Kent' co-refer and the sentences are identical in all other respects, the proposition expressed by (3b) is different from the proposition expressed by (3a). Nevertheless, TCP remains faithful to the Principle of Semantic Innocence because none of the words that appear in the scope of the epistemic operator in the sentences in (3a) or (3b) changes either its character or its content. The difference in propositional content is accounted for by a primary pragmatic process that supplies a different mode of presentation constituent in the two cases (Clark Kent presented as 'Clark Kent', Clark Kent presented as 'Superman'). Thus our strong intuition that (3b) cannot be validly inferred from (3a) is accounted for. Furthermore, the TCP account does a better job of accounting for intuitions than the IT account, since the intuition is that (3b) is simply false (indeed, that is an assumption of the Superman story), that is, our intuition of falsity concerns what is said and not what is conversationally implicated and so, in accordance with the Availability Principle, the pragmatic component is to be located within 'what is said'. (The superiority of the TCP account over the IT account is all the more evident when more complex examples, in which belief sentences fall within the scope of logical connectives, are considered. See Recanati 1993: chapter 17.)

At first glance, the Innocence Principle according to which the meaning of expressions remains constant no matter what linguistic structure they appear in, including the scope of an intensional operator, might seem to be at odds with the contextualist viewpoint that virtually all words are context-sensitive and that the proposition expressed by an utterance is a function of pragmatic processes that are receptive to the specific context of use. Given that both claims have intuitive support and arguments in their favour, however, we would want to maintain both of them, if possible. Innocence seems to be required in order to account for how we learn and understand language, to explain some of our intuitions about how language works and, from a methodological point of view, it allows for simpler and more elegant semantic theories. At the same time, processes of 'free' pragmatic enrichment (recovery of unarticulated constituents and *sense modulation*, as Recanati (2004a) calls pragmatic adjustments to word meaning), which contribute to truth-conditional content, seem to be required to account for pervasive intuitions of speakers and addressees. This is especially evident when metarepresentational operators and logical connectives are at issue, but it is really a much more general phenomenon, occurring whenever the meaning of a word or phrase is fine-tuned to fit the situation in which it is used, whether narrowed or loosened in meaning, or projected onto a distinct concept, as in the case of metonymy. Recall again the modulation of the sense of 'stop' in example (1) and the supplying of a specific temporal constituent in (2). It also seems clear, on the other hand, that words should not change their meanings (in particular their character or expression-type meaning) from one context to the next, if we are to explain how it is that human communication is very often a successful enterprise.

As shown above, with regard to propositional attitude contexts, Recanati has found a way of accommodating the insights of both Semantic Innocence and Contextualism by taking advantage of the notion of unarticulated constituents that he has borrowed from Perry (1986/93). Certain linguistic contexts, such as 'Lois Lane believes that . . . ', are particularly susceptible to the pragmatic process of free enrichment, so that the operator 'believes that' might shift to a new operator 'so-believes that' and the propositions expressed by the sentences/utterances in (3a) and (3b) might, therefore, incorporate the mode of presentation under which Lois Lane thinks of Clark Kent. When this situation arises, the path from (3a) to (3b) is no longer valid, but this does not conflict with, or require any modification to, a uniform account of the *semantics* of names, here the Kripkean view of proper names as rigid designators. In fact, the resources of Contextualism serve the cause of Semantic Innocence.

An alternative analysis has it that metarepresentational prefixes such as 'X believes that' and 'In the story/film' are context-shifting operators. On such an account, the operator 'believes that' in (3a) and (3b) causes the embedded sentence to be interpreted not in the current context of utterance but in the context of Lois Lane's 'belief world', where Superman is one entity and Clark Kent another. This sort of analysis might seem preferable to the free enrichment account for cases where the embedded sentence includes empty singular terms, such as 'Santa Claus' or 'Sherlock Holmes', which refer to nothing in the context of utterance but have referents in the appropriate belief and story worlds. However, such an account clearly violates Semantic Innocence, since the content of the names is different depending on the linguistic environment in which they appear. Kaplan (1977/89: 511) has dubbed context-shifting operators 'monsters' and claimed that there are none in English, a position for which Recanati (2000) provides a detailed defence. While he accepts that context-shifting does occur in metarepresentations he insists that it is not something imposed by the metarepresentational prefixes themselves. Rather, they provide an environment that is hospitable to various pragmatic processes (specifically, free enrichment and 'deference', a kind of pragmatic context-shift) and it is these that are responsible for the frequent but not inevitable opacity of metarepresentational sentences. When monsters do seem to appear, they belong to the realm of pragmatics. The TCP framework is thus semantically innocent though perhaps pragmatically suspicious.

These four interconnected domains are central to François Recanati's philosophy of language, and each of the chapters that follow addresses one or more of them. Here is a little more detail on each of the chapters:

Robyn Carston examines Recanati's distinction between primary pragmatic processes, which contribute to the truth-conditional content of an utterance, and secondary pragmatic processes, which include those processes that result in conversational implicatures. She questions the adequacy of Recanati's associative account of primary processes with its 'coherence' criterion, arguing instead for a relevance-based account, and she casts doubt on Recanati's claim that secondary pragmatic processes, but not primary ones, are explicitly and rationally reconstructible by those cognitive agents in whom they have occurred as fast, spontaneous, tacit online processes.

Jerôme Dokic distinguishes the issue of unarticulated constituents as applied to (a) language and to (b) thought. His analysis requires a modification to the notion of situation as used by Recanati, a notion which originated in Situation Semantics. He considers unarticulated constituents from the perspective of their inferential relevance and argues that, if it is to be inferentially effective, an apparently unarticulated constituent in thought must in fact be articulated somehow – otherwise it is inferentially inert. He takes Recanati's stress on the situated nature of representations further, connecting representations thus considered with *ad hoc* concepts and disassociating them from the notion of non-persistent fact.

Manuel Hernández Iglesias analyses Recanati's notion of literal meaning, rejecting Recanati's diagnosis that the problem with it lies in the failure of theorists to isolate its several different levels of interpretation. Hernández shows that the difference between the everyday notion of talking literally and the technical notion as used by the semanticist is neither clear-cut nor exhaustive. In his view, Recanati's classification of kinds of literality should not be applied either to sentences or to utterances, but rather to layers of meaning. His conclusion is that '*the* notion' of literality cannot be refined by any analysis, Recanati's included, because there is no single notion, or a single pair, literal/nonliteral, to refine. Rather, there is a complex of useful dichotomies, with, we may assume, some analogical links among them.

Stephano Predelli contests the claim that the notions of saturation and free enrichment are novel and originate with Truth Conditional Pragmatics. His point is that Recanati's views on underarticulation can be accommodated by the traditional picture of truth-conditional semantics. The clue to developing a traditional explanation *à la* Kaplan of the relative roles of unarticulated constituents and saturation in cases of predicates (the cases that mark out the borderline between any kind of literalism and Recanati's contextualism) is provided by the distinction between demonstratives and the demonstration related to them. Demonstrations relate demonstrative components of expressions to the relevant contextual features that allow their complete interpretation.

Philippe de Brabanter discusses the topic of metalinguistic demonstrations. He offers support for the view that metalinguistic demonstration is not a homogeneous phenomenon that always refers to expression types. His argument is that some acts of metalinguistic demonstration unconventionally point to tokens. Adding reference to tokens would require some modifications of Recanati's system.

Paul Egré explores the borderlines between semantics and pragmatics through discussion of Recanati's theory of belief reports and opacity phenomena. Recanati subscribes to the Principle of Semantic Innocence, which states that a sentence embedded in a belief report expresses the same proposition it expresses when not embedded. In Recanati's analysis, Semantic Innocence involves two components: semantic constancy and direct reference. Egré submits that a theory that would get rid of direct reference could still preserve semantic constancy and provide a semantically innocent account of substitutivity failures. Egré argues further that a multi-referential analysis of attitude verbs, in the style of Hintikka, which Recanati presents as departing from semantic innocence, can be made compatible with the program of truth-conditional pragmatics.

Recanti's treatment of imaginary situations and belief ascriptions is dealt with in Pelletier's contribution. According to Pelletier, Recanati follows David Lewis in considering imaginary situations as hyperinsulated from the actual world and from one other. Pelletier's comment is that Recanati's conception of the logic of imaginary situations makes it difficult, if not impossible to make sense of fictions within fictions. Concerning Recanati's conception of belief ascriptions and his claim that metarepresentations are intrinsically simulative, Pelletier suggests that they rely on an empathetic conception of simulation. Only such a conception can motivate Recanati's 'transparency thesis' – that is, the claim that metarepresentations do not constitute an opaque interface between the ascriber and the ascribee's thoughts.

Voltolini distinguishes between absolutely empty names (names that do not refer to anything in any context) and fictional names (names that refer to fictional characters in fictional situations). Recanati treats both types together, maintaining that the sentences in which they appear have primarily fictive truth conditions and that a fictive ascription of a singular belief amounts to a factive ascription of a pseudo-singular belief. By means of the above distinction, Voltolini urges that it is paradigmatically when embedding absolutely empty proper names that metarepresentational sentences have fictional truth-conditions. Moreover, he insists that, for such cases, fictional truth-conditions are the only truth-conditions those sentences possess.

Luis Fernandez Moreno addresses the issue of semantic externalism, specifically the topic of the direct referentiality of natural kind terms, along the lines of Putnam and Kripke. Although Recanati expresses himself from time to time as if he identified the meaning of natural kind terms with their extensions, there are texts (1988, 1993) that allow for an interpretation of them that is closer to that of singular referential names. Thus, although Recanati does not treat the topic in detail, extending his view on referential singular terms to cover general nouns as well would be consistent with his wider programme.

María J. Frápolli discusses the compatibility between Recanati's open adherence to externalism and the Principle of Availability that he has inherited from his Gricean beginnings. Externalism unfastens semantics from epistemology. Concepts are individuated by the surrounding world, either natural or social, to which speakers only have external, not introspective, access. Maintaining at one and the same time that the proposition expressed by an utterance is a part of the speaker's meaning, and that the speaker always has the last word about its composition, as the Principle of Availability requires, seems at first sight to be at loggerheads with the main point of externalism. Frápolli's main focus is the topic of deference.

Esther Romero and Belén Soria endorse Recanati's Contextualism, his thesis that what is said is a part of the speaker's meaning, and his defence of metaphor as involving a primary pragmatic process. They point out that Recanati does not develop a coherent theory of metaphor. Indeed, in (1993) and (1995) Recanati considers metaphor as transfer and in *Literal Meaning* (2004) as loosening. Romero and Soria acknowledge the insights that support his second treatment, but argue that metaphor involves transfer. They claim, unlike Recanati, that transfer depends on a type of context-shift, a type of language-shift, prompted by the identification of a metaphorical use of language.

As we have attempted to point out in this introduction and as the range of issues addressed in the 11 chapters indicates, Recanati's theory of language, meaning and communication encompasses central concerns in philosophy of language, pursues many of them to great depth and has implications that go well beyond pure philosophy into cognitive science. Inevitably, a project on this scale raises many questions, even some misunderstandings. The unifying purpose of the contributions to this volume is to analyse, criticise, and attempt to clarify this fine-grained and highly sophisticated body of work. This purpose is greatly furthered by the fact that François Recanati has provided a short response to each of the contributions.

Note

1. We are grateful to George Powell, N. Burton-Roberts and Neftalí Villanueva for comments on a previous version and very useful discussion of the issues, and also to Jean Stephenson for her help with aspects of the English of an early draft.

References

Carston, R. (1988) 'Implicature, Explicature and Truth-theoretic Semantics'. In R. Kempson (ed.), *Mental Representations: The Interface between Language and Reality*. Cambridge: Cambridge University Press, pp. 155–81.

Donnellan, K. (1966) 'Reference and Definite Descriptions'. *Philosophical Review* 75: 281–304.

Frege, G. (1892) 'On Sense and Meaning'. In P. Geach and M. Black (eds) (1988), *Translations from the Philosophical Writings of Gottlob Frege*. New Jersey: Barnes & Noble Books, pp. 56–78.

Grice, P. (1975/89) 'Logic and Conversation'. In P. Cole and J. Morgan (eds), *Syntax and Semantics 3: Speech Acts*. New York: Academic Press, pp. 41–58. Reprinted in H.P. Grice (1989), *Studies in the Way of Words*. Cambridge. MA: Harvard University Press, pp. 22–40.

Kaplan, D. (1977/89) 'Demonstratives'. Paper read at the American Philosophical Association 1977. Printed in J. Almog, J. Perry, and H. Wettstein (eds) (1989), *Themes from Kaplan*. Oxford: Oxford University Press.

Kripke, S. (1972/80) 'Naming and Necessity'. In: D. Davidson and G. Harman (eds), *Semantics of Natural Language*. Dordrecht: Reidel, pp. 253–5, 763–9. Reprinted as S. Kripke, (1980) *Naming and Necessity*. Oxford: Blackwell.

McKay, T. (1981) 'On Proper Names in Belief Ascriptions'. *Philosophical Studies* 39: 287–303.

Perry, J. (1986/93) 'Thought without Representation'. *The Aristotelian Society Supplementary* 60: 137–51. Reprinted in J. Perry (1993), *The Problem of the Essential Indexical and Other Essays*. New York: Oxford University Press, pp. 205–26.

Putnam, H. (1970/77) 'Is Semantics Possible?' In H.E. Keifer and M.K. Munitz (eds), *Language, Belief and Metaphysics*. New York: State University of New York Press, pp. 50–63. Reprinted in S.P. Schwartz (ed.) (1977), 102–18.

Putnam, H. (1973/77) 'Meaning and Reference'. *The Journal of Philosophy* 70: 699–711. Reprinted in S.P. Schwartz (ed.) (1977), pp. 119–32.

Putnam, H. (1975) 'The Meaning of "Meaning"'. In K. Gunderson (ed.), *Language, Mind and Knowledge: Minnesota Studies in the Philosophy of Science*, vol. 7. Minneapolis: University of Minnesota Press, pp. 131–93. Reprinted in H. Putnam 1975. *Philosophical Papers, vol. 2: Mind, Language and Reality*. Cambridge: Cambridge University Press, pp. 215–71.

Recanati, F. (1979) *La Transparence et l'Enonciation*. Paris: Editions du Seuil.

Recanati, F. (1981) *Les Enoncés Performatifs*. Paris Minuit.

Recanati, F. (1987) *Meaning and Force: The Pragmatics of Performative Utterances*. Cambridge: Cambridge University Press.

Recanati, F. (1988) 'Rigidity and Direct Reference'. *Philosophical Studies* 53: 103–17.

Recanati, F. (1993) *Direct Reference: From Language to Thought*. Oxford: Blackwell.

Recanati, F. (1995) 'The Alleged Priority of Literal Interpretation'. *Cognitive Science* 19: 207–32.

Recanati. F. (2000) *Oratio Obliqua, Oratio Recta: An Essay on Metarepresentation*. Cambridge, MA: MIT Press.

Recanati, F. (2001) 'What is Said'. *Synthese* 128: 75–91.

Recanati, F. (2004a) *Literal Meaning*. Cambridge: Cambridge University Press

Recanati, F. (2004b) 'Pragmatics and Semantics'. In L. Horn and G. Ward (eds), *The Handbook of Pragmatics*. Oxford: Blackwell, pp. 442–62.

Salmon, N. (1986) *Frege's Puzzle*. Cambridge, MA: MIT Press.

Schwartz, S.P. (ed.) (1977) *Naming, Necessity and Natural Kinds*. Ithaca and London: Cornell University Press.

1

How Many Pragmatic Systems are There?[1]

Robyn Carston

1.1 Introduction: Grice, Recanati and Relevance Theory

An important component of recent pragmatic theorizing is the view that the linguistically encoded meaning of an utterance often falls far short of determining the proposition that a speaker explicitly communicates and that the gap between the two is bridged by highly context-sensitive pragmatic processes. Crucially, processes of 'free pragmatic enrichment', that is, processes that are not dictated by elements of linguistic form, mediate the transition from linguistic meaning to explicit propositional content. This 'contextualist' position is vigorously defended by François Recanati (1989, 1993, 2002a, 2004a) and by relevance theorists (Sperber and Wilson 1986/95; Carston 1988/91, 2002b), among others. In this respect, Recanati and Relevance Theory (hereafter RT) differ from Paul Grice (at least on most people's reading of Grice),[2] who appears to recognize only a minimal pragmatic contribution in the determination of 'what is said': the provision of an occasion-specific value for referring expressions and the selection of a single sense in cases of ambiguity. In his brief discussion of these processes, Grice (1975) indicates that his conversational principles (hence considerations of speaker m-intentions) play no role in them.

Recanati calls the pragmatic processes that contribute to determining 'what is said' (or 'explicature' in RT terms) 'primary' pragmatic processes and those that are responsible for the derivation of conversational implicatures 'secondary' pragmatic processes. These are useful labels, which I have adopted in my own RT work, but for Recanati they are much more than that: the two kinds of pragmatic processes are of quite distinct kinds, only the secondary ones being properly inferential, the primary ones being more akin to associative processes.

Hence, on Recanati's view, linguistic communication is not fundamentally inferential, that is, addressees can, and standardly do, recover the explicit propositional content of utterances without any recourse to maxims concerning rational communicative behaviour or metarepresenta-tional premises concerning mental states of the speaker, and, in fact, without the mediation of any properly inferential process at all (whether reflective or unreflective). So, despite Recanati's strong contextualist stance, his posi-tion on primary pragmatic processes is, in certain respects, a very Gricean one; indeed, his account can be seen as a 'cognitivized' version of Grice's view that the pragmatic processes needed for a full identification of 'what is said' do not involve anything like his working-out schema for implicature derivation but that 'context is a criterion' that settles the outcome of these processes.

Although first and foremost a philosopher of language, Recanati has taken significant steps toward developing an on-line cognitive account of primary pragmatic processes (see his 1995; 2004a: chapter 2). He has, so far, provided nothing comparable for secondary pragmatic processes. Rather, his main concern has been to emphasize the Gricean point that secondary pragmatic processes are to be understood as part of a more general theory of human action interpretation and so as having the philosophically central prop-erty of being rational, personal-level (as opposed to subpersonal) processes. Closely linked to this is his claim that secondary pragmatic processes, but not primary ones, meet the 'Availability Condition'; that is, for any given utterance, we have conscious access to its explicature ('what is said') and its implicature(s), and to the inferential process that mediates them.

In his most recent work, however, Recanati (2004a: 46–7) has endorsed the relevance-theoretic view that a unitary, on-line pragmatic processing system derives explicit content and conversational implicatures in parallel. This account makes crucial use of a mechanism of 'mutual adjustment', from which it follows that a hypothesis about an implicature can both precede and shape a hypothesis about an explicature. On the face of it, Recanati's approval is baffling, for it seems to imply that one and the same process (implicature derivation) is both a personal-level, explicit, reflective, inferential process and also one of the tacit, unreflective processes performed by a single, presumably subpersonal, system.

In this chapter, I focus on Recanati's account of primary and secondary pragmatic processes. First, I consider his non-inferential, activation-based account of primary processes, comparing it with the relevance-based account of Sperber and Wilson, and attempt to assess its adequacy in dealing with the full range of primary processes, which include the supplying of linguistically unarticulated expressions and the interpretation of various kinds of non-literal uses of language, including metaphor and irony. Second, I consider some issues that turn on the primary/secondary pragmatic process distinc-tion, in particular, on the claims about conscious accessibility, and the ques-tion of how these two kinds of processes can interact with, and affect, each other, while having a fundamentally different status (associative *vs* inferen-tial, subpersonal *vs* personal). Finally, I observe some empirical consequences of Recanati's claim that a capacity for explicit, reflective inference is intrinsic to implicature derivation and suggest how these might be tested.

1.2 Utterance comprehension and the primary/secondary distinction

Despite their common cause of contextualism, there are some important differences between Recanati's view of pragmatic processes and the relevance-theoretic view. I will start by giving a brief indication of how utterance comprehension works on the RT account and use this as a comparative reference point in looking at Recanati's ideas.

According to the RT account, explicatures and implicatures are derived in parallel and there is often a process of mutual adjustment between them in which not only does explicit content influence the implicatures derived, but implicatures can affect elements of explicatures, such as the choice between word meanings in the case of ambiguity or the occasion-specific meaning taken to have been expressed by an unambiguous word (Wilson and Sperber 2002, 2004). Before showing an example of this, here is a very brief description of the central claims of relevance-theoretic pragmatics. Relevance is a property of inputs to cognitive processes quite generally: the more cognitive effects the input has, the greater its relevance; the more mental resources and effort expended in processing it, the lower its relevance. Unlike most other inputs, an utterance comes with a presumption that it is optimally relevant, that is, that (a) it is sufficiently relevant to warrant the addressee's attention, and (b) it is maximally relevant *modulo* the speaker's abilities and preferences. Given this, an utterance automatically triggers quite specific expectations of relevance in its addressee, that is, expectations concerning both the quantity and the kind of cognitive effects (implications) it will yield if optimally processed. The addressee (or, at least, his comprehension system) follows a path of least effort in accessing interpretative hypotheses and stops as soon as he arrives at one that satisfies his expectations of relevance.[3] In somewhat truncated form, the relevance-driven process of deriving explicatures and implicatures is demonstrated in (1) where the utterance under scrutiny is Bob's response to Ann:

(1) Ann: I expected Jane to be here by now.
    Bob: She missed her coach.

(a) Output of linguistic decoding of Bob's utterance:
    SHE$_x$ MISSED HER COACH$_1$ COACH$_2$
    where: 'SHE$_x$' indicates the requirement to assign a referent
    'COACH$_1$' = instructor, 'COACH$_2$' = bus

(b) Input to the pragmatic system:
    Bob has said SHE$_x$ MISSED HER COACH$_1$/COACH$_2$
    [Decoded logical form is embedded in a description of the ostensive act]

(c) Ann expects Bob's utterance to be optimally relevant to her
[General expectation of relevance triggered in the addressees of utterances]

(d) Bob's utterance will achieve relevance by explaining why Jane hasn't arrived yet.
[Specific expectation of the kind of cognitive effects the utterance will have]

(e) MISSING A DESIGNATED COACH$_2$ IS A REASON FOR A PERSON NOT ARRIVING WHEN EXPECTED
[Highly accessible assumption in the context which, together with other appropriate premises, might satisfy expectation (d)]

(f) JANE MISSED HER COACH$_2$
[Highly accessible development of the logical form of Bob's utterance which can combine with (e) to lead to the satisfaction of (d)]

(g) JANE ISN'T HERE YET BECAUSE SHE MISSED HER COACH$_2$
[Inferred from (e) and (f), satisfying (d)]

(h) JANE MAY STILL ARRIVE AT A LATER TIME
[Inferred from (g) plus background knowledge about Jane and transport possibilities, etc. One of several further cognitive implications which, together with (g), satisfy expectation (c)]

This is a very incomplete rendering of the pragmatic processes involved in Ann's likely interpretation of the utterance: for instance, the verb 'miss' can be understood in several ways, only one of which is relevant here, and the possessive relation in 'her coach' needs to be specified (Jane doesn't own the coach), etc. All that's shown here is how the process of disambiguating 'coach' is influenced by the expectation of a certain kind of cognitive effect: an explanation of Jane's non-arrival, which is the implicature shown in (g). The choice of COACH$_2$ for the explicature in (f) is a result of a process of developing the decoded logical form of the utterance in such a way that, together with highly accessible contextual assumptions such as that in (e), it warrants the implicated conclusion in (g).

Here are some points to note about this account. All aspects of utterance comprehension (apart from linguistic decoding) fall under a single procedure of looking for the most accessible interpretation which meets particular expectations of relevance, a strategy licensed by the presumption of optimal relevance which accompanies all utterances (and acts of ostensive communication quite generally). The processes involved are claimed to be entirely a matter of (non-demonstrative) inference, with linguistic meaning providing crucial guiding evidence, and some of the inferences, such as that leading to the choice between the two 'coach'-concepts, are backwards inferences geared to providing a sound basis for expected implications. Evidently, on an approach such as this, the distinction between pragmatic contributions to explicit content (primary) and implicatures (secondary) does not entail any fundamental difference in the kind of process, mechanism, or system involved, nor in the procedure followed or the criterion to be met.

As well as disambiguation, the pragmatic tasks contributing to the explicit level (hence, falling under the label of primary pragmatic processes) include reference assignment, other cases of saturation and/or propositional completion, free enrichment (whether in the form of modulation of a linguistically-encoded concept or the supplying of a linguistically-unarticulated conceptual constituent), metaphor interpretation and metonymic transfer. Some of these, in particular the latter two, may fall within the construal of one of the others, but I won't concern myself with that here. The properties that Recanati takes to be characteristic of primary processes are the following:

Input: decoded linguistic meaning

Output: explicit utterance content ('what is said' or explicature)

Type of process: local, associative (not properly inferential)

Guiding criterion: accessibility (highest degree of activation in a conceptual network)

Consciousness status: unconscious (and may be inaccessible to consciousness)

Attribution of speaker mental states: none in the premises or inferential steps (only the output is understood as speaker intended)

Disambiguation offers perhaps the clearest example of how such primary processes work:

(2) *Utterance*: I'm going to the bank now to get some cash.

Linguistic decoding provides two candidate senses for the position in the evolving representation of explicit content marked out by the form /bank/: BANK$_1$ (=financial institution) and BANK$_2$ (=river side). Let us suppose that, for whatever reason, at the point of accessing the lexical form /bank/, it is BANK$_2$ that is the more highly activated candidate and so is initially assigned to the position. However, by the end of the utterance, the relative degree of activation of the two concepts will have changed (this is what Recanati calls an 'accessibility shift'). At this point, BANK$_1$ is more highly activated than BANK$_2$ because it has received an activation boost, via a mechanism of spreading activation, from the associated concept CASH which has been activated by the lexical form /cash/, and perhaps, in addition, from a mentally represented stereotypical frame or script for 'GETTING MONEY FROM A BANK$_1$'. So, ultimately, and in accordance with our off-line intuitions, the winning candidate is BANK$_1$. See Recanati (1995, 2004a: 30–1) for a similar sort of account of a reference assignment process involving two candidates.

Now, consider the contrasting properties of secondary pragmatic processes:

Input: the speaker has said that *p* (where *p* is 'what is said' or 'explicature')
Output: the speaker has implicated that *q*
Type of process: properly inferential (global, propositional, explicit)
Guiding criteria: Gricean maxims (norms of rational communicative behaviour)
Consciousness status: both the input and output representations, and the fact that there is an inferential link between them, are conscious or, at least, accessible to consciousness.
Attribution of speaker mental states: integral to the interpretation process (appearing as premises in the reasoning process)

The deep difference that Recanati sees between primary and secondary processes is most evident in his following statement:

> The determination of what is said [explicit content] takes place at a *subpersonal* level, like the determination of what we see or hear. But the determination of what the speaker implies takes place at the *personal* level, like the determination of the consequences of what we see or hear. (Seeing John's car, I infer that he did not leave; hearing the doorbell ring, I infer that there is someone at the door.) (Recanati 2002a: 114)

He takes this view to be backed by a number of other philosophers, in particular Ruth Millikan, who has taken a strong position against Gricean reflective reasoning being any 'kind of "mechanism" that drives ordinary language use and understanding' (Millikan 1984: 68; this view is developed further in her 2004 book).[4] She recognizes that mature communicators do have the ability to reflect on how linguistic communication works, to interrupt and 'tinker with the mechanisms of normal language flow' and to 'rise above these automatic mechanisms if necessary' (Millikan 1984: 69). Recanati (2002a: 114; 2004a: 39) takes it that this is what goes on in what he calls 'special' cases and that the secondary process of retrieving conversational implicatures is such a special case, requiring reflective capacities that are not exercised in the 'normal language flow'.[5]

In the next two sections, I look in more detail at each of the two kinds of process in turn, but before doing so, let me mention, in order to set it aside, an issue that might seem to arise here. In earlier work (Carston 2002a), I took it that a consequence of these views of Recanati was that the two kinds of process are sequential, that is, that the derivation of implicatures takes place after the derivation of what is said (explicature). This is a conclusion that has continued to be greatly encouraged by quite recent statements made by Recanati: 'No implicature can be computed at a sublocutionary level. We have to compute truth conditions first, so as to ascribe a definite content to the speaker's speech act, before we can infer anything from that speech act.' (Recanati 2003a: 300); 'the interpretation of indirect speech acts (and other kinds of conversational implicatures) is a two-step procedure. The interpreter *first* determines the utterance's primary meaning, *then* infers some additional meaning' (Recanati 2004a: 74, my emphasis). It is encouraged further by the repeated use (2004a: 42–3; 2004b: 50–1) of the analogy with perception (first I hear the doorbell ringing, then, on that basis, I infer that there is someone at the door).

Apparently, however, it is a mistake to draw this conclusion: although what is said is *logically* prior to implicatures (that is, it functions as a premise in an inferential process which issues in implicature) it is not, Recanati insists, to be taken as *temporally prior*: 'I deny that my view commits me to a "sequential model"' (Recanati 2004a: 47). To back up this denial, he goes on to discuss briefly and endorse the phenomenon of 'parallel mutual adjust-ment' between implicature and explicature ('what is said'), an important component of the RT account, as outlined above. If this mechanism really does play a crucial role in the interpretation process it follows that there is no generalization to be made about which of the two kinds of commu-nicated assumption is recovered first and functions as input to the recovery of the other; the parallel adjustment process entails that neither is wholly temporally prior to the other. Recanati expresses his agreement with this, maintaining that it is quite compatible with his account of primary and secondary processes.

So let us accept that the primary/secondary distinction as characterized does not entail sequential processing. What we face now, though, is a new set of questions and gaps. First, presumably, the analogy with perception breaks down at this point: except for quite unusual circumstances, one does not arrive at the judgement that the doorbell is ringing by a process of *adjusting one's auditory perception* to an antecedent hypothesis that someone is at the door. Second, it is unclear how Recanati can maintain both his view of the deep differences between primary and secondary processes, on the one hand, and his endorsement of the parallel mutual adjustment mech-anism, on the other. Within relevance theory, this is a mechanism which operates in the pursuit of an overall interpretation of an utterance which meets specific expectations of relevance (that is, expectations concerning effort expenditure and cognitive gain) and which, all going well, is the speaker's meaning. Although Recanati is not explicit about how much of RT he wants to take on board, I assume he does not (cannot) accept the relevance-based comprehension procedure (which applies to all aspects of pragmatic interpretation), given his entirely accessibility-based account of primary processes. As for the secondary processes of implicature deriva-tion, they appear to be regulated by consciously available norms of rational communication. The obvious and pressing question is: *how* can these two quite distinct types of process (local, associative, unconscious, subpersonal, in the one case; global, inferential, consciously accessible, person-level, in the other case) interact in such a way as to effect adjustments to each other's content? Specifically, how can implicatures, whose derivation takes 'what is said' as its input, affect the content of 'what is said'? Recanati (2004a) does have an answer to this, which I'll look at in section 1.4, though what that answer entails is that while he offers an account of the online cognitive processes involved in deriving primary utterance meaning (explicature, what is said), he does not, after all, provide any account of the online derivation of secondary utterance meaning (implicatures). It turns out that the personal-level inferential account of implicatures is construed not as an account of actual 'occurrent' processes, but as a matter of rational reconstruction. Before considering this, however, let's take a closer look at the account of primary processes.

1.3 Primary processes: associative relations and least effort

Summing up his account of primary processes, Recanati (2004a: 32) says: 'In the framework I have sketched, the interpretation ['what is said'] which eventually emerges and incorporates the output of various pragmatic processes results from a blind, mechanical process, involving no reflection on the interpreter's part. The dynamics of accessibility does everything and no "inference" is required. In particular, there is no need to consider the speaker's beliefs and intentions.'

I will raise two questions about the adequacy of this sort of account. The first concerns cases where a candidate concept is the most highly activated one throughout and results in an interpretation which is both coherent and highly relevant, but which, according to strong offline intuitions, would not be the one chosen by the addressee. Consider the following scenario. I'm walking along with one of my students, Sarah, who turns to me and utters the sentence in (3). Let us suppose I know two people called 'Neil', one of whom is my young son, $NEIL_1$, the other a colleague in the linguistics department where I work, $NEIL_2$. So there are two candidate referents here, both of them activated when the name 'Neil' is uttered.

(3) Neil has broken his leg.

Suppose further that I am worried about my son, who tends to get into a lot of trouble – he is constantly on my mind. In other words, my $NEIL_1$ concept is more highly activated than my $NEIL_2$ concept, and so, given the blind mechanical nature of the primary process of reference assignment, $NEIL_1$ is the winning candidate. The resulting interpretation is consistent with my knowledge (I haven't seen the boy for several hours), perfectly coherent (Recanati sometimes alludes to a search for coherence in interpretation (Recanati 2004a: 36)) and highly relevant (it has many cognitive effects for me), though considerations of relevance appear not to enter into Recanati's account. Nevertheless, this is not the interpretation I give to the utterance – for the simple reason that I know that the speaker (one of my students) does not know anything about my family life, while she does know that I have a colleague, Neil, who teaches her syntax. So, even if initially my highly activated $NEIL_1$ concept is the first one accessed, it is soon replaced by $NEIL_2$. This interpretation is also coherent and sufficiently relevant.

This is explained quite straightforwardly within the RT approach, whose concept of optimal relevance includes as a crucial component of interpretation considerations of the speaker's abilities (which include her knowledge of the world) and preferences. Recognizing that the student does not *know* (or *believe*) that I have a son called 'Neil', I take it that she did not (could not) *intend* to refer to him. Recanati's account of primary processes, on the other hand, precludes consideration of the speaker's mental states (beliefs, intentions) so, unless there is some other mechanism for altering the relative accessibility of the two $NEIL$ concepts, I seem to be stuck with my first most accessible referent. There is one possibility here: cognitive schemas (frames, scripts) play an important role in Recanati's activation-based account, so is there some schema or script that could plausibly be thought to bring about the necessary accessibility shift in this example? A schema is an abstract representation of a situation type which may be evoked by the words used or by other salient features of the speech situation.[6] Thus, it could be argued here that, given the situation in which the exchange took place, a 'university lecturer and student' or perhaps, a 'linguistics department' schema is evoked, which may contain within it slots for various different lecturers, one of whom is $NEIL_2$, so that the result is that this is the more highly activated of the two $NEIL$ concepts and is thereby (correctly) selected as the referent. I find it implausible that there is any such schema (though the constraints on what constitutes a schema have yet to be specified) or that, if there is, it would necessarily be activated in the utterance situation as given above or that, if it was, any activation it provided would outdo that of my highly activated $NEIL_1$ concept. But even supposing this account goes through for the example as described so far, we can change the speech situation so that it does not make salient university departments, lecturers or subjects like syntax. Suppose I run into Sarah at the local supermarket, and after some chat about the merits of organic vegetables, she says to me, 'I hear that Neil's broken his leg'. Given the high activation of my $NEIL_1$ concept and the absence of any frame to effect an accessibility shift, the prediction of the automatic, non-reflective associative account seems to be that (contrary to intuitions) I will take her to have said that $NEIL_1$ has broken his leg.[7]

My second question is a more general one, concerning how the account works for cases where there is no linguistic mandating of the pragmatic process: cases of free enrichment, meaning modulation, concept transfer and, as in the case of irony, 'staging'. Setting aside the problem just discussed, one can see how the accessibility account is thought to work for disambiguation and saturation (including reference assignment), that is, those minimalist pragmatic processes allowed by Grice. In such cases, there is a pre-given set of candidate concepts – linguistic senses in the case of ambiguity, contextually available referents that meet the linguistically-encoded constraint in the case of referring expressions (MALE PERSON for 'he', PERSON CALLED 'NEIL' for the name 'Neil', etc.) – and the one among them that is the most highly activated wins out. But it is much less obvious how this automatic, low-level ('dumb') mechanism can account for cases of free enrichment or meaning modulation, processes which are optional and constructive, and which may result in a concept that is entirely ad hoc and one-off. Recanati says: 'If we assume that what undergoes semantic composition is the most accessible of the candidate senses associated with a given constituent, we can explain how a derived sense resulting from free enrichment (or loosening, or transfer) can be selected and undergo composition in lieu of the literal meaning from which it is derived' (Recanati 2003b: 2.3). Even supposing that, given a set of candidate senses (some literal, some derived), the accessibility-based story can account for the process of selecting one of them, there is a pressing antecedent question: where do the non-literal (unencoded) candidate senses come from, how are they brought into the scene so as to become candidates? It begs the question to say that they are derived by free enrichment or concept modulation, since the issue precisely is how those very primary processes work, what it is that drives them, on this wholly accessibility-based account.

Recanati provides an answer to this in the case of the famous metonymic use of 'The ham sandwich' in (4a):

(4) a. The ham sandwich left without paying.
     b. The ham sandwich is being eaten.
     c. The ham sandwich needs some mustard.

The choice of THE GUY WHO ORDERED THE HAM SANDWICH as referent is accounted for by a combination of schema activation and encoded linguistic meaning. A café/restaurant schema is evoked and this provides several candidates for the referent of 'the ham sandwich': the sandwich itself, the plate with the sandwich on it, the person who ordered the ham sandwich, perhaps the person responsible for assembling the ham sandwich, and so on. Initially, when only the subject noun phrase has been processed, it is likely that the concept of the sandwich itself is the most highly activated, but further down the line, the processing of the predicate 'left without paying' ensures that the concept of the orderer of the ham sandwich is the most highly activated, since this is the one that coheres best with both the predicate's requirement of a human subject and the participant roles in the café schema. Similar accounts can be given for the choice of the food itself in (4b) and the several possibilities in (4c) (unresolvable without further contextual specification).

Note that, in this metonymic case, the candidate referents are all components of a single schema evoked by the situation of utterance (probably a café setting with the utterance made by a waiter) and the encoded concept HAM SANDWICH. I doubt that this is very often the case for metaphors. Rather, the conceptual content that results from a metaphorical use and which, on this sort of account, is composed into the primary meaning of the utterance is often not a component of any existing schema at all, but is new (ad hoc), consisting of 'emergent features or properties', as it is put in the literature (Becker 1997; Gineste *et al.* 2000; Vega-Moreno 2004), that is, the derived concept has properties which are not associated with the metaphor vehicle. Let's consider some quite ordinary examples, avoiding any extra questions that might be raised by very creative or extended metaphors:

(5) a. The ATM swallowed my credit card.
     b. Don't let that surgeon operate on you. He's a butcher.
     c. Mary is a bulldozer/block of ice/butterfly.

The first example is discussed briefly by Recanati (2004a: 26, 76–7), who describes it as involving the construction of an ad hoc concept (call it SWALLOW*) which can apply both to creatures that do actually swallow and to ATMs (non-biological entities) that do not. This is achieved by an unreflective process of 'relaxing the conditions of application for "swallow"' (p. 26). Based on Recanati's comments on 'partial schematicity'[8] (pp. 76–7), let me try to extrapolate how an account solely in terms of associations between concepts and spreading activation might work in this case. The encoded meaning of the verb 'swallow' activates a schema about the process of swallowing, with specifications of the kind of bodily organs that perform this function, the kinds of things on which it is performed (mostly foods of one sort or another), and the normal upshot of the process (permanent disappearance of the food, its decomposition, etc.). Much of this schema cannot apply to ATMs and credit cards; the activation level of those bits that can apply (principally, the disappearance of the thing swallowed, maybe also its decomposition) is enhanced by activation that spreads associatively to them from the schema for ATMs and credit cards, and the rest is deactivated (perhaps actively suppressed, as suggested in some of the psycholinguistic literature; see Rubio-Fernandez 2005). According to Recanati, what motivates this, and primary pragmatic processes quite generally, is 'the search for coherence in interpretation' (p. 36). So, in this case, it seems that the concept conveyed by the metaphor may be quite directly extractable from the schema evoked by the linguistic meaning of 'swallow'.

Consider now the nominal metaphor in (5b). What this utterance attributes to the surgeon concerned is a property (label it BUTCHER*) which is roughly paraphraseable as 'lacking skill, careless, dangerous, likely to cause damage and pain to those he operates on'. The problem here is that these attributes are not associated with the metaphor vehicle; they are not aspects of the standard schema for butchers going about their usual business, in which they are represented as expertly cutting animal carcasses into pieces and causing no damage or pain to anyone. This is not to deny that we have a pretty clear sense of how the metaphor works – we imagine the live human body on the butcher's block being hacked at with a meat cleaver – but it is to question how this can be accounted for simply in terms of different levels of activation of concepts which are either linguistically encoded or made available through the schema associated with the metaphor vehicle, BUTCHER. It seems that something more is needed, whether something akin to a mapping between the domains (aspects of the butcher domain are mapped onto aspects of the surgeon domain), or a process of blending of the two domains to create a new one (surgeon with meat cleaver hacking at live person on block), or a relevance-driven inferential process in which the addressee considers what components of a butcher's behaviour, if applied to a surgeon, would explain why she should not let that surgeon operate on her. For the first two of these possibilities, domain-mapping and blending, it seems likely that relevance-based inference would also be required, in order to account for, in the one case, which components of the one domain are mapped onto which of the other, and, in the other case, which components of the two domains are blended to make a new domain.[9]

This problem seems to be a quite general one (although it may not arise for the ATM example and a few others). Consider the various predicates in (5c). Allowing that there will be interpretive differences across contexts and individuals, the property of being a BULLDOZER* can be roughly para-phrased as being 'obstinate, insensitive, uninterested in other people's opin-ions and feelings', and that of being a BLOCK-OF-ICE* as being 'emotionally unexpressive, self-contained, unfriendly bordering on hostile'. Pretty clearly, these concepts are not going to be found in the encyclopaedic entries or the schemas attached to the linguistically encoded concepts BULLDOZER and BLOCK-OF-ICE, to which the communicated properties do not (cannot) apply, so that again some process or mechanism other than, or additional to, the activation (and deactivation) of existing concepts or parts of schemas is required. The process is, in a real sense, a constructive one, so unlikely to be effected by a passive dumb mechanism in which 'the dynamics of accessib-ility does everything and no inference is required' (Recanati 2004a: 32).[10]

Let us now consider how Recanati's framework deals with a very different kind of non-literal language use, that of irony, focusing on the primary meaning of ironical utterances. He discusses just the rather standardized example 'Paul is a fine friend' (Recanati 2001: 272–3; 2004a: 71, 77–8) but it seems clear that the account is intended to apply to novel instances of irony too. It builds on Grice's (1978/89b: 54) few remarks about ironical utterances, that they involve (transparent) pretence and have a secondary meaning (conversational implicature): 'By pretending to say of Paul that he is a fine friend in a situation in which just the opposite is obviously true, the speaker manages to communicate [by implicating] that Paul is everything but a fine friend' (Recanati 2004a: 71). So what is the primary meaning here and how is it to be accounted for on the associative, accessibility-based account of pragmatic processes? Recanati says that at the primary level one must recognize that 'the act of asserting that Paul is a fine friend is staged or simulated rather than actually performed. And that means that one must discern two "layers" within the primary meaning of the utterance: the surface speech act which the speaker pretends to perform, and the ironical act of staging the performance of that act' (Recanati 2004a: 77). He emphasizes that this layering, which is typical of a wider class of 'staged communicative acts", is internal to the primary meaning of the utterance. But what of the primary *process* responsible for deriving this complex primary meaning? Recognition that an apparent assertion is being staged is clearly a matter of a global pragmatic inference, and one which appears to depend on some pragmatic principle or other concerned with rational communicative behaviour, whether a Gricean Maxim of Truthfulness or something more like the Sperber/Wilson Communicative Principle of Relevance. Recanati gives no indication of how primary processes, as he has characterised them, could account for this dual-layered primary meaning. We may, of course, agree that both of the concepts FINE FRIEND and LOUSY FRIEND will be highly activated, the former due to linguistic encoding and the latter to salient features of the situation under discussion, but that alone cannot account for the conclusion that the speaker is simulating a speech act. It is equally compatible with interpreting this as a pun or as a case of miscommunication; something is missing from an account entirely in terms of levels of concept activation and that something seems to require considerations of rational communicative behaviour which are precluded from the 'blind, mechanical, local and entirely accessibility-based' account of primary processes.

I leave non-literal uses now and turn briefly to cases of free enrichment which involve an unarticulated constituent. In such cases, a primary pragmatic process is not only responsible for the concept understood but also brings about a structural change in that there was no linguistic constituent (overt or covert) in the position occupied by the concept.[11] Cases frequently discussed, by Recanati and others, are given in (6), where the concept in brackets, which is a component of what is said, has no linguistic correlate in the sentence uttered.[12]

(6) a. I haven't had breakfast [TODAY]
    b. It's raining [IN LONDON]
    c. She took out her key and [THEN] opened the door [WITH THE KEY]
    d. She insulted him and [AS A RESULT] he left the room

As before, the issue is whether and, if so, how the account of primary pragmatic processes in terms of differential levels of concept activation can explain how these cases work. In this regard, there is very little to go on in Recanati's discussion, which concentrates on cases of reference assignment and disambiguation. The usual talk of competing candidates doesn't seem to make much sense when the constituent is not linguistically articulated – what would they be competing for? Since there is no variable or slot in the structure requiring that a value be provided, there seems to be nothing to motivate the process. An interpretation of (6a) as saying that the speaker (referent having been assigned) hasn't had breakfast *tout court* may not be very plausible or relevant, but considerations of plausibility and/or relevance are not supposed to play any role in primary processing. Such an interpretation would be highly accessible (since it involves little more than straight decoding and one very simple instance of reference assignment) and it is perfectly coherent. Similar comments could be made about the other examples. In each case, it is difficult to see how an interpretation which involves the linguistically unmotivated addition of a constituent of content could be more accessible than one that does not.

It is perhaps significant that it is with regard to examples such as these that Recanati expresses his approval of the RT mutual adjustment mechanism, whereby explicit utterance content can be enriched so as to provide inferential warrant for independently motivated hypotheses about implicatures (Recanati 2004a: 47). So, for instance, in (7), B indirectly communicates (via implicature) that she doesn't want a meal at that time, but this is only warranted by what she has said (her explicature) if it is enriched with the constituents shown in brackets (or similar ones):

(7) A: Will you have supper with me now?
   B: I've eaten [A MEAL] [THIS EVENING]

This does indeed provide a basis for explaining how the recovery of unarticulated constituents is motivated and it makes good sense in the context of the RT account where the fundamental goal of comprehension is taken to be the derivation of sufficient cognitive implications, at a low enough processing cost, to satisfy the expectation of relevance raised by the utterance. This expectation guides the interpretation process, allowing a substantial element of backward inference from hypotheses about intended implications (implicatures) to premises (including the explicature) that might yield those implications. It is much less clear how it can be integrated into an account like Recanati's, according to which the recovery of the components of what is said is simply a matter, for any given constituent location in the structure, of the most highly activated concept taking the position – a process, apparently, not constrained by any bid for relevance or by any other conversational maxims or principles.[13] In short, it remains to be demonstrated how, on this associative account, linguistically absent constituents of propositional content can be recovered.

Finally, although these non-inferential processes are not governed by Gricean maxims or by any other principles of rational communicative behaviour, Recanati does briefly advert to a search for coherence in arriving at primary meaning (what is said): 'the tendency to prefer coherent interpretations (with a high degree of fit between the various semantic values)' (Recanati 2004a: 36) and he cashes this out in terms of a preference for interpretations which instantiate available cognitive schemata. He doesn't seem to view the search for coherence as having the status of a pragmatic principle in his 'accessibility-based framework', but rather as a quite general cognitive proclivity, which plays a central role in determining the most accessible interpretation. Whether or not this framework proves able to explain the specific processes of free enrichment, staging, concept transfer, etc., there is a more general and basic question concerning what, on this account, motivates the utterance interpretation process in the first place. Utterances (and other ostensive stimuli) are attention pre-empting in a way that most other environmental phenomena are not. What is it about utterances that almost inevitably triggers attentional focus and the expenditure of some processing effort? On the RT account, it is that such stimuli carry a presumption of their own optimal relevance, that is, a presumption that effort expended will be offset by cognitive effects gained. Mere accessibility, even coherence-based accessibility, doesn't seem to be sufficient to motivate the automatic investment of attention and effort typical of our cognitive response to utterances. What is the cognitive benefit of a coherent, highly accessible interpretation which is nonetheless irrelevant, that is, does not connect up with existing assumptions and thoughts? Without the prospect of benefit, there seems to be little foundation for ongoing effort.

1.4   Secondary versus primary pragmatic processes: conscious (un)availability

At least since his 1989 paper, Recanati has maintained that what is crucial about conversational implicatures is that the secondary pragmatic process by which they are derived is a global, inferential process which is consciously available to all individual speakers and hearers who are capable of producing and comprehending implicatures – that is, the process is a personal-level one. In this regard, Recanati sees himself as very much a Gricean:

> Grice said that 'the presence of an implicature must be capable of being worked out' (Grice, 1989, p.31). For an implicature to be worked out, two conditions must be satisfied: (i) both what is said and what is implied must be grasped, and (ii) the inferential connection between them must also be grasped. Many followers of Grice have (wrongly) interpreted this

as requiring that *the theorist* be capable of working out whatever conversational implicature is posited to explain a given semantic phenomenon; but Grice clearly had in mind the participants in the talk-exchange themselves: it is the speaker and hearer who must be capable of working out the implicatures... (Recanati 1993: 245)

He emphasizes that 'we have *distinct conscious* representations for "what is said" and for "what is implicated" by a given utterance' and 'the inferential connection between these representations is as consciously accessible as the representations themselves' (Recanati 1993: 245). This Availability Condition distinguishes secondary processes from primary processes, which, he claims, do not meet it.

There seem to be two slightly different ways of construing this condition, at least on the basis of the quote above, one stronger than the other. As is well known, Grice provided a general schema or pattern for the working out of implicatures, starting with the premises that the speaker has said that p and that the speaker is observing the conversational maxims (or at least the Co-operative Principle), then moving through a number of steps of reasoning involving the attribution of mental states to the speaker, some of them quite metarepresentationally complex (e.g. 'she intends me to think, or is at least willing to allow me to think, that q'), ending with the conclusion that the speaker has implicated that q (Grice 1975/89b: 31). It is the capacity to reconstruct a line of reasoning of this sort that a number of followers of Grice have taken to be a requirement on the theorist. What is not entirely clear is whether Recanati's *Availability Condition* includes a requirement that hearers be consciously aware of performing such inferential steps as these, or it is the less demanding requirement of awareness that 'what is implicated' is inferentially grounded in, or justified by, 'what is said' (without awareness of the inferential steps). This second, weaker interpretation is supported by passages in later work (Recanati 2002a: 118; 2004a: 42). If that is the right interpretation, then there still is a distinction between what is required of the theorist, who has to be able to provide a step-by-step 'working out' of an implicature, and of the speaker/hearer, who (merely) has to be aware that there is an inferential connection.

However, the picture is altered when Recanati (2004a: 49–50) responds to the question of how it is possible to reconcile his acceptance of the RT mechanism of mutual adjustment of explicature (what is said) and implicature with the very distinct types of pragmatic process (primary and secondary) that he claims to be responsible for them. This would be pretty near impossible if the conscious availability of the inferential secondary process was taken to be a requirement on the process *as it occurred* (that is, while interacting with local primary processes that are unavailable). Drawing on some ideas from Garcia-Carpintero (2001), Recanati distinguishes between two kinds of personal-level inferences: those that are conscious explicit *occurrent* inferences, 'reasonings which we make by carefully going through their steps', and those that, although they may occur as spontaneous, tacit (unconscious) processes, are such that "the cognitive agent to which [they are] ascribed . . . is *itself* capable of making the inference explicitly and of rationally justifying whatever methods it spontaneously uses in arriving at the "conclusion" ' (2004a: 50). Recanati's proposal, then, is that secondary processes are personal-level inferences of this second sort, that is, although they are usually not explicit or consciously available as they occur (on-line, as the psychologists put it), the individual must have the off-line 'reflective capacities for making the inference explicit'. This reflective capacity is, he emphasises, *constitutive* of the capacity to derive conversational implicatures (but not of the capacity to derive what is said). This does take us some way to seeing how he can embrace processes of mutual adjustment in deriving what is said and what is implicated, although there is now a gap in the account: we are given no idea of how the actual tacit online process of implicature derivation works, that is, what the 'methods spontaneously used' might be (presumably, they are not associative as the primary processes are claimed to be).

While this move from occurrent to (merely) *dispositional* reflective inference is clearly a weakening of the conscious Availability Condition, it is also, in another respect, a strengthening in that it seems that not only must the individual be able to become consciously aware that there is an inferential connection between what is said and what is implicated, but she must also be able to make the inferential steps explicit, that is, to provide a rational reconstruction of the inferential link between premise and conclusion. So, what many followers of Grice have taken to be a task for the theorist really is, for Recanati, a requirement on individual speaker/hearers: they must be able to construct a pattern of reasoning from what is said to what is implicated which goes (roughly) along the lines of Grice's working out schema.

I would like now to consider two particular components of Recanati's Availability claims, bearing in mind the weaker dispositional construal of conscious accessibility. First, as regards primary pragmatic processes, the claim is that only their output (what is said) is consciously available, so neither the processes themselves nor the decoded linguistic meaning and elements of background information which provide the input to the processes are available to consciousness (Recanati 1993: 247; 2004a: 14, 19–20). Second, given that what is said is consciously available as a *distinct representation* from what is implicated, within overall speaker meaning (what is communicated), Recanati takes it that speaker-hearers have reliable intuitions about what is said and that these intuitions can be called on as support for his contextualist position as against various minimalist positions. Let's consider these points in order.

Is it true that linguistic (expression-type) meaning and the extralinguistic contextual information on which primary processes depend are unavailable to speaker-hearers? Consider again the metonymic use in (8a), which, for Recanati, has the explicit content (what is said) given in (8b) (and, we may suppose, an implicature such as (8c)):

(8) a. The ham sandwich is getting impatient.
   b. THE PERSON WHO ORDERED A HAM SANDWICH IS GETTING IMPATIENT.
   c. THE WAITER SHOULD SERVE PROMPTLY THE PERSON WHO ORDERED A HAM SANDWICH.

In comprehending (8a), the process that takes us from the literal concept of the item of food to the person who ordered it is highly transparent (available to conscious reconstruction). In fact, for people who haven't met this kind of use before, it's not only consciously available, but actual conscious reasoning may be necessary in order to derive the intended meaning. Its availability is reflected in the perfectly coherent, albeit deliberately uncooperative or playful, response by B in (9):

(9) A: The ham sandwich is getting impatient.
   B: Don't be silly – sandwiches can't get impatient.

The situation is similar for a range of other primary processes, including metaphorical transfers, recovery of unarticulated constituents, strengthenings and loosenings of word meanings. Consider the exchange in (10), where, again, the idea is that B understands the metaphor perfectly well, but his response shows his awareness of the literal meaning of A's utterance:

(10) A: Juliet is the sun.
    B: Oh right, full of hydrogen and helium is she?

Recanati (2004a) considers some metaphorical uses where the relation between the literal and the figurative meaning is transparent; he describes them as 'cases in which there is a felt duality *internal to the primary meaning of the utterance*', a duality which is importantly different from the primary/secondary (or *external*) duality because 'normal interpreters are aware of the (secondary) processes through which the secondary meaning is derived, but they are not aware of the (primary) processes through which the primary meaning is derived.' Recanati (2004a: 79). This raises a number of questions. First, it is debatable that normal speaker-hearers have no (dispositional) awareness of the primary process involved in cases of transparent metaphor – given awareness of the duality of meaning of, for instance, 'the sun' in (10) (and, of course, awareness that Juliet is not literally the sun), a speaker-hearer is surely highly likely to be capable of consciously recognising that one meaning is derived from (grounded in) the other. Second, on the usual assumption that the literal meaning of a metaphor is not speaker-meant, there is a tension between this account of (transparent) metaphor and Recanati's insistence that the primary meaning of an utterance (what is said) is a component of speaker meaning. And, third, even if the explanation does work for certain cases of extended metaphor (and/or irony, to which he also applies it), it does not carry over to the transparent metonymic case – the speaker did not mean that the bread-and-meat object was getting impatient – nor to the next group of examples, (11)–(12), which are cases where a quite ordinary (non-figurative) process of pragmatic enrichment appears to be consciously available.

(11) A: Everyone came to my party.
     B: That's rubbish. Tony Blair didn't come, nor did Madonna or Osama Bin Laden, and, anyway, your house couldn't fit every single person.
(12) Mother to young child just before bedtime: Have you brushed your teeth?
     Child (grinning): Yes I have – [*pause*] – last night.

In the case of (11A), it will be obvious to any normal hearer that the speaker intended to communicate that everyone in some specific group (say, all the members of her pragmatics class) came to her party. The deliberately obtuse response in (11B) indicates the availability of the input (i.e. the unqualified quantifier) to the pragmatic process which supplies the quantifier domain[14] and quite probably also an ability to provide some justificatory reconstruction of how the intended primary meaning is derived. The example in (12) is an attested case where a child of four shows his awareness both of the primary meaning the mother intended and of the linguistic input to the pragmatic process (the open temporal parameter), and perhaps also of the process itself (certainly there is awareness *that* there is some process of fixing the relevant time).

An interesting case here is Grice's (1975/1989b: 32) 'open garage' implicature example, which Recanati (2004a: 46) reanalyses as a case of sense modulation, a primary process, as follows:

(13) A: I am out of petrol.
     B: There's a garage round the corner.
     What is said: THERE'S A GARAGE* ROUND THE CORNER
     [where GARAGE* = garage that is open and has petrol to sell]
(14) I didn't say the garage was open – I just told him where it was.

Queried later, a disingenuous B could respond as in (14), showing the (at least dispositional, perhaps even occurrent) availability of the linguistic meaning of 'a garage'. Just as Grice required (and demonstrated when discussing this example), the process that takes us from the literal meaning of 'a garage' to 'a garage that is open and selling petrol' (or his more tentative: 'a garage that is, at least as far as B knows, open, etc.') is explicitly reconstructible as a rational inferential process, with a premise that the speaker is observing the Maxim of Relation, and inferential steps concerning what she must, therefore, have intended the hearer to think on the basis of her utterance. On Recanati's reanalysis, however, this is a primary process and so is predicted to not be available to consciousness.

In arguing that primary processes do not meet the Availability Condition, Recanati (2002a: 118) says: 'The interpreter is not aware that his judge-ment, to the effect that the speaker has said that *p*, is inferentially derived from a prior judgement, e.g. a judgement to the effect that the speaker has uttered sentence S.' What this entails is that global *sentence meaning* is not consciously accessible, which is almost certainly right. Given the early onset (as soon as the first utterance sounds impinge) and speed of pragmatic processing, it is very unlikely that a hearer ever forms a representation of pure sentence meaning as a whole (even subpersonally). But what the discus-sion above suggests is that quite a lot of the lexical or phrasal meaning, which is the input to primary processes, is available to ordinary speaker-hearers, and they are well aware that there is some process (whether it is to be thought of as inferential or not) that goes from elements of conventional linguistic meaning to elements of explicitly communicated content. So, at the very least, there is a lot more to be said here than simply that secondary processes are (dispositionally) available to consciousness while primary ones are not, a statement that seems to leave primary pragmatic processes lumped in with linguistic processes, like lexical access and syntactic parsing, which are indeed inaccessible to consciousness (tacit, sub-doxastic). The current observations call for some finer-grained distinction within the realm of avail-ability: perhaps a distinction between availability as a global process and availability as a local process. The examples above seem to indicate that (at least some) primary pragmatic processes are (at least dispositionally) consciously available as local processes. Given that they *are* local processes – very often the result of a specific constituent adjustment made in aid of providing inferential support for an implicature hypothesized on the basis of expectations of relevance – it is hardly surprising that what we are aware of is not a global mapping from sentence meaning (logical form) to what is said (explicature) but rather a variety of local mappings from linguistic constituents to communicated concepts.

On the basis of the examples so far considered, it might seem that among primary processes, it is the optional, non-minimal ones (i.e. various kinds of 'free' enrichment) that are available; that is, precisely those cases which Grice would have treated as conversational implicatures and so would have expected to meet his calculability requirement (that is, to be rationally reconstructible by the *speaker-hearer*, on Recanati's interpretation of Grice). What about the minimal processes of disambiguation and reference assign-ment? Trying to follow the pattern of the previous examples, let's suppose the exchange in (15) has taken place and is followed, some time later, by the exchange in (16). Here, B's response to A's challenge is odd, scarcely coherent:

(15) A: Who won the election?
     B: [*looking at Tom*] He did.
(16) A: You were wrong. It was Sam, not Tom, who won the election.
     B: I only said HE won the election – I didn't say TOM did.

Presumably, the difference between this case and the earlier examples is due, at least in part, to the obligatory nature of the process of reference assignment and the fact that without it no fully propositional entity can be derived. (There must be more to it than this, though, given that other, apparently obligatory, cases of saturation – of which (12) might well be one – do not lead to the incoherence of (16).)

However, what is significant here is that nothing seems to follow concerning the (un)availability of the process of reference assignment. The inputs to the process (linguistic meaning and extra-linguistic contextual information) are certainly not inaccessible to consciousness (contrary to Recanati 1993: 247; 2004a: 14). Naïve native speakers (for instance, students in their first week of a linguistics programme) have no problem in giving a fair rendering of the expression-type meaning of 'he', 'she', 'here', 'there', etc. There is also no difficulty in making explicit the basis on which a tacit process of reference fixing has been made. For instance: if asked why they think that a speaker was referring to Tony Blair (rather than Cherie Blair or Jacques Chirac), they will respond that they know this because the speaker said [= uttered] 'he' [rather than 'she'] while pointing at (or demonstrating in some other ostensive way) Tony Blair and that this behaviour only makes sense if the speaker intended to be understood as referring to Tony Blair. They thereby show that their referential hypothesis has a rational basis and that they are (dispositionally) aware of the hypothesis itself, and of the evidence on which it is based, and are able, on reflection, to make the connection explicit. Recall that one property that primary and secondary pragmatic processes are widely acknowledged (and certainly by Recanati) to have in common is their reliance on background information, or what is sometimes called 'wide context'. How odd, then, that in the case of primary processes the relevant contextual facts are claimed to be only tacitly known (sub-doxastic, subpersonal) while they are consciously accessed (or at least accessible) in the case of secondary processes (Recanati 1993: 247; 2004a: 20, 46). With regard to reference assignment, it's not that the contextual information is only tacitly known, but rather that it's so obvious that hearers are likely to find it weird to be asked how they know who the speaker is referring to (only an academic would ask that!).

At the least, we can conclude that the availability of the ingredients of primary processes distinguishes them from the subpersonal processes of linguistic decoding (or visual perception), which are neither occurrently nor dispositionally available, but have to be investigated by more indirect scientific methods. Now, it might be that Recanati would be prepared to concede these points about primary processes, while insisting that they make no difference to what, in the end, is the fundamental claim in his 2004 book, which is that it is *constitutive* of conversational implicatures that they meet the Availability Condition while it is not constitutive of 'what is said' (explicature). So, even if the pragmatic processes involved in deriving 'what is said' can be rationally reconstructed, that is a contingent matter – the ability to understand utterances by performing these primary processes in no way *depends* on having the reflective capacity for making elements of the processes explicit. In the case of secondary utterance meanings, on the other hand, the claim is 'that there would be no conversational implicature if the interpreters did not have that reflective capacity' (Recanati 2004a: 50). As it stands this is mere stipulation, but it does appear to have some testable empirical consequences.

Young children (below the age of four) who lack a fully developed explicit concept of belief (as investigated by standard false belief tasks), presumably, do not have the reflective capacity in question, so the issue to investigate is whether they are or are not able to produce and comprehend implicatures. Unfortunately, there is remarkably little research on this question and what there is seems equivocal. It has been repeatedly shown that children who are otherwise quite communicatively competent tend not to derive scalar 'implicatures', such as the inference from 'some of the F' to 'not all of the F' (see summary in Noveck 2004). But there are just too many unresolved issues around the process of scalar inference to make it a good test case for the current question; for instance, it's not even clear yet whether it is a secondary or a primary pragmatic process (a point discussed a little more below), and it may be that it requires a metalinguistic ability, that is, an ability to compare linguistic forms ('she said "some" when she could have said "all", so . . . '), which may develop relatively late. There is some meagre evidence that children between 2 and 3 years old can produce and understand indirect requests (Newcombe and Zaslow 1981; Papafragou 2002), but, while most pragmatists would treat these as cases of implicature, it can be argued (and several developmentalists have done so) that they are really cases involving established routines of some sort (e.g. 'when I say I'm hungry mummy gives me something to eat'). There are, then, two areas of research needing attention here: the development of a typology of conversational implicatures detailing the different cognitive demands of the different kinds, and the testing of young children's ability to comprehend the different types (in tandem with tracking the development of their capacity for explicit reflective reasoning). Only when these investigations are sufficiently advanced will it be possible to test Recanati's 'constitutiveness' claim. For the moment, it remains an interesting but unsubstantiated hypothesis.

Let's move now to the second of the consequences of Recanati's Availability view under consideration. As he points out, the availability of 'what is said' follows from Grice's characterization of it as a variety of non-natural meaning, an aspect of (overtly intentional) speaker meaning. On this basis, Recanati formulates his Availability Principle (as distinct from the Availability Condition), 'according to which "what is said" must be analysed in conformity to the intuitions shared by those who fully understand the utterance – typically the speaker and the hearer, in a normal conversational setting' (Recanati 2004a: 14). He takes this principle to work against the minimalist (or literalist or semantic) view of what is said which does not, or so he claims, conform to speaker-hearers' intuitions.[15]

How can we theorists tap these intuitions? Recanati assumes that 'whoever fully understands a declarative utterance knows which state of affairs would possibly constitute a truth-maker for that utterance, that is, knows in what sort of circumstance it would be true' (Recanati 2004a: 14) and suggests that the way to elicit intuitions concerning what is said (truth-conditional content) is to present 'subjects with scenarios describing situations, or, even better, with – possibly animated – pictures of situations, and to ask them to evaluate the target utterance as true or false with respect to the situations in question' (Recanati 2004a: 15). This method has, in fact, been employed by Ira Noveck and colleagues in a series of experiments on people's understanding of scalar terms such as 'some', 'or' and 'might' (for a survey of the experiments, see Noveck 2004). The focus is on the pragmatic process of 'scalar inference', as mentioned above, which goes from 'some of the F' to 'not all of the F', from 'P or Q' to 'not both P and Q', and from 'x might be F' to 'x might not be F' (leaving aside number terms which are now widely thought to work differently from other scalar cases). The issue that concerns us here is whether this process does or does not contribute to the intuitive truth-conditional content ('what is said') of the utterance (although this was not generally the issue concerning the experimenters). In one of the many experiments on this, one of the test utterances was 'Some of the turtles are in the boxes', presented to subjects with a number of accompanying scenarios, including one in which some of the turtles are in the boxes and some are lying outside the boxes, and another one, the crucial case, in which all of the turtles are in the boxes. Presented with an utterance-scenario pair, adult subjects[16] were asked to judge the utterance as 'true' or 'false', where the response 'false' in the test case (where all the turtles are in the boxes) should, according to Recanati's principle, indicate that the scalar inference ('not all of the turtles') is contributing to truth-conditional content ('what is said'). The problem for the Availability Principle is that adult responses were very far from univocal. In this particular experiment, 53 per cent responded positively, 47 per cent negatively (Noveck 2004: 308) and this result is consistent with the findings across a wide number of other experiments carried out on such scalar terms. In short, the pretheoretic intuitions of ordinary speaker-hearers concerning the truth-conditional content (hence 'what is said') of utterances involving scalar terms (presented with scenarios which strongly encourage the pragmatic inference) are highly divergent.

It could reasonably be objected that the pragmatics (and semantics) of scalar terms is a particularly contentious area and therefore not one which should lead us to abandon a principle or a methodology which is otherwise sound. However, doubt about the utility of the principle which enjoins respect for intuitions coupled with the suggested method for eliciting intuitions is not confined to scalar cases. For cases of metaphor and metonymy, there are a number of complications: first, how to set up appropriate scenarios for the intended content is unclear (Juliet with light radiating from her?) and second, it seems quite likely that 'The ham sandwich is getting restless' coupled with a picture of an animated ham sandwich, or 'Juliet is the sun' with a picture of Juliet's face peering out of the sun, will elicit 'true' responses (hence not reflect what the speaker has said, on the contextualist position). There are also quite banal cases where it seems that truth-conditional intuitions vary, some people being naturally more literal-minded (or rigorous) than others when asked to focus on truth. Consider the example in (17), adapted from Travis (1989: 18–19), where the contextualist view is that what B explicitly communicates ('says') by her utterance incorporates the conceptual narrowing represented by MILK*.

(17) A: Let's have some coffee.
    B: Okay, there's milk in the fridge.
    What is said: THERE'S MILK* IN THE FRIDGE
    [where MILK* = milk suitable for coffee]

Now suppose, employing Recanati's favoured method for eliciting intuitions concerning 'what is said', subjects are presented with the utterance (fully contextualized) and a picture of the open fridge which has a half-full bottle of milk on one of its shelves, and are asked to evaluate the truth of the utterance with respect to the situation depicted. Subjects will, no doubt, judge it to be true. But how will they respond when the utterance is presented together with a picture (a close-up photograph, perhaps) of the open fridge containing no bottle, carton or jug of milk but with a few drops of spilt milk clearly visible on the bottom shelf? Some may say the utterance is false (after all, this does not constitute milk in the intended sense), but others will surely say it is (strictly speaking) true in the pictured situation. If allowed to elaborate, they might explain themselves along the following lines: 'Well, of course, it doesn't mesh with what the speaker intended or what the hearer would take her to have meant, but strictly speaking the utterance is true – there *is* milk in the fridge in this scenario, but not milk that is of any use for making coffee which is what really matters to the conversational participants. It's true but irrelevant and misleading.' Berg (2002: 353) discusses this example, regarding which he has the latter sort of intuition, and talks of the 'slugfest of intuitions' into which theoretical debate about such cases among minimalists and contextualists is apt to descend. In the case of ordinary folk with no theoretical axes to grind, there isn't any fight but, I believe, their untutored intuitions are likely to be equally divergent. Judgements of truth/falsity will depend on what a given individual takes as the object to be evaluated, whether some element of conventional linguistic meaning or some aspect of what the speaker meant.[17]

Given the availability (of many instances, at least) of literal lexical meaning, as argued earlier in this section, it is hardly surprising that intuitions about the truth of an utterance might pull away from (intuitions about) what a speaker meant (explicitly) by the utterance. Acceptance of the *relevance-driven* mechanism of mutual adjustment, which affects (speaker-meant) explicit utterance content as well as implicature, should also deter us from expecting truth judgements to always coincide neatly with judgements about what constitutes a level of pragmatically enriched content ('true but not relevant' being a very reasonable sort of judgement to make). In fact, we might wonder whether any particular purpose is served by the concept of 'the truth-conditional content of *an utterance*'. From a communication-theoretic (or speaker meaning) perspective, what matters is what is communicated and how it is communicated. For good reasons, this splits into two kinds of communicated assumptions – explicature (what is said), which is developed out of the decoded logical form of the utterance, and implicature, which is wholly inferred – and, of course, each of these has its own truth conditions. On the Fodorian 'psychosemantic' view (Fodor 1987), adopted by relevance theorists, the primary bearer of truth conditions is not utterances (much less sentences) but propositions or thoughts, so any talk of the truth conditions of utterances is purely derivative and not of any obvious use.

I'm not sure that these considerations invalidate the Availability Principle itself, but they make it effectively unusable because of the problem of eliciting intuitions of the right sort. I agree with Recanati (2004a: 14–15) that directly asking people what a speaker has said, as opposed to implied, is hopeless, but asking them for truth value judgements doesn't seem very much better. So analysing 'what is said' in conformity with the intuitions of ordinary speaker-hearers does not, alone at least, provide clear support for the contextualist over the minimalist. Perhaps the theorist has to adopt a more roundabout approach. It may be that people's pretheoretic intuitions about what a speaker has implied (and clearly not said) could provide a better starting point. Then, given theoretically motivated constraints such as that (a) what is said is a pragmatic development of the encoded linguistic meaning, and (b) it must provide inferential warrant for the implicature (what the speaker has clearly implied), we may be able to reason our way to a decision about what she can be taken to have explicitly communicated ('said'). In practice, this is pretty much how contextualists like Recanati and relevance theorists have proceeded in getting at explicit utterance content.

1.5 Conclusion: pragmatic processes and reflective reasoning

There are (at least) three striking aspects to Recanati's pragmatics: (1) his radical contextualism, which incorporates into 'what is said' many elements of speaker meaning that Grice treated as conversational implicatures; (2) his account of the pragmatic processes that contribute to 'what is said' in terms of conceptual associations and levels of activation; (3) his claim that it is constitutive of the (secondary) processes responsible for conversational implicatures that they are (dispositionally) consciously available and reconstructible by the speaker-hearer. I have raised some questions about the second and third aspects. It remains to be shown, and there is some reason to doubt, that the approach in terms of differential levels of concept activation can explain the proposed primary meaning of metaphorical and ironical utterances or account for the recovery of unarticulated constituents. At present, it appears better able to support a minimalist than a contextualist position. As regards the availability claims, the components of many primary processes (metonymy, recovery of unarticulated constituents, some instances of saturation) seem to be as readily available as those of secondary processes, and at present there is no empirical evidence that could enable assessment of the 'constitutiveness' assertion as regards secondary processes.

The relevance-theoretic approach to utterance comprehension offers a unitary account of the pragmatic processes that deliver explicatures and implicatures. It makes no strong claims about the conscious availability or unavailability of particular subprocesses or the inputs to them. In particular, it does not assume that speaker-hearers' intuitions about explicit content or the truth of utterances can play a criterial role in the delimitation of explicature (what is said). However, if and where there is some uniformity of judgement (perhaps for a subset of declarative utterances), that is valuable evidence to be used along with other considerations and constraints. One such constraint is that, as Recanati insists, an essential property of explicature ('what is said') is that it is speaker-meant (part of what is communicated). Any retreat from that to some more semantically-oriented notion of 'what is said' (for instance, in Bach 1994) simply entails that the explicit/implicit distinction *within speaker meaning* arises under some other labelling ('implicature'/implicature for Bach). A second constraint shared by Recanati and RT is the requirement that the outcome of the comprehension process should be such that any implicated conclusions are properly warranted. One of the premises on which an implicature depends is the explicature (what is said), which may have to be enriched or otherwise adjusted so as to provide the required inferential soundness. These considerations may well be sufficient to secure the contextualist position on explicature (what is said).

Finally, then, what role does the capacity for explicit reflective reasoning play in communication/comprehension? It *can* be employed for the rational reconstruction of a spontaneous pragmatic process (whether primary or secondary), though this is not an exercise that people perform much off their own bat. Its most likely role is as a backup mechanism when something goes wrong with the automatic intuitive mechanisms of utterance understanding. This seems to be the view of Campbell (1981) in a passage, which, oddly enough, Recanati often cites as support for his position on the essential involvement of reflection in implicature (see Recanati 2004a: 12; 2004b: 47): 'A macropragmatic process is one constituted by a sequence of explicit inferences governed by principles of rational cooperation. A micropragmatic process develops as a cryptic [= unconscious] and heuristic procedure which partially replaces some macropragmatic process and *which defaults to it in the event of breakdown*' (Campbell 1981: 101 [my emphasis]).[18] As far as I can see, this is also very much in keeping with Millikan's (1984: 69) discussion of the conditions under which Gricean reflective reasoning enters into communication: 'The truth in Grice's model is that we have the ability to interrupt and prevent the automatic running on of our talking and our doing-and-believing-what-we-are-told equipment, and assume others have this ability too. We interrupt, for example, when we have happened to look under the hood and discovered evidence that the conditions for normally effective talking . . . are not met.'

Notes

1. Many thanks to Deirdre Wilson for valuable discussion and encouragement. Thanks also to Alison Hall, Mark Jary, George Powell, Rosa Vega-Moreno and Vladimir Zegarac, who have all, in different ways, aided and abetted me in the writing of this chapter. I am particularly grateful to María J. Frápolli, editor of this volume, for patience and support way beyond the call of duty.
2. Not everyone agrees with this reading of Grice as a 'minimalist' rather than a 'contextualist' with regard to what is said (see, for example, Wharton 2002). One of the main pieces of evidence used to support a possible contextualist orientation to Grice's thinking is his discussion of cases of 'dictiveness without formality' in Grice (1989b: 361). However, it seems very likely that Grice assumed that the gap here is bridged, not by pragmatic inference, but by instances of what he would have thought of as conventions of linguistic behaviour. For very helpful discussion of Grice on social convention and of the Gricean programme more generally, see Garcia-Carpintero (2001).
3. For a much more detailed account of these ideas and their motivation, see Wilson and Sperber 2004.
4. In fact, very few people these days would take a 'Gricean mechanism' stance on utterance comprehension. On the relevance-theoretic account, pragmatic inferences are the domain of a fast, automatic modular system and the default ('naïve') strategy of the system involves no reasoning over attributed mental states (Sperber and Wilson 2002; Wilson 2005). And various other frameworks posit systems of default, or short-circuited, or routinized pragmatic inferences that bypass considerations of speakers' mental states. Grice himself probably did not take these complex metarepresentational reasoning schemes to be what speaker/hearers

actually employ in online processing, recognizing that implicatures 'can in fact be intuitively grasped' (Grice 1975/89b: 31), and that there is both a laborious effortful way of making inferential moves, and a 'quick way, which is made possible by habituation and intention', the latter being desirable as often as possible, given its much lower demands on time and energy (Grice 2001: 17).

5. I do not believe that the distinction Millikan makes between the automatic mechanisms of the normal language flow and the reflective, 'tinkering' capacity matches up with Recanati's distinction between primary and secondary processes, but I do not argue the point in this chapter.

6. A good example of a schema evoked by the words used and responsible for an accessibility shift is given by Recanati (2004a: 36–7) in discussing the assigning of a referent to the pronoun 'he' in the process of comprehending an utterance of 'John was arrested by a policeman yesterday; he had just stolen a wallet'. Suppose that initially when the pronoun is uttered the representation of the policeman is more highly activated than the representation of John; still, by virtue of the 'stealing something and being arrested' schema evoked by the predicates, *John* becomes more highly accessible than *the policeman* due to activation received from the linked participant roles in the schema [person who did the stealing and person who was arrested]. Thus, and in accordance with offline intuitions, *John* is the winning candidate for referent of 'he'.

7. On the relevance-theoretic account, there are, in fact, several manifestations of the comprehension strategy mentioned in section 2.1 above, differing in the degree of metarepresentational complexity they require (Sperber 1994). The simplest (naïve) strategy involves no consideration at all of the speaker's mental states and is likely to be pursued by young children (under four years old), whose theory-of-mind capacity is not yet fully matured. On such a strategy, the addressee will accept the first accessible interpretation that she finds relevant, so, in comprehending an example like (3) above, she would choose the most highly accessible referent whether or not it fell within the competence of the speaker to have intended it. More complex strategies develop subsequently on which the pragmatic inferential process may employ premises concerning the speaker's beliefs and preferences. Using one of these more sophisticated strategies, the addressee won't necessarily choose the first relevant referent; in an example like (3) above, her understanding of the speaker's state of knowledge will lead her to the intended referent. It looks as if, on Recanati's account, we remain forever egotistic children (whatever is most accessible to us is what we take the speaker to have referred to).

8. At the point in the text where Recanati discusses this notion (Recanati 2004a: 76–7), his objective is not to give any kind of detailed demonstration of how the primary process works, but to account for the fact that metaphorical use is sometimes transparent to addressees, that is, they are aware of the discrepancy between it and the literal content of the utterance. He explains this in terms of an ongoing above-threshold activation of aspects of the literal meaning which are at odds with the metaphorical meaning.

9. See Vega-Moreno (2004) for a relevance-based inferential account of this example and Vega-Moreno (2005) for discussion of a wider range of cases involving emergent properties and of some problems for the blending account of how these properties arise.

10. Note that I am not claiming here that the inference need involve considerations of the speaker's mental states. However, it has been suggested by Happé (1995), on the basis of her work testing the comprehension capacities of autistic

people, that the understanding of metaphor requires a theory-of-mind capacity (the ability to pass first-order false belief tasks), something which is not necessary for the understanding of corresponding similes or literal language generally. If this is right, then the associative account with its blindness to speaker's mental states cannot be right. (My own guess at this stage is that some metaphorical understanding requires reflective inference and some does not).

11. In his paper called 'Unarticulated Constituents', Recanati's (2002b) objective is to argue for the existence of unarticulated constituents against those who deny there is such a thing, specifically Stanley (2000). In that paper, Recanati distinguishes between a 'semantic' and a 'syntactic' construal (or variety) of free enrichment, and he focuses there on the semantic construal. In the current context of a discussion of primary pragmatic processes, I take it that the relevant conception is the syntactic variety, whereby an addressee recovers a conceptual constituent on entirely pragmatic grounds and incorporates it into his mental representation of what the speaker has said.

12. Some cases involving unarticulated constituents may be reconstrued as instances of meaning modulation (*ad hoc* concept construction). Recanati (2004a: 25) mentions example (6c) as a case in point, saying that instead of involving the linguistically unarticulated constituent [WITH THE KEY], it could be a matter of pragmatically narrowing the encoded general concept OPEN to the more specific concept OPEN-WITH-KEY. However, it is not clear to me that, having effected this conceptual narrowing, we wouldn't still need to supply the unarticulated constituent in order to represent the intended meaning that she opened the door *with the key mentioned in the first conjunct* (Recanati 2004a: 23–4). Consider in this regard: 'He picked up the hammer and vigorously hammered in the nail', where the verb 'hammer' encodes HIT-WITH-HAMMER but still the meaning intended – that he hammered in the nail *with the hammer mentioned in the first conjunct* – has to be pragmatically inferred.

13. A reasonable riposte here would be that we should suspend judgement on this until we have considered Recanati's account of the secondary pragmatic process of implicature-derivation. However, as will be discussed in the next section, his concern is with certain conditions on that process (principally its availability to consciousness) rather than with how the actual spontaneous, tacit on-line process works, so we do not get any idea of how it might interact with the associative primary processes.

14. Examples (9) and (11) are adapted from Stanley (2005), who uses them for his different purpose of trying to establish which aspects of intuitive content are, and which are not, genuinely semantic (in his terms).

15. When it was first presented (Recanati 1989: 309–10; 1993: 248), the Availability Principle was put to a slightly different use: as a criterion for deciding, for any pragmatically determined aspect of utterance meaning, whether it is part of what is said or an implicature.

16. The experiments conducted by Noveck and colleagues were primarily focused on the development in children of the ability to make scalar inferences, the data from adults being used mainly for comparative purposes. The general finding is that children are less likely than adults to derive scalar inferences and so more likely to find scalar utterances acceptable in any scenario compatible with the literal (logical) meaning of the scalar term.

17. As Deirdre Wilson has pointed out to me, there is a further range of factors that are likely to confound intuitions about the truth of utterances, including folk ideas about literal vs figurative meaning (some people simply have a robust

intuition that metaphors and metonymies are false, others don't), the effects of linguistic form on the way utterance information is presented (foregrounding vs backgrounding, parentheticals, subordination vs coordination, stress placement, etc.) and cases where the main point of the utterance doesn't coincide with the contextualist 'what is said' (e.g. an utterance of 'I lied' whose main point may be to communicate 'I admit that I lied', or an utterance of 'I think I'll leave now' whose main point is 'I'll leave now').

18. As noted by Wilson (2005: 1135) in a discussion of the communicative and pragmatic characteristics of people with Asperger's syndrome, it looks as if '[they] use general-purpose reflective reasoning to make up for a lack of the spontaneous intuitive ability [to interpret utterances]'. She demonstrates this with the case of a woman who uses explicit reasoning to try to figure out what someone meant by his use of the word 'sad', so a case of lexical meaning adjustment (or sense modulation).

References

Bach, K. (1994) 'Conversational Impliciture'. *Mind and Language* 9: 124–62.

Becker, A.H. (1997) 'Emergent and Common Features Influence Metaphor Interpretation'. *Metaphor and Symbolic Activity* 12(4): 243–59.

Berg, J. (2002) 'Is Semantics Still Possible?' *Journal of Pragmatics* 34: 349–59.

Campbell, R. (1981) 'Language Acquisition, Psychological Dualism and the Definition of Pragmatics'. In H. Parret, M. Sbisa and J. Verschueren (eds), *Possibilities and Limitations of Pragmatics*. Amsterdam: Benjamins, pp. 93–105.

Carston, R. (1988/91) 'Implicature, Explicature and Truth-theoretic Semantics'. In R. Kempson, (ed.) 1988. *Mental Representations: The Interface between Language and Reality*. Cambridge: Cambridge University Press, pp. 155–81. Reprinted in S. Davis (ed.) 1991. *Semantics: A Reader*. Oxford: Oxford University Press, pp. 33–51.

Carston, R. (2002a) 'Linguistic Meaning, Communicated Meaning and Cognitive Pragmatics'. *Mind and Language* 17(1/2): 127–48.

Carston, R. (2002b) *Thoughts and Utterances: The Pragmatics of Explicit Communication*. Oxford: Blackwell.

Fodor, J. (1987) *Psychosemantics*. Cambridge, MA: MIT Press.

Garcia-Carpintero, M. (2001) 'Gricean Rational Reconstruction and the Semantics/ Pragmatics Distinction'. *Synthese* 128: 93–131.

Gineste, M., Indurkhya, B. and Scart, V. (2000) 'Emergence of Features in Metaphor Comprehension'. *Metaphor and Symbol* 15: 117–35.

Grice, H.P. (1975/89b) 'Logic and Conversation'. In P. Cole and J. Morgan (eds), *Syntax and Semantics 3: Speech Acts*. New York: Academic Press, pp. 41–58. Reprinted in H.P. Grice (1989b), pp. 22–40.

Grice, H.P. (1978/89b) 'Further Notes on Logic and Conversation'. In P. Cole (ed.) *Syntax and Semantics 9: Pragmatics*. New York: Academic Press, pp. 113–27. Reprinted in H.P. Grice (1989b), pp. 41–57.

Grice, H.P. (1989a) 'Retrospective Epilogue'. In Grice, H.P. (1989b), 339–85.

Grice, H.P. (1989b) *Studies in the Way of Words*. Cambridge, MA: Harvard University Press.

Grice, H.P. (2001) *Aspects of Reason*. Oxford: Clarendon Press.

Happé, F. (1995) 'Understanding Minds and Metaphors: Insights from the Study of Figurative Language in Autism'. *Metaphor and Symbolic Activity* 10(4): 275–95.

Millikan, R. (1984) *Language, Thought, and Other Biological Categories*. Cambridge, MA: MIT Press.

Millikan, R. (2004) *Varieties of Meaning*. Cambridge, MA: MIT Press.

Newcombe, N. and Zaslow, M. (1981) 'Do 2.5-Year-Olds Hint? A Study of Directive Forms in the Speech of 2.5-Year-Olds to Adults'. *Discourse Processes* 4: 239–52.

Noveck, I. (2004) 'Pragmatic Inference Related to Logical Terms'. In I. Noveck and D. Sperber (eds), *Experimental Pragmatics*. Basingstoke: Palgrave, pp. 301–21.

Papafragou, A. (2002) 'Mindreading and Verbal Communication'. *Mind and Language* 17(1/2): 55–67.

Recanati, F. (1989) 'The Pragmatics of What is Said'. *Mind and Language* 4: 295–329.

Recanati, F. (1993) *Direct Reference: From Language to Thought*. Oxford: Blackwell.

Recanati, F. (1995) 'The Alleged Priority of Literal Interpretation'. *Cognitive Science* 19: 207–32.

Recanati, F. (2001) 'Literal/Non-literal'. *Midwest Studies in Philosophy* 25: 264–74.

Recanati, F. (2002a) 'Does Linguistic Communication Rest on Inference?' *Mind and Language* 17(1/2): 105–26.

Recanati, R. (2002b) 'Unarticulated Constituents'. *Linguistics and Philosophy* 25: 299–345.

Recanati, F. (2003a) 'Embedded Implicatures'. *Philosophical Perspectives* 17(1): 299–332.

Recanati, F. (2003b) 'Analytical Table of Contents for *Literal Meaning*'. Available at: http://jeannicod.ccsd.cnrs.fr/documents/disk0/00/00/03/26/index.html.

Recanati, F. (2004a) *Literal Meaning*. Cambridge: Cambridge University Press. Available at http://www.institutnicod.org

Recanati, F. (2004b) ' "What is Said" and the Semantics/Pragmatics Distinction'. In C. Bianchi (ed.), *The Semantics/Pragmatics Distinction*. CSLI Publications, pp. 45–64.

Rubio-Fernandez, P. (2005) *Pragmatic Processes and Cognitive Mechanisms in Lexical Interpretation: The On-Line Construction of Concepts*. PhD dissertation, University of Cambridge.

Sperber, D. (1994) 'Understanding Verbal Understanding'. In J. Khalfa (ed.), *What is Intelligence?* Cambridge: Cambridge University Press, pp. 179–98.

Sperber, D. and Wilson, D. (1986/95) *Relevance: Communication and Cognition*. Oxford: Blackwell. Second edition 1995.

Sperber, D. and Wilson, D. (2002) 'Pragmatics, Modularity and Mind-reading'. *Mind and Language* 17(1/2): 3–23.

Stanley, J. (2000) 'Context and Logical Form'. *Linguistics and Philosophy* 23: 391–434.

Stanley, J. (2005) 'Semantics in Context'. In G. Preyer and G. Peter (eds), *Contextualism in Philosophy: Knowledge, Meaning and Truth*. Oxford: Oxford University Press, pp. 221–53.

Travis, C. (1989) *The Uses of Sense*. Oxford: Oxford University Press.

Vega-Moreno, R. (2004) 'Metaphor Interpretation and Emergence'. *UCL Working Papers in Linguistics* 16: 297–322.

Vega-Moreno, R. (2005) *Creativity and Convention: The Pragmatics of Everyday Figurative Speech*. PhD dissertation, University of London.

Wharton, T. (2002) 'Paul Grice, Saying and Meaning'. *UCL Working Papers in Linguistics* 14: 207–48.

Wilson, D. (2005) 'New Directions for Research on Pragmatics and Modularity'. *Lingua* 115: 1129–46.

Wilson, D. and Sperber, D. (2002) 'Truthfulness and Relevance'. *Mind* 111: 583–632.

Wilson, D. and Sperber, D. (2004) 'Relevance Theory'. In L. Horn and G. Ward (eds), *Handbook of Pragmatics*. Oxford: Blackwell, pp. 607–32.

Recanati's Reply to Carston

Carston distinguishes three aspects in my pragmatics: (i) my radical Contextualism (i.e., my rejection of Minimalism), (ii) my account of primary pragmatic processes in terms of activation and association (rather than inference), and (iii) my claims about 'availability' as one of the contrasting features distinguishing secondary from primary pragmatic processes. She has no quarrel with (i), but questions both (ii) and (iii). Following her discussion, I will deal with these two aspects in turn.

Carston's main objection to my account of primary pragmatic processes in terms of activation and association is that it makes them too dumb. A similar concern has been voiced by Sperber (*personal communication*) and Breheny (2002: 178–80). There, allegedly, lies the superiority of the RT approach. For relevance theorists, utterance interpretation, whether at the primary or secondary level, is a smart, 'all-things-considered' inferential process that pays due regard to the speaker's intentions and whichever factor may be relevant for getting the speaker right.

Carston provides the following counterexample (see p. 25 example 3) to show that primary pragmatic processes are not dumb. Sarah says 'Neil has broken his leg' in a context in which (i) the addressee (Robyn) knows two people called 'Neil', one of whom is her young son, $Neil_1$, the other a colleague in the department where Robyn works, $Neil_2$, and (ii) Robyn is currently worried about her son, so that her $Neil_1$ concept is more highly activated than her $Neil_2$ concept. Given the blind, mechanical nature of the primary process of reference assignment as I construe it, Carston says that $Neil_1$ ought to be the winning candidate, on my account. But if we add to the context the fact that (iii) Robyn knows that Sarah does not know anything about Robyn's family life, while she does know that John has a colleague, $Neil_2$, who teaches her syntax, then the actual interpretation of the utterance will be quite different from that which (according to Carston) my account predicts: $Neil_2$ will be the winning candidate. As she points out, 'this is explained quite straightforwardly within the RT approach, whose concept of optimal relevance includes as a crucial component of

49

interpretation considerations of the speaker's abilities (which includes her knowledge of the world) and preferences'.

To a large extent I have already addressed this sort of concern in previous work. Thus I made the following reply to Sperber's analogous objection:

> Sometimes the first interpretation that comes to mind (the most accessible one) turns out not to be satisfactory and forces the hearer to backtrack. According to Sperber, the possibility of such garden-path effects shows that success, for a candidate semantic value, cannot be equated with sheer accessibility. This objection is misguided, I think. The most accessible interpretation at some stage s in the interpretation process may well turn out to be unsatisfactory at some later stage s', thereby resulting in a garden-path effect and the need to backtrack. This does not show that interpretational success cannot be cashed out in terms of accessibility. At any given stage, the most accessible interpretation will be the winning one (at that stage). In garden-path utterances we have *two* successive stages to consider. Some interpretation is the most accessible one, hence wins, at s, but that interpretation fails to fit some schema, hence loses, at a later stage s'. In an accessibility-based framework, this means that this interpretation's accessibility at s' is no longer sufficient for it to be the winning candidate (at s'). Another candidate (which was less accessible at s, but turns out to be more accessible at s) takes over, hence the garden path effect. The distinction between successive stages of interpretation, together with the notion of an accessibility shift, is sufficient to account for garden path effects within the accessibility-based framework. (Recanati 1995: 227; 2004: 32)

This is exactly what happens in the 'Neil' example. As Carston herself puts it, $Neil_1$ is initially the most accessible candidate, so it is initially the winning candidate (at stage s). This means that the first interpretation that comes to the mind of the speaker (for whom $Neil_1$ is very salient) is mistaken and has to be corrected at stage s' when the hearer realizes that the speaker cannot be referring to $Neil_1$. Here stage s' corresponds to what we might call *the externalization of the explicature*, i.e. the step when the primary meaning is embedded within the meta-representational schema 'The speaker says that . . . ' At that stage, an accessibility-shift occurs, for the following reason: Sarah (the speaker) is unconnected to $Neil_1$, while she's got some connection to $Neil_2$. As a result of this, $Neil_2$ becomes the most accessible candidate at stage s'. That is so because, owing to the connection between them in the knowledge base of the interpreter, the concept of Sarah and the concept of $Neil_2$ mutually reinforce their activation, so that the winning interpretation at s' (the externalization stage) is *Sarah tells me that $Neil_2$ has broken a leg*. This is very similar to the other sorts of accessibility-shift I have described in the works Carston refers to. To be sure, there is something special about the accessibility-shift in this example, as opposed to e.g. the stolen wallet example (Recanati 1995: 225–6; 2004: 30–1). There are actually two differences, which go a long way towards explaining why Carston believes I should have trouble here. The first difference is that the accessibility-shift occurs when the explicature is externalized, that is, when the interpreter starts paying attention to the fact that the speaker is saying what she is saying. There is something metarepresentational in this sort of case, as opposed to other cases (like the stolen wallet example, where the shift occurs before externalization). The second feature has to do with the role of schemata or scripts in examples like the stolen wallet example. Schemata or scripts are an instance of *general* world-knowledge as opposed to *particular* world knowledge (such as John's knowledge that Sarah does not know $Neil_1$ while she is acquainted with $Neil_2$).

As far as the second feature is concerned, let me say straightaway that I do not believe (and I never claimed) that *only* general world-knowledge can trigger the sort of accessibility shifts I talk about. Particular world-knowledge can play exactly the same role, and the crucial notion of associative 'links' between representations applies to representations at both levels. So, contrary to what Carston seems to assume, I do not have to start looking for relevant schemata or scripts before I can apply the notion of accessibility-shift to the Neil example.

Still, the Neil example involves metarepresenting the speaker as saying something, and ruling out interpretations that conflict with what we know of the speaker and what she might or might not be saying. This sort of example, insofar as it involves metarepresentational capacities on the part of the interpreter, seems to contradict my claim that:

> The interpretation which eventually emerges and incorporates the output of various pragmatic processes result from a blind, mechanical process, involving no reflection on the hearer's part. The dynamics of accessibility does everything and no 'inference' is required. In particular, *there is no need to consider the speaker's beliefs and intentions.* (Recanati 2004: 32; my current emphasis)

Indeed, the last sentence (that I have italicized) goes too far. At some point the explicature is externalized, and the externalization process itself may contribute to shaping the explicature, as in the Neil example. This means that the interpretation process may involve some metarepresentational component even at the primary level. It may, but it need not: that is presumably sufficient to ground the difference between the primary and the secondary level. (The secondary level is *essentially* metarepresentational: to understand conversational implicatures, you have to be sensitive to the fact that the speaker is saying what she is saying). What I have said about the Neil example shows that my 'dumb' processes of activation and association may well mimic the smart, inferential processes posited by Relevance Theory. In view of that fact, it may be that the difference between the two frameworks reduces to a difference in the level of description. Indeed, whatever takes place in the brain has got to be dumb at an appropriately low level of description, however smart the behavior that is thereby made possible. If this is right – if the smartness of an inferential system can be implemented in a dumb associative system, as I claim – then what happens to the contrast I insist on between, on the one hand, secondary processes that are inferential and smart and take place at the 'personal' level, and primary processes that are sub-personal, associative and blind? Am I not making a category mistake when I contrast these processes, since I clearly provide different levels of description for them? That is how I understand Carston's main line of criticism. As Sperber once put it (in conversation), 'everything is subpersonal' at the appropriate level of description. If, therefore, we focus on a single level of description (as we should if we are to understand mechanisms like mutual adjustment), it is unclear that there will remain any substantial contrast between the two types of process. Even secondary processes like the inferential derivation of conversational implicatures will turn out to be underpinned by dumb processes of the subpersonal variety.

In response, let me say first, that there *would* remain a substantial difference between the two types of process even if the personal/subpersonal distinction collapsed, namely the difference between processes that are global and (essentially) metarepresentational, and processes that are neither. Second, I do not think the personal/subpersonal distinction collapses. Yes, in a certain sense, 'everything is subpersonal'. Does this entail that there is no difference betweens subpersonal and personal processes? No. Whatever their subpersonal underpinning personal processes are *consciously available*. That is a feature they have which 'mere' subpersonal processes don't have. In all likelihood, there is something which, at the subpersonal level, is responsible for that feature, but whatever that is, secondary pragmatic processes have that feature (I claim) while primary pragmatic processes don't. This we can express, as in the following table, by saying that although primary and secondary pragmatic processes alike take place subpersonally, still secondary pragmatic processes are distinguished by their 'personal' quality – their conscious availability – to which nothing corresponds on the primary side.

	Primary pragmatic processes	Secondary pragmatic processes
Personal	–	+
Subpersonal	+	+

But Carston objects to my notion that secondary pragmatic processes are consciously available, in contrast to primary pragmatic processes. She points out that the availability issue is quite complex: 'there is a lot more to be said here than simply that secondary processes are (dispositionally) available to consciousness while primary ones are not... The current observations call for some finer-grained distinction within the realm of availability.' I agree: the issue *is* complex, and a series of rather subtle distinctions have to be made. I have made some of them, but more, and finer-grained, distinctions are undoubtedly needed. Among those I have made are the following:

- First, there is the distinction between occurrent and (various types of) dispositional availability. Note that for me, contrary to what Carston suggests, the inferential connection between the explicature and the implicature has to be occurrently grasped, even though this may be done intuitively rather than by going through an explicit inference. In other words the interpreter must only be *capable* of making the inference (dispositional availability), but the fact *that* an inference is involved must be occurrently grasped.
- Second, there is the distinction between accidental and constitutive availability. Owing to that distinction, it's not true that a primary pragmatic process, on my account, is 'predicted to not be available to consciousness': a primary pragmatic process need not, but it may, be available to consciousness. Carston says that the constitutiveness claim is hard to test experimentally, and she may be right, but that is an issue I cannot go into here.
- Third, there is a distinction between two kinds of constitutive availability: that which derives from what I called the 'external duality' displayed by secondary pragmatic processes, and that which derives from the 'internal duality' displayed by some primary pragmatic processes, namely those which are responsible for 'above-threshold' (transparent) metaphors and metonymies (and, possibly, for certain scalar implicatures). That distinction has only been briefly sketched in *Literal Meaning* (Recanati 2004) and much more needs to be said about it, and about 'transparency' more generally.

On the whole, I think I agree with Carston: to support my availability-based account of the primary/secondary distinction in the face of phenomena (such as 'accidental availability' or 'transparency') which blur the distinction, we need to elaborate ways of testing intuitions that are much finer-grained than anything currently available. The need for finer-grained ways of testing intuitions goes well beyond my availability-based account, however – Relevance Theory faces the same problem. The 'transparency' which characterizes certain primary pragmatic processes is such that in some cases, the speaker/hearer is aware that the meaning-ingredient which results from the process is extraneous to the semantic core of the utterance (even though that meaning-ingredient satisfies the Scope Principle). This awareness can be and has been used to argue that the pragmatic processes at issue do not really affect the utterance's intuitive truth-conditions, appearances notwithstanding (see e.g. Stanley 2005b: 230–1, 248–51, and Marti, 2006). In the same spirit, Stanley has argued that in many cases what Relevance Theorists construe as explicatures (because the relevant meaning-ingredients intuitively seem to affect the utterance's truth-conditions) ought to be construed by them as implicatures or at least as external to semantic content because the relevant meaning-ingredients do not satisfy the Scope Principle (Stanley 2005a: 368). Faced with such challenges, the contextualist approach (in whatever clothing) can only be sustained by drawing 'finer-grained distinctions within the realm of availability'.

References

Breheny, R. (2002) 'The Current State of (Radical) Pragmatics in the Cognitive Sciences'. *Mind and Language* 17(1/2): 169–87.

Marti, L. (2006) 'Unarticulated Constituents Revisited'. *Linguistic and Philosophy* 29(2): 135–66.

Recanati, F. (1995) 'The Alleged Priority of Literal Interpretation'. *Cognitive Science* 19(2): 207–32.

Recanati, F. (2004) *Literal Meaning*. Cambridge: Cambridge University Press.

Stanley, J. (2005a) 'Review of Carston, *Thoughts and Utterances*'. *Mind and Language* 20(3): 364–8.

Stanley, J. (2005b) 'Semantics in Context'. In G. Preyer and G. Peter (eds), *Contextualism in Philosophy*. Oxford: Oxford University Press, pp. 221–53.

2

What to Say on What is Said: Some Remarks on Recanati's Views on Semantic Contextuality[1]

Stefano Predelli

In this chapter, I discuss some aspects of François Recanati's views on semantic interpretation, contextuality, and the notion of 'what is said'. I focus on some motives of disagreement between me and Recanati: a few pages devoted to my critical remarks are undoubtedly preferable to the list of issues on which I agree with Recanati – for such a list would indeed be a long one.

I thus refrain from discussing Recanati's complex and important semantic approach in its entirety, and I remain silent not only on many questions playing a central role in Recanati's philosophy, such as the role of inferential processes within pragmatics or the Principle of Availability, but also on a variety of issues more immediately linked with my topic in what follows. Rather, I focus on the extent to which Recanati's considerations about 'what is said' do indeed pose a threat to traditional semantic approaches, such as those in Kaplan (1977) or Lewis (1980), as persistently suggested by both the letter and the spirit of Recanati's writings. More precisely, in section 2.2, I concentrate on Recanati's views on saturation, and on his distinction between traditional, 'automatic' forms of saturation, and allegedly not sufficiently appreciated alternative forms of saturation. In section 2.3, I turn to free enrichment, truth-conditional pragmatics, and underarticulation. As for saturation, I insist that Recanati's views are by no means inconsistent with a traditional, widely accepted approach to indexicality; regarding free enrichment, I argue that the evidence put forth in favour of so-called truth-conditional pragmatics is in fact compatible with customary (fully-articulated) semantic analyses.

2.1 Semantics and representations

The task of a semantic theory is to provide a systematic account of certain presumably semantically interesting properties of particular utterances, in a way that respects competent speakers' intuitions, modulo certain independently motivated considerations regarding the scope and reliability of such intuitions. Suppose, for instance, that our inclinations to regard an utterance of 'I am hungry now' as true on certain occasions are deemed to be worthy of semantic recognition, that is, suppose that they are interpreted as providing an important constraint for the assignment of truth conditions to that utterance; then, what is required of any empirically adequate semantic theory is that it yields a systematic explanation of why utterances of that sentence on those occasions are associated with a semantic profile of that kind. However, not unlike a variety of different theoretical enterprises, theories to this effect are typically developed in terms of structures that do not immediately take as input the items about which they eventually intend to produce a verdict. Although what is ultimately at issue is the explanation of the semantic behaviour of utterances, the theoretical systems developed for this aim are typically centred around theoretical artefacts of a very different type – say, labelled trees, discourse representation structures, or, in the approach considered in this chapter, pairs consisting of particular syntactic constructs and a collection of parameters, hereinafter labelled an index. What is fairly uncontroversially recognized as relevant for the semantic analysis of an utterance is thus the need for a process of representation of that utterance in a theoretically tractable format, that is, as a pair of that kind. What, exactly, is the type of representation required from a particular point of view is, of course, dependent upon the level of semantic regularity one desires to unveil. Since in what follows questions of syntactic structure play at best a marginal role, I shall here rest satisfied with the simple-minded notion that the constructs under evaluation are English sentences, and that the indexes under consideration are relatively unstructured n-tuples, including (but, of course, not limited to) an agent, a time, and a location. It is representations of this kind that are mapped to semantically interesting results by one's favourite semantic theory. Clearly, and uncontroversially, the justification of a particular representational choice is not the immediate responsibility of the semantic apparatus itself, even though the results yielded by that apparatus with respect to given hypotheses of representation may well be taken into account. For instance, that my utterance of:

(1) In 1998 the President was a Democrat

is to be represented in terms of a structure roughly along the lines of

(2) [In 1998 it was the case that][there is a unique President and he is a Democrat]

is a decision that may not be motivated within a semantic theory for, say, definite descriptions, temporal operators, and scope ambiguities. It is, rather, a conclusion justified on the basis of factors such as (negotiably) my intentions, or the fact that our discussion pertained to twentieth-century presidential history, rather than on George W. Bush's political biography. Although the plausibility of choices at this level may well appeal, among other things, to the results that a theory of descriptions or temporal operators may yield when applied to alternative syntactic constructs, the indisputable fact remains that a variety of contextual, and, if you prefer, pragmatic factors must come into play at this stage.

This much is by no means a controversial, innovative conclusion, one potentially dismantling the traditional understanding of the confines separating semantic considerations from other fields of inquiry. The need for what has traditionally been called a process of pre-semantic regimentation has in fact been a recurrent theme in philosophical semantics. For instance, to cite one among many, Quine rather explicitly warned that:

> ... it would be folly to burden a logical theory with quirks of usage that we can straighten ... on the one hand there is theoretical deduction and on the other hand there is the work of paraphrasing ordinary language into the theory. The latter job is the less tidy of the two ... (Quine 1960: 158–9)

As I indicated, the type of items appropriate for the kind of semantic analyses I aim for here involve, together with some sentence, what I called an index. Both items, of course, need to be interestingly related to some aspects of the utterance under analysis. That my utterance is suitably represented by means of, among other things, a clause such as (2) has to do both with the fact that I uttered a certain sentence, and that I had certain intentions when doing so. Similarly, that my utterance of

(3) I am hungry now

is suitably represented by means of, among other things, an index including myself in its agent coordinate has to do with the fact that it was I who spoke, rather than, say, George Bush. Uncontroversially, decisions pertaining to the choice of the index involved in the representation for an utterance may not be justified by appealing solely to the resources internal to the semantic apparatus one intends to employ. It would be folly to demand that a systematic account of the semantic behaviour of, say, (3), be able to list, for any particular utterance, the kind of index appropriate for its interpretation. Rather, 'pre-semantic' considerations, such as information pertaining to the identity of the speaker, need to be provided to the module responsible for semantic evaluation independently from, and logically prior to, that module's structure and content.

In many typical cases, and for a variety of purposes, the choice of the appropriate index is far more straightforward than the identification of the syntactic construct appropriately representing the uttered sentence. Instead of pondering the intricacies of scope relations, co-indexed nouns, or mechanisms of ellipsis, what suffices in this case is the identification of the speaker, or of the spatiotemporal location at which her speaking takes place. Still, although such straightforward methodology may well be appropriate for 'run of the mill', exceedingly simple instances, more controversial issues are inevitably raised by the representational process leading to the identification of the appropriate index, for at least two reasons. Firstly, in a variety of cases involving simple sentences, it may be independently questionable that the speaker and the utterance's spatiotemporal location provides the adequate parameters for the evaluation of indexical expressions. For instance, at least according to some accounts of historical narratives, such as a discourse involving my utterance of

(4) It is 1945; the allied troops are now ready

the co-ordinates appropriate for the interpretation of 'now' and the present tense, that is, the temporal parameter in the appropriate index, appear to be distinct from the time of utterance or inscription (on these issues see, for instance, Corazza *et al.* 2002; Predelli 1998, 2002; and Romdenh-Romluc 2002). Secondly, and even less controversially, important and by no means straightforward issues may be raised by more complex instances, at least according to theories appealing to less immediate forms of indexicality. Take for instance the view that attitude predicates such as 'believes' are indexical expressions, sensitive to (roughly) a contextually salient representational-type, or the widespread approach to comparative adjectives, according to which, say, 'small' is sensitive to a contextually appropriate comparison standard. (For very different versions of the former view, see among many Richard (1990), Crimmins (1992), and Schiffer (1992); regarding comparative adjectives, see for instance Heim and Kratzer (1998)). The identification of such parameters is clearly less immediate and straightforward than processes such as the identification of who is speaking, or of the location at which that utterance has taken place.

My point here is not the defence of indexicalist approaches to 'believes' or 'small', or a discussion of examples such as (4) above. What is important is that, on pretty much anybody's view, these are intelligible proposals, and that, consequently, on pretty much anybody's view, questions pertaining to the identification of the index for the representation of a particular utterance is a non-trivial, possibly controversial process – in particular, one which may well need to be attuned to 'pragmatic' questions such as those pertaining to the salience of certain items under particular conditions. In a nutshell: on an understanding of context as the concrete, multicoloured and complex setting in which an utterance takes place, it is relatively uncontroversial that the relation between a context and an index is a pre-semantic question worthy of attention. Widespread consensus on this conclusion may well be masked by the equally widespread tendency to refer to indexes as 'contexts', as in, say, Kaplan (1977), yet, the formally precise definition that inevitably accompanies the use of that term leaves no doubt as to its structure, or to the role it plays in the semantic account of an utterance.

2.2 Saturation

So much for background. On the basis of certain hypotheses of representation, traditional semantic approaches assign certain semantic results to particular utterances, typically results in terms of intensions, in turn interpretable as conclusions regarding that utterance's truth-conditional content – that is, conclusions pertaining to 'what that utterance says' (more on this later). On the basis of, among other things, such conclusions, one may then proceed to the discussion of that utterance's communicative effects, for instance, by taking into consideration the well known Gricean mechanisms for the calculation of conversational implicatures. When it comes to questions of 'what is said', and to the interface between the process of semantic interpretation and pragmatic regularities, Recanati finds fundamental shortcomings in the traditional approach. According to him:

> ... there is a single notion of what is said, and that is a pragmatic notion: saying, as Grice claimed, is a variety of non-natural meaning, characterized by the role which the conventional meaning of the sentence plays in the hearer's intended recognition of the speaker's communicative intention. (Recanati 2001: 87)

Most importantly for my aim here, it follows for Recanati (2001: 85) that 'there is something deeply wrong with the standard picture' of the interface between semantics and pragmatics, and with the notion of 'what the sentence says'. What, exactly, went wrong?

A few preliminary exegetic caveats are in order at this stage. Recanati does not wish to deny that the notion of conventional meaning does play an important role in the systematic analysis of an utterance. In fact, at least as far as present considerations go, Recanati appears more than willing to grant an understanding of such meaning along the traditional lines of Kaplanesque characters (although he may well wish to question, correctly, the appropriateness of such an understanding for purposes not immediately relevant here). Recanati does also explicitly recognize the distinction between 'what is said' and merely pragmatically imparted information, a distinction he explains in terms of primary vs secondary contextual processes (see, for instance, Recanati 1993 or 2001). What he questions is rather the availability of a notion of semantic content insensitive to pragmatic considerations, a notion he apparently judges to be inherent in what he calls the 'standard picture'.

The analysis of Recanati's view of primary processes, that is, the processes presumably responsible (together with conventional meaning) for the establishment of 'what is said', is thus of immediate relevance. According to Recanati, there are two types of primary processes, saturation and free enrichment. It is on saturation that I focus in this section; some comments on free enrichment are proposed in section 2.3. Some instances of saturation are apparently unexciting: everybody and his dog know that 'I' depends on context. Yet, according to Recanati, questions such as the interpretation of 'I' do not exhaust the import of saturation. In the case of 'I' or 'now':

> ... the contextual assignment is automatic and rule-governed. Thus the reference of 'I' is determined automatically on the basis of a linguistic rule, without taking the speaker's beliefs and intentions into consideration. Recanati (2002: 299)

Allegedly of greater interest, and apparently problematic from the traditional point of view, are other, presumably more pragmatically oriented cases. A recurrent example is provided by instances involving genitive constructions such as 'John's car', which Recanati interprets in terms of an expression containing a free relation-variable, roughly along the lines of 'the car that bears relation R to John'. He writes:

> The free variable must be contextually assigned a particular value; but that value is not determined by a rule and is not a function of a particular aspect of the narrow context. What a given occurrence of the phrase 'John's car' means ultimately depends upon what the speaker who utters it means (Recanati 2001: 85; see also Recanati 2002: 299).

Given the very wide array of possible interpretations for the variable in question (the car John owns, the car he drives, the car in which he bet, the car on which he is sitting ...), the contextual dependence affecting possessive constructions seems to Recanati of a fundamentally different type than that relevant for 'I' or 'now':

> ... the type of context-dependence exhibited by (pure) indexicals has nothing to do with the radical form of context-dependence which affects speaker's meaning. The hallmark of the more radical form of context-dependence is the fact that any piece of contextual information may be relevant. But the context that comes into play in the semantic interpretation of indexicals is ... a very limited context which contains only a few aspects of the pragmatic context: who speaks, when, where, and so forth. (Recanati 2001: 85)

I am perplexed with respect to the relevance of Recanati's distinction. What exactly is at issue? One difference is undeniable, namely that in a variety of typical instances involving the use of 'I' one may easily determine who the referent is: if it is granted that the contextually salient agent is the speaker, establishment of reference is thus automatic, as long as one knows who the speaker is. When it comes to the interpretation of possessive constructions (or comparative adjectives, or attitude predicates, etc.) the process may well be less straightforward: pragmatic questions of salience, and in particular the discussion of the speaker's communicative intentions, undoubtedly play a role. Yet, leaving such practical differences aside, it is equally the case that, as long as one knows what the salient relation (comparison class, representation type, etc.) is, semantic interpretation is as 'automatic' here as for 'I' or 'now'. Representational questions may well be easier, and less dependent upon speaker meaning, for 'I' and 'now' than for other instances (though I would challenge even this weaker claim). But why should such a presumed difference be problematic for the traditional approach to semantics and its interface with pragmatics? Demonstratives provide fairly explicit evidence for my suspicion that the presumed 'radical form of context dependence' assessed by Recanati is by no means incompatible with customary approaches, though widely recognized to occupy a level importantly different from that pertaining to the relationship between indexes and semantic interpretations. For instance, in that epitome of traditionalism that is Kaplan 1977, questions pertaining the profile of a demonstrative within the module responsible for compositional analysis are firmly distinguished from the issue of the structure and role of a demonstration – so much so that Kaplan, one of the most outspoken critics of a Fregean theory of singular terms, sympathetically (even if only temporarily) entertains a Fregean theory of demonstrations. Yet, Recanati writes, when it come to demonstratives, traditionalists:

> ... will add to the narrow context a sequence of 'speaker's intended referents', in such a way that the n-th demonstrative in the sentence will refer to the nth member of the sequence. Formally that is fine, but philosophically it is clear that one is cheating. We pretend that we can manage with a limited, narrow notion of context of the sort we need for handling indexicals, while in fact we can only determine the speaker's intended referent ... by resorting to pragmatic interpretation and relying on the wide context. (Recanati 2001: 86)

I am unsure what the distinction between fine formalism and philosophical cheating amounts to. What is perfectly intelligible is another distinction, namely that between the role played by indexes within traditional semantic structures, and the pragmatically driven appeals to 'wide context' determining the choice of the index within the representation for an utterance. But there is no reason for believing that the latter is incompatible with anyone's accounts of the semantic profile for a demonstrative expression.

2.3   Free enrichment

Recanati's comments on saturation constitute only a preliminary first stab at the traditional conception of the role and structure of semantic theories. Far more spectacular in this respect are Recanati's views on free enrichment, and the associated defence of what he aptly calls 'truth-conditional pragmatics'. Truth-conditional pragmatics is a semantic programme: it is not presented as an interpretation, an embellishment, or an enriched version of customary semantic approaches, but as an alternative picture, grounded on principles incompatible with certain assumptions allegedly characteristic of the traditional view. What seems to go importantly wrong, in particular, is the traditionalists' commitment to the so-called principle of full-articulation, according to which any component of truth-conditional content is to be traced to the semantic contribution of a syntactic item.

It is this polemical aspect of truth-conditional pragmatics that I intend to question in what follows: the evidence customarily presented in favour of underarticulation, so I explain, is perfectly compatible with the traditional picture within mainstream truth-conditional semantics. On a certain understanding of full articulation and truth-conditions, traditional accounts provide fully articulated analyses consistent with the intuitively desired truth-conditions. On a different understanding of these terms, on the other hand, the presence of unarticulated constituents would indeed be problematic from the traditionalist's point of view, but is by no means supported by the evidence typically put forth.

As I indicated in section 2.1, the evidence with which empirically adequate semantic accounts need to be compatible pertains to competent speakers' reactions regarding the semantic profiles of certain utterances. In that section, I focused on issues pertaining to the input appropriate for the application of customary semantic approaches to the objects under analysis: although it is utterances which eventually need to be mapped to appropriate semantic results, what the apparatus of compositional evaluation traditionally takes into consideration are representations of such utterances, for instance in terms of sentence–index pairs. What is important for the purpose of this section is a closer scrutiny of a complementary relationship between semantic theories of the customary kind and the type of evidence constraining their results, namely the relationship holding between the output they produce and our verdicts along truth-conditional lines.

On the basis of the semantic contribution provided (with respect to i) by the expressions occurring in s, and only by them, and taking into consideration the syntactic structure for s, the apparatus of fully-articulated compositional modules eventually assigns objects of a certain type to the sentence-index pair $< s, i >$. These objects are distributions of truth-values across parameters of an appropriate kind, customarily called points of evaluation. Such distributions are typically understood as functions from points to truth-values, that is, as intensions. Modulo the hypotheses of represent-ation of the kind discussed in section one, these results may be applied to utterances: an utterance u is assigned the intension associated with the sentence-index representing it. In a sense, a result of this kind may be inter-preted as a conclusion pertaining to the conditions required for the truth of the utterance under analysis: my utterance of, say, 'this is red', taking place in a context in which o is being demonstrated, turns out to be true at all and only at those points at which o partakes within the extension of 'is red', that is, more colloquially, true as long as o is red. The question that needs to be addressed is whether an apparatus developed along these lines gives the right results of truth-conditions. Consider the following case. My copy of Recanati's *Direct Reference* is wrapped in red paper. I ask: 'Could you pass the red book on the shelf?' intending to direct your attention to it. Holding the book in my hand, I remark, apparently truly: 'This is red'. But take now my conversation with Jones, who insists that books in philosophy inevit-ably appear in garish, tasteless red hues. I disagree, and indicate my copy of Recanati's *Direct Reference* as a counterexample: 'This is not red', I say, truly. An utterance of 'This is red', perfectly appropriate in the first scenario, would now be treated as false. Since my book did not undergo any relevant change in the time separating my utterances, it follows that the alternative utterances of 'This is red' envisioned above have intuitively distinct truth-conditions: one is true, the other false, given one and the same condition of my copy of *Direct Reference*. Can all this be compatible with fully articulated analyses of my utterances?

For Recanati, the answer is unequivocally negative. As far as saturation goes, so it may be pointed out, one and the same object is provided in either case as the semantic interpretation for 'this', namely my copy of *Direct Reference*. Barring unjustified appeals to ambiguity, unmotivated postulations of hidden syntactic distinctions, or non-immediately relevant questions of vagueness, it also appears that one and the same sentence figures in the representation of my utterances. But, so it is concluded, if one and the same syntactic item is being supplied to the process of semantic evaluation, and if the parameters required for the saturation of its components are identical, it follows that the desired conclusion of truth-conditional discrepancy may be obtained only on the basis of semantic enrichment, that is, only on the basis of a process incompatible with the structures presented in traditional accounts.

There is a good deal that is correct in the foregoing reasoning. I have little sympathy for non-independently justified tampering at the syntactic level, that is, for suggestions that the semantic discrepancy between my utterances be explained either in terms of distinct syntactic items, or in terms of hidden, differently saturated expressions. I take it moreover to be the task of an empirically adequate semantic theory that it be compatible with our intuitions of truth-value, in particular, with the notion that the different utterances of 'this is red' considered above differ in truth-value *vis-à-vis* one and the same state of affairs. In this sense of truth-conditions, then, truth-conditional content does indeed involve enrichment: the truth-value of an utterance of 'This is red' depends on contextual factors that are not traceable to the semantic contribution of any of the uttered expressions. It is, incidentally, in this sense of truth-conditional content that the notion of underarticulation had originally been motivated in John Perry's seminal 'Thought Without Representation' (Perry 1986): what motivates the assumption of the location's constituency within the truth-conditional profile of 'It is raining' is, for instance, the appropriateness of behaviour of a certain type, such as your cancelling a tennis match in Palo Alto while refusing to take an umbrella in Murdock. By the same token, if asked to make my utterance of 'That is red' true, performed while pointing at Recanati's book, you may need to inquire about further aspects of the occasion on which I spoke: in one scenario you may have to persuade Blackwell's printers, in the other you merely need to provide an adequate wrapping.

Where I disagree with the defender of the free enrichment programme is in the conclusion typically drawn from such evidence of truth-conditions, together with the aforementioned, eminently plausible assumptions pertaining to the representations of my utterances. It is true that traditional, fully articulated semantic theories, when applied to the sentence-index pair apparently appropriate for either of my utterances, yield one unique result of truth-conditions, in the sense of one unique distribution of truth-values across points of evaluation. But the further tenet that such a result must clash with our intuition that the utterances in question have distinct truth-conditions is grounded on a fallacious equivocation, namely in the confusion between the sense of truth-conditions to which our semantic intuitions are attuned, and the sense in which customary compositional evaluation yields truth-conditionally relevant results.

Take 'is red', a predicate which, on anybody's view, pertains to a certain colour, say, ignoring questions of vagueness, the actual colour of fire trucks. On the basis of this hypothesis, and on the basis of some rather uncontroversial tenets pertaining to simple demonstratives and the subject-predicate form, it follows from straightforward, fully articulated accounts that an utterance of 'this is red' while pointing at my wrapped copy of *Direct Reference* is true if and only if the demonstratum is one among the red objects. So, is my copy of *Direct Reference* red or not? And if it isn't, what would you have to do in order to render my utterance true? The answer, it seems, is highly contextually dependent. For some purposes, say, for the purpose of directing your attention to an object on the shelf, my book qualifies as a red object; on this occasion, the contextually appropriate requirement for being red demands that a sufficiently large portion of its visible surface be the actual colour of fire trucks (or something along these lines). For other purposes, however, my book does not count as one among the red items: given the criteria operative during a discussion on printing techniques, what matters is the hue originally chosen by the printer for the book's cover, regardless of the tint of the paper in which I wrapped it. It is precisely such contextuality that affects our intuitive appraisal of my utterances of 'is red'. An utterance presumably saying that the book is red is pre-theoretically assessed as true in the former scenario because, on that occasion, that item is indeed included among the objects that are red. An utterance conveying that same claim is on the other hand assessed as false in the latter setting because, given the purpose of that exchange, my book does not deserve inclusion within the list of red things.

If this is the case, then the phenomenon of contextual dependence highlighted by the evidence typically presented against full articulation is perfectly consistent with an account of the traditional type. What such an account renders is the (correct) conclusion that utterances of 'This is red' put forth a certain requirement about the demonstratum's relation to redness: truth is obtainable only at points where that object belongs in the appropriate extension. Which way things need to be in order to satisfy a requirement of this kind is a further question, one likely to receive different answers with respect to different interpretations of the situation at hand. A semantic theory's output of 'truth-conditions', in the sense of distributions of truth-values to points of evaluation, may thus be understood in terms of truth-conditions, in the customary sense of the term, only as long as the appropriate contextual effects are taken into consideration. Unsurprisingly, utterances sharing their truth-value at any point may end up being evaluated differently *vis-à-vis* one unique condition of the world, as long as the respective contexts differ in significant manner.

Recanati's (and common sense's) intuitions are, of course, correct: one utterance of 'is red' provides a true description of my book, the other does not. My insistence that such intuitions are compatible with 'unenriched' semantic analyses is not an *ad hoc* attempt at salvaging the old-fashioned apparatus we were taught at school. To the contrary, the distinction between the type of contextuality affecting my utterances of 'This is red' and the kind of context sensitivity most naturally incorporated within a semantic apparatus indirectly indicates that the taxonomy emerging from a customary account is on the right track. (For a discussion of what I called the 'post-compositional' role of context, see Predelli 2004.) The conclusion to be drawn is not that, in my view, semantic analysis ends up being disentangled from conclusions of truth-conditions. The point is rather that semantics' truth-conditional commitments are geared towards what has always been traditional semantics' main aim: a systematic analysis of the conditions for truth, derived from the meaning of the expressions under investigation – that is, in the customary jargon, an analysis of the requirements for 'truth in virtue of meaning', i. e., logical truth. The colour of my book, printed with a white cover, wrapped in red paper, illuminated by fluorescent light, or set in any other imaginative scenario you may wish to concoct, hardly presents an insurmountable difficulty in this respect.

Note

1. Many thanks to the participants at the 13th Inter-University Worshop on Philosophy and Cognitive Science, Granada, Spain, 25–28 February 2003, and in particular to François Recanati, for their comments and feedback. I have only recently discovered that the title of the present paper overlaps with Isidora Stojanovic's title for her Stojanovic 2003; my apologies for this unintentional duplication

References

Corazza, E., W. Fish, and J. Gorvett (2002) 'Who Is I?'. *Philosophical Studies* 107: 1–21.

Crimmins, M. (1992) *Talk About Beliefs*. Cambridge, MA: The MIT Press.

Heim, I. and A. Kratzer (1998) *Semantics in Generative Grammar*. Oxford: Blackwell.

Kaplan, D. (1977) 'Demonstratives'. In J. Almog, J. Perry, and H. Wettstein (eds), (1989), *Themes from Kaplan*. Oxford: Oxford University Press.

Lewis, D. (1980) 'Index, Context, and Content'. In S. Kanger and S. Öhman (eds) (1981), *Philosophy and Grammar*. Dordrecht: Reidel. Reprinted in D. Lewis (1998), *Papers in Philosophical Logic*. Cambridge: Cambridge University Press.

Perry, J. (1986) 'Thought Without Representation'. *Proceedings of the Aristotelian Society*, suppl. 60: 137–52.

Predelli, S. (1998) 'Utterance, Interpretation, and the Logic of Indexicals'. *Mind and Language* 13(3): 400–14.

Predelli, S. (2002) 'Intentions, Indexicals and Communication'. *Analysis* 62: 310–16.

Predelli, S. (2004) 'The Lean Mean Semantic Machine'. In C. Bianchi (ed.) (2004), *The Semantics/Pragmatics Distinction*. CSLI Publications, pp. 13–26.

Quine, W.V.O. (1960) *Word and Object*. Cambridge, MA: MIT Press.

Recanati, F. (2001) 'What is Said'. *Synthese* 128: 75–91.

Recanati, F. (1993) *Direct Reference: From Language to Thought*. Oxford: Blackwell.

Recanati, F. (2002) 'Unarticulated Constituents'. *Linguistics and Philosophy* 25: 299–345.

Romdenh-Romluc, K. (2002) 'Now the French Are Invading England!' *Analysis* 62: 34–41.

Richard, M. (1990) *Propositional Attitudes: An Essay on Thoughts and How We Ascribe Them*. Cambridge: Cambridge University Press.

Schiffer, S. (1992) 'Belief Ascription'. *The Journal of Philosophy* 89: 499–521.

Stojanovic, I. (2003) 'What to Say on What Is Said'. In Blackburn *et al.* (eds), *Modeling and Using Context: 4th Int. and Interdisciplinary Conference*, Context 2003. Berlin: Springer-Verlag.

Recanati's Reply to Predelli

Stefano Predelli objects to my admittedly polemical remarks on 'traditional semantic approaches' and their ways of handling (or ignoring) context-sensitivity. Those approaches, he argues, can easily accommodate the phenomena I adduce against them.

First, Predelli points out that there is an important distinction between pre-semantic processes such as disambiguation or the determination of the relevant contextual index, and the semantic mechanism which, given a disambiguated sentence and a contextual index, determines the truth-conditions of the sentence with respect to that index. The former, but not the latter, may be fully pragmatic and involve the hearer's holistic appraisal of the speaker's meaning. Once such a distinction is made, the existence of semantically underdeterminate expressions whose semantic value depends upon what the speaker means can no longer be considered as raising a problem for traditional approaches. What is automatic and independent of speaker's meaning, for those theories, is only the semantic determination of truth-conditional content. The pre-semantic share of the work can be as pragmatic and messy as you please. So Predelli rejects my claim that the form of saturation triggered by semantically underdeterminate expressions is problematic from the traditional point of view.

With free enrichment, things are subtler. Here Predelli admits that there is a *prima facie* problem for traditional accounts: the truth-value of an utterance of, say, 'this is red' depends on contextual factors that are not traceable to the semantic contribution of any of the uttered expressions. But, he suggests, nothing prevents a traditional theorist from attempting to account for free enrichment, by adding to the theory a new layer of analysis: the 'post-compositional' layer. In this way progress can be made within the traditional framework, just as progress was made when the distinction between extension and intension, or that between content and character, was originally introduced.

In response, let me say, first, that I do not think there is any substantial disagreement between Predelli and me, as far as I can understand. With respect to free enrichment, his account is not detailed enough for me to say whether I can accept it or not, but I have no doubt that some story can be told, by adding a new layer of analysis. The only clear point of disagreement concerns the history of ideas. Am I fair, or I am unfair, to the semantic tradition – the tradition that began with Frege and took a new start with Montague – when I criticize it in the way I do? Predelli says I am unfair, and I want to defend myself.

I take the semantic tradition to be deeply committed to a (tacit) philosophical view that I call 'Literalism'; it is that view which I criticize. To say that the tradition is committed (by default, as it were) to a mistaken view is not to say that it is worthless, however; on the contrary, I think the semantic tradition has been tremendously (and unexpectedly) successful in dealing with natural language in the last thirty years. But to the extent that it has been successful, it has had to give up some of the basic literalist assumptions which it started by presupposing. This evolution away from Literalism and towards Contextualism was gradual and is still unfinished (I claim).

According to me, four stages can be discerned in the historical development of the semantic tradition. The first two or three stages undoubtedly belong to the past, and Predelli does not want to defend the views that were then held. The first of these views is Proto-Literalism, according to which context-sensitivity is a defect of a natural language, to be ignored in theorizing about language. (This view was held at a time when logicians and formally minded philosophers were not, or only marginally, interested in natural language.) Then came Eternalism, which holds that indexicality is a practical convenience rather than an essential feature of natural language. According to Eternalism, indexicality is not a defect – we could hardly communicate if natural language did not have that feature – but it is 'in principle' eliminable so that we can ignore it in theorizing about language.

Next came Conventionalism. This view acknowledges the extent (and ineliminability) of context-sensitivity, but it draws a sharp contrast between the content of a sentence (with respect to context) and the content of the speech act performed by uttering that sentence. The content of the speech act depends upon the multicoloured context in all its richness and it can only be determined on a pragmatic basis, by appealing to factors such as mutual beliefs, speaker's intentions, etc. Things are different with regard to the content of the sentence. It is the linguistic conventions, rather than the speaker's intentions (or the hearer's beliefs regarding the speaker's intentions), which fix the content of the sentence with respect to context. Thus what determines the content of an indexical expression is not what is in the head of the language users, but a linguistic rule – the rule that constitutes the conventional meaning of that expression.

Predelli argues that the determination of the index with respect to which an indexical sentence is interpreted is pre-semantic, hence it may involve pragmatic factors such as the speaker's intentions without threatening the claim that the meaning of the sentence automatically fixes its content (with respect to an appropriate index). But this liberal stance is not acceptable from a Conventionalist point of view. Conventionalism rests on the idea that the truth-conditions of a disambiguated sentence are fixed by its linguistic meaning independent of speaker's meaning. This determination is relative to some index, whose determination is indeed pre-semantic, but *the determination of the index cannot itself depend upon what the speaker means on pain of falsifying the central conventionalist assumption.* So when Predelli says that the traditional framework is compatible with the facts of semantic underdetemination, what he really means is that the traditional framework is not committed to Conventionalism (understood as I do).

In a sense, I agree: Like Proto-Literalism and Eternalism, Conventionalism was but one step in the development of the semantic tradition. Conventionalism replaced Eternalism when the Eternalization Principle was abandoned. Contrary to Eternalism, Conventionalism still has advocates today; but it is no longer the dominant position. It is widely acknowledged that the speaker's meaning has a role to play in fixing the truth-conditions of indexical sentences. On this, Predelli and I agree. We agree that semantics must take input from pragmatics, not only as far as disambiguation is concerned, but also when it comes to determining the relevant 'index'. The index cannot be read off the context: it must be pragmatically determined.

So there has been a misunderstanding. I never said that what Perry calls 'intentional indexicals' (as opposed to 'automatic indexicals') raise a problem for current views, such as Predelli's. The traditional framework constantly evolves, and it seems to me that most reasonable semanticists nowadays give up Conventionalism and accept that semantics needs an input from pragmatics even if we set disambiguation aside. But Conventionalism has been replaced by a new way of drawing the distinction between the content of the sentence and the content of the speech act. That new view, which dominates the scene today, is Minimalism. In the minimalist framework, the semantic content of the utterance departs only minimally from the linguistic meaning of the sentence type (hence the name 'Minimalism'); it departs from it only when the meaning of the sentence itself requires that some contextual value be assigned to a context-sensitive word or morpheme, or to a free variable in logical form. Now I think Minimalism must be given up in order to account for free enrichment, just as Conventionalism had to be given up to account for semantic underdetermination.

My claim, then, is this: the semantic tradition has its roots in the study of artificial languages, and it is historically committed to Literalism. Literalism, in general, minimizes context-sensitivity, which is a characteristic feature of natural language. Still, the semantic tradition has managed to deal with natural language, and has achieved considerable success in that endeavour. Inevitably, in the process, the literalist prejudice had to be given up. But the departure from Literalism has been slow and progressive. It is only recently that Conventionalism has been given up (some theorists still hold that sort of view) and I hold that some work has still to be done in this area – the *aggiornamento* is not completed yet: we still have to account for free enrichment and similar matters. Predelli seems to agree; he himself attempts to show what such an account might look like.

So what is the difference between Predelli and me? I do not deny that the semantic tradition can evolve and adapt itself to the facts of natural language. It has done so in the past, and it continues to do so today. So I am optimistic. On the other hand, as a philosopher I point out that this tradition has consistently tried to minimize context-sensitivity by adhering to whichever version of Literalism seemed defensible at the time, given the evidence then available. What the historical development of Literalism reveals is a gradual weakening of Literalism: from Proto-Literalism to Eternalism to Conventionalism to Minimalism. The question that naturally arises is: How far can we go in this direction? Where will this tendency ultimately lead us? And the obvious answer (for me) is: to Contextualism. I find nothing in Predelli's argument that challenges this conclusion.

3
Externalism, Deference and Availability[1]

María J. Frápolli

3.1 Introduction

In his dispute with Minimalism, Recanati uses the Availability Principle as the main weapon on his side, being thus the touchstone on which his truth-conditional pragmatics (TCP) is built. The speakers might not be aware of the minimalist proposition, Recanati argues, which often needs to be abstracted from the pragmatically modified information that speaker and hearer exchange. Moreover, the result of the primary pragmatic processes accepted by Minimalism, i.e., saturation (Recanati 1993: 263) and sense selection (Recanati 1995: 210), might not produce the suitable proposition. In several places, Recanati argues for a stronger thesis: that without adding unarticulated constituents, no proposition can be expressed. According to Contextualism, it cannot be a level of meaning that is truth-evaluable and not affected by top-down processes (Recanati 1993: 254 n. 13, 260; 2002f: 6). The disagreement between minimalists and maximalists or contextualists has to do with how much information is included in the proposition, in what is said, in contrast to what is implicated. Both minimalists and maximalists accept contextual processes in the determination of content, being the difference that minimalists consider that the contribution of the context to what is said is made only through bottom-up processes, in contrast to the top-down ones acknowledged by maximalists. So, it might occur that the 'minimalist proposition' is not even a complete truth-bearer (Recanati 1993: 258).

In *Literal Meaning* (2004) Recanati offers a more sophisticated classification of theories according to the weight given to context in the determination of content. He distinguishes five positions, from Literalism to Contextualism, and seems to endorse the fifth, Contextualism. In many places in his work he argues that there is no such thing as what a sentence 'says', not just in (2003). In particular, he defends that semantic interpretation does not result in complete propositions (2001: 85), and thus that the very notion of minimal proposition is devoid of sense.

As I see it, the main disagreement between Minimalism and Recanati's view concerns the role of unarticulated constituents required to obtain a proposition, and in fact to obtain the proposition intended by the speaker. Which these unarticulated constituents are in each case depends on the context of the utterance and, according to Recanati, the speaker has the last word about what she has said by it. This is the import of Recanati's Availability Principle.

The Availability Principle establishes a relation between the speaker and an entity, what is said, which is the content of the utterance produced by the speaker in the particular context. And what the principle says is that the speaker is aware of the proposition expressed. She knows what she has said and consciously distinguishes it from what has been pragmatically conveyed as the result of secondary pragmatic processes by her saying it.

On the one hand, Recanati subscribes the main features of the Gricean tradition in philosophy of language (although Grice, as Recanati acknowledges, was a minimalist). On the other hand, following some widely accepted implications of a theory of direct reference for singular terms such as his, Recanati also endorses the general background that has been the natural setting of direct reference theories, i.e, Externalism, and offers a sophisticated version of a two-component view of content which, he contends, makes his Externalism compatible with his eclectic (in part Fregean and in part Russellian) view of semantics.

In what follows I would like to discuss the alleged compatibility between a fully-fledged Availability Principle, with a philosophically interesting version of Externalism. As I see it now, to guarantee this compatibility, further thinking on the notions of 'availability', 'what is said' and 'externalist proposition' is called for.

The tension I see between propositional awareness and Externalism shows itself dramatically in deferential beliefs and for this reason I will discuss how, according to Recanati, the deferential operator works and I will pay some attention to his account of the externalist topic of imperfect mastery.

The chapter is structured as follows. First, I will deal with the different formulations of the Availability Principle that appear in Recanati's work. Then, I will try to determine what is this entity of which speakers are aware, what exactly is 'what is said'. Thereafter, I will analyse Recanati's Externalism and determine whether his two-component view is an acceptable way out for the compatibility problem. And finally, I will apply the results to his treatement of deference and incomplete mastery.

3.2 The Availability Principle

Recanati formulates his Availability Principle from different perspectives all throughout his work. Here I present three of them, two formulations from (1993), another from (2001).[2]

In (1993) there is a quite weak formulation, as follows:

> Availability Principle: In deciding whether a pragmatically determined aspect of utterance meaning is part of what is said, that is, in making a decision concerning what is said, we should always try to preserve our pre-theoretic intuitions on the matter. (1993: 248)

and a bit further on, one reads: 'What is said and what is implicated thus remain distinct, and are consciously available as distinct' (loc. cit.). The first version seems to be only a regulative principle, a sort of methodological recommendation. But under the name of 'Availability Principle' or 'Availability Hypothesis' Recanati sometimes defends the second formulation intended as an empirical hypothesis.

In (2001: 80) he expresses it as follows:

> Hence my 'Availability Principle', according to which 'what is said' must be analysed in conformity to the intuitions shared by those who fully understand the utterance – typically the speaker and the hearer, in a normal conversational setting

The context in which the Availability Principle is put at work is the debate between semantic Minimalism and pragmatic Maximalism. The central point of this debate is whether 'what is said' by an utterance can be determined only by reference to the linguistic meaning of the sentence type and saturation of linguistically given slots or whether there is something else. I will not reproduce the arguments and counterarguments on both sides of the dispute. I will only mention those theses of Recanati's that are relevant for the aim of this chapter.

Recanati's point is the following: the linguistic meaning of the sentence type underdetermines what is said, which must serve as input to the secondary pragmatic processes. This is expressed in (2001: 87) as: 'There is no such thing as "what the sentence says" [. . .]. There is a single notion of what is said, and that is a pragmatic notion.' In order to apply these secondary processes, something has to be said that might be more complex than what is strictly derived from linguistic meaning plus saturation and sense selection. There are other processes at work, which are also primary (they do not require that something has been said) but that are not mandatory, as saturation is. Typically there are processes of free enrichment that, in Recanati's view, are optional and do not depend on any syntactic constituent of the sentence. These are what Recanati calls 'unarticulated constituents'. Recanati also accepts transfer and loosening as primary pragmatic processes, but in what follows I will focus on free enrichment. Then, what is said, i.e., the input from which speakers derive implicatures through secondary pragmatic processes, includes the result of the application of several primary pragmatic processes, among which saturation is just one. There are three main arguments that Recanati (1993: 269–74) uses for his point, and against Minimalism. One of them, about which I will say only a couple of words at the end of the chapter, is that the enriched proposition, which he identifies with 'what is said', falls under the scope of logical operators. A second argument is that it may be that saturation is not enough to complete linguistic meaning so that the resulting entity is not evaluable for truth or falsity (2002f: 6). The third is that, in a Gricean setting, ' "saying" is a variety of non-natural meaning' (2001: 80), and that, as a matter of intention-recognition, it has to be consciously available (loc. cit.). The minimalist proposition, if there is something like that, is not directly accessible for the subject, and it cannot be what the speaker says.

Availability being a relational principle that connects the speaker to what is said, and what is said being the touchstone that divides the two conflicting views, it would be illuminating to have a look at the kind of entity that Recanati identifies with 'what is said'. In Recanati's words: 'What is said in the maximalist sense corresponds to the intuitive truth-conditions of the utterance, that is, to the content of the statement as the participants in the conversation themselves would gloss it' (2001: 80). It is the proposition expressed (2001: 75), the explicit content of the utterance (2001: 79). The same account is offered in Recanati (1993). A proposition, Recanati says there, is *'the truth condition of the utterance as it is presented by the utterance itself'* (1993: 33, his italics).

Although Recanati expresses his adherence to a Kaplanian view of meaning and, in fact, his *Oratio Obliqua* is the development of a Kaplanian thesis, he does not identify the entity of which the speaker is aware with the character of the expression uttered. If what is said is not character, it might be content. And it is, but not Kaplanian or semantic content. What is said is a pragmatic notion, affected by all these primary pragmatic processes that distinguish Recanati's Truth Conditional Pragmatics (TCP) from Minimalism. This pragmatic what is said is part of the speaker's meaning (2001: 87) and so far is a perfect mate for an Availability Principle to have.

Meaning underdetermines what is said, and for this reason Recanati is contextualist in a very strong manner: even rejecting the Principle of Expressibility (2002e), linguistic meaning together with primary pragmatic processes (mandatory and not-mandatory) conform what is said, which is identical to the expressed proposition.

3.3 Externalism

Contextualism and Externalism make different points. Contextualism, for instance, is opposed to Literalism and Indexicalism and is a view about how much influence the context of the utterance has in the proposition expressed. Externalism is in opposition to Internalism and both are views about the nature of concepts and meanings. Availability plays an essential role in the dispute that Recanati maintains with Indexicalism. The dispute is thus between all sorts of Minimalism and TCP. Nevertheless, once put to work, it has a place in other controversies and may have unwanted consequences for the overall picture. The Availability Principle might lead us to think that Recanati rejects the externalist principle that speakers might not be aware of the content of some of their mental states. However, discussing Deferentialism (2000: 275) he explicitly affirms the opposite. If speakers 'do not, in general, "know" the propositional contents of the representations which they accept' (loc. cit.), in which sense, one might ask, is what is said by these representations available to them?

The lesson of Externalism is that a speaker does not need to know what she says by her utterances in order to actually say it. Putnam taught us that there exists in natural languages what he called a Division of Linguistic Labor, which transfers to experts the responsibility for the content of words. Burge and Sperber have followed the same path, and both have dealt with the phenomenon of deferential belief, which I will touch upon in the next section.

Recanati deals extensively with Externalism in (1993). His version of it is highly sophisticated. In what follows I will present its basic claims and comment on them. Recanati accepts a two-component picture of Externalism and answers some well-known objections against it, particularly those raised by Evans and McDowell. Why a two-component picture? Well, the reason is that it is an answer to the difficulties of a Russellian account of propositions in explaining our mental life and our behaviour. An externalist view on propositions takes them 'out of the head' and implies that the speakers might not be aware of the content of their beliefs, utterances etc. A two-component view promises the best of both worlds: it allows for an externalist proposition, public and shareable, and at the same time maintains the advantages of a more Fregean view in which senses make the suitable bridge between the proposition and what the speaker knows. This is the rationale behind the several versions of a two-component view that have come to the fore in the last decades of the twentieth century. Recanati's is one of them, although not the most typical kind. Let's have a look at the features that make it a markedly different proposal. He grants critics of the two-component picture that it is hardly consistent. If contents are always relational, Cartesian contents cannot exist. Contents are environment-dependent entities, so Externalism implies and Recanati accepts, and narrow contents should be environment-independent. Thus, apparently, Externalism precludes the existence of such solipsistic entities. Nevertheless, environment independence can be understood in two different ways. I will come back to this distinction in a while.

One of the morals of Putnam's Twin Earth story is that unless the speaker's environment contains samples of H_2O, she cannot posses the concept WATER.

A concept, and thus the content of one's mental states, is dependent on the environment in this causal sense. Our interaction with samples of water prompts our WATER concept. Inside this paradigm, Cartesian contents make no sense. If we were brains in a vat, we would not possess genuine concepts, and the idea that even in this situation we might have thoughts which would be indistinguishable from our actual thoughts contradicts the main externalist thesis. The alleged brain-in-a-vat thoughts have what some externalists would consider as narrow content. And this kind of 'content', Recanati argues, is incompatible with Externalism. Interpreting what is in the head as solipsistic, Cartesian concepts render Putnam's thought-experiment inconsistent. Agreement with the externalist view of concepts forces the rejection of narrow contents thus explained. Nevertheless, there is a weaker way of understanding narrow contents and their independence from the environment. We acquire our concept WATER in virtue of our having an experience of H_2O, or deferring our use to those who have experience of it. In this sense, no WATER concept can exist without contacts with water. Once we have the concept, though, we can use it to have water thoughts in front of water, in front of XYZ, or in front of a cleverly designed hologram. Particular water thoughts are independent of the actual environment in which they are produced. In this weak sense, they are context-independent. And this picture is wholly compatible with Externalism. Recanati's two-component view amounts to saying this: that contents are context-dependent in their origin. But once the normal relations with the surroundings are fixed, contents remain constant in cases of correct representation, of misrepresentation and in the empty case. And Recanati continues:

> Corresponding to two notions of narrow content, there are two versions of the two-component picture. One version uses the strong, individualistic notion of narrow content, and is inconsistent with Externalism. Another – that which I am defending – uses the weak notion and is consistent with Externalism. One may thus take content to be inherently relational, in accordance with Externalism, while maintaining that there are two types of content, a type of content which does, and one which does not, depend upon the *actual* environment of the thought episode. (1993: 217)

Recanati's point is that this version of a two-component view of content is consistent with Externalism. And it is. But only because it *is* Externalism, the classical one-component version. If I am right, we do not have here a two-component view and so we do not have here a way out for the problems that Externalism poses for the philosophy of language, mind and action. In Putnam's story, an earthling who travelled to Twin Earth would have WATER thoughts in front of the stuff whose chemical composition was XYZ. This would be a case of misrepresentation. But earthian concepts, those that have been introduced in front of earthian stuffs in acts of baptism, become attached to these stuffs and refer to them in any circumstance. Only contents of indexical expressions depend on the actual environment. And natural kind terms do not work as indexicals in this sense, although it has been sometimes so interpreted. The myth that externalists use to explain the dependence on the environment possessed by natural kind terms is the initial baptism. Terms were introduced in front of a particular sample of a particular stuff, and the term then will apply to any sample that bears the relation 'the same stuff as' with the original stuff. Thus, natural kind terms depend for their content on the normal environment and not on the actual one. In this sense, natural kind terms, like 'water', are rigid not indexical, although Putnam himself says that they have an indexical component, the indexical component is bearing a 'certain similarity relation to the water *around here*' (Putnam 1973: 131).

For this reason I cannot see in which useful sense Recanati's Externalism presents a two-component picture. Only indexicals are dependent on the actual environment, other terms are dependent on the normal one. Concepts are always relational, and their contents always depend on how the world, independently of the mind, is. My daughter and I both have the concept WATER, as any other normal human being on Earth. And psychology does not need to postulate special contents, apart from the usual, relational concepts, in order to establish species-wide laws. The Burgean patient who thinks that she has arthritis in her thigh was using the concept ARTHRITIS, and she had genuine ARTHRITIS thoughts, false thoughts in this case, although she was not in front of a case of arthritis. There is no difference here between Burge's one component picture and Recanati's two-component one.

Interpreted weakly, this version of the two-component picture makes perfect sense, although Putnam's version amounts to much more, and Recanati is well aware of it. My Doppelgänger in Twin Earth and I use the same word 'water' to refer to some stuff present in both worlds. Or so it seems. For there is no single stuff which is responsible for the concepts that my Doppelgänger and I express by the word 'water'. Appearances notwithstanding, there is nothing in common between my concept of the liquid I drink when I am thirsty, and the concept my Doppelgänger resorts to in similar circumstances. Nevertheless, Recanati insists that it might be useful to possess a notion of content that accounts for the intuitive similarities between my mental state when I think that I am thirsty and my Doppelgänger's thinking (apparently) the same thing. This is what Recanati calls second-order narrow content. Arguments for the usefulness of narrow content in the weak sense can be automatically addressed for the utility of second order narrow contents, as Recanati sees it. And to support both, weak narrow contents and second order narrow contents, Recanati appeals to what he dubs the 'Cartesian intuition' (1993: 213).

Let's have a look at this 'Cartesian intuition'. It apparently applies smoothly to his two-component view, so we need to explain what cases of misrepresentation have in common with the felicitous cases, i.e., why the subjective experience I have when I see an apple can be qualitatively identical to the experience I have when I see a pear that I mistakenly take for an apple even when hallucinating. And its extension to cover second-order narrow contents is designed to explain how my Doppelgänger and I can have indistinguishable subjective experiences, she in front of XYZ and I in front of H_2O. Although Recanati considers that the role of the Cartesian intuition is the same with respect to these two phenomena, there are significant features that make them relevantly different from each other. In the first case, the case of misrepresentation, the explanation of why we can have the same kind of experience in front of an apple and in front of a badly illuminated pear is just that in both situations we have genuine APPLE thoughts, because we possess the concept APPLE in our repertoire of concepts. When we misrepresent a pear as an apple we put at work our APPLE concept, not a diluted version of it and here there is no need to resort to Descartes' teachings, this 'Cartesian intuition' is an externalist anti-Cartesian position.

To extend, on the other hand, the Cartesian intuition to second-order narrow contents has, as I see it, the air of *petitio principii*. It is as question-begging as the third argument for the two-component picture that Recanati criticizes in (1993: 200). That my Doppelgänger and I have the same subjective experiences is a postulate of Putnam's story, not a fact that can be accounted for. And I agree with Recanati that, as Recanati expounds it, Putnam's story is incoherent. The incoherence lies in the use of solipsistic concepts together with relational ones. Then, the issue now is whether there might be two-component versions of Externalism that would escape from this inconsistent *fatum*. Recanati holds that there are possible ways out and his holistic Externalism is one of them. Recanati's holistic Externalism rests on the assumption that there is a horizontal dimension of some concept 'WATER' that my Doppelgänger and I share. Concepts are related to each other and thus even if the external links of some of them are severed, the whole is still grounded provided there remain some concepts with their normal connections to the external world. This holism explains content using conceptual roles. Although my Doppelgänger's WATER* is not related to water, and were we to sever its connections to XYZ it would become empty, it might borrow some content from its relations to other concepts which have not been ungrounded. And so, considering the conceptual role, one might say that my Doppelgänger and I have something in common. As regards holist Externalism, I have a more pessimistic view, which might be expressed in a nutshell as follows: if the discrepancy between my Doppelgänger and me is only punctual, classical Externalism has an answer. This is an instance of a word referring to two different natural kinds, or if you prefer of two homonymous words. This does not seem to be the case of Twin Earth. There the discrepancy between my Doppelgänger and me is much wider and therefore the net will hardly work. If the only difference between my Doppelgänger and me is the meaning of our words 'water', we can do without holism (although sharing a stereotype does not prevent us from equivocation). But if the divergence is bigger than that, the holistic net that Recanati proposes is of no use either. And the divergence is bigger, as Putnam makes clear. Besides natural kind terms, Putnam also adds to the list names of sensible qualities, and Kripke mentions adjectives of other kinds (Putnam *loc. cit.* and Kripke 1980). Other words can be defined through necessary and sufficient conditions, of course, but a relevant number of words are essentially related to *this world*.

My uneasiness with this argument lies in the fact that, as Putnam's story goes, most of my concepts refer to Earth, and most of my Doppelgänger's concepts refer to Twin Earth. In order to find something in common between my Doppelgänger and me it does not suffice to unground the concept expressed by the homonym word 'water' in each case, but rather it is necessary to unground most of our concepts – at least, with our natural kind concepts, and with our empirical concepts, which depend on the actual structure of our world. I do not think that in Putnam's experiment 'a single concept is logically ungrounded' as Recanati says in (1993: 225). Rather, Putnam's point is that subjective experiences might be exactly the same even if the surroundings were essentially diverse. And this cannot be accounted for by appealing to a sort of conceptual network, for this network will be ungrounded itself. A holistic account of meaning rests on the meanings of words where these meanings are related to the outer world through some kind of ostensive definition. This is the way in which words acquire content according to Externalism, which is a science-oriented, and so naturalistic, account of meaning. If the only difference between my Doppelgänger and me is reduced to a single concept, then the situation is the same as the cases of jadeite and nephrite, an isolated point of misunderstanding that can easily pass unnoticed. Nevertheless, if Putnam's story has a philosophically interesting point, it must be the possibility of having a Doppelgänger qualitatively indistinghishable from me in a surrounding superficially identical to Earth, although completely disparate in deep structure. In this situation my Doppelgänger and I cannot communicate even though we speak languages that are formally identical. And here the Cartesian intuition does not need to be accommodated because it is inconsistent.

Let us return to Recanati's picture. He supports Externalism and a two-component theory of content, understanding 'narrow content' in a weak sense. He also accepts second-order narrow contents, which manage to avoid being schematic by borrowing some content from their relations to genuine contents. All the three types have in common that they are not solipsistic and that somehow they all are relational. From their respective definitions they seem to be different; in one case content depends on the actual environment, in the second case on the normal environment and in the third case on its relations to other contents that manage to be grounded by reference to external stuffs. I have argued that the first two kinds are the same and that the third is either a case in which two people use a homonym word without noticing it or else a case of complete equivocation. Then, what Recanati presents in (1993) is the classical one-component Externalism, if it has to be consistent. The relevance of this point is that if we do not have here a two-component view of content (or two kinds of content), then one single entity has to carry the burden of being the externalist proposition, the externalist 'what is said' (epistemologically incomplete, as Recanati defends against Sperber in (2000: 274)), and the entity of which speakers are aware, according to the Availability Principle.

3.4 Deferential beliefs and imperfect mastery

One topic where one needs to take into account semantics and epistemology together is deferential belief. Deferential beliefs, as plain beliefs, have content, although these contents incorporate a constituent that is unknown to the believer. An example of conscious deference is Recanati's (1),

(1) the teacher says that Cicero's prose is full of 'synecdoches' used by a student who does not know what synechdoche is.

A related topic is imperfect mastery. Believers often entertain thoughts that they have not fully mastered. Externalism foregrounded the issue of imperfect mastery by adhering to the principle of Division of Linguistic Labor (see Putnam 1973: 125). We all think with concepts whose content we do not need to know. It is up to the experts to decide whether our GOLD concept only applies to samples with the atomic number 79.

There might arguably be two separate issues with their own peculiarities here. The first might be how to deal with conscious deferential uses of words and the second how to explain imperfect mastery of concepts. The first kind of phenomenon is particularly common in learning, but the second, other lesson of Externalism, is much more widespread. In fact, according to Externalism, we do not need to master any of our concepts in order for us to have genuine attitudes involving them. This would require particularly unlikely circumstances, but it strictly follows from Externalism. Nevertheless, Recanati identifies them in (2000: 262). The phenomena are not exactly similar, as he recognizes in his answer to Woodfield, but the difference between them is syntactic, not semantic: in cases of imperfect mastery the deferential operator can work as an unarticulated constituent (2000: 282). The identification of imperfect mastery with deferential use of concepts has deep philosophical consequences, because, according to Externalism, imperfect mastery occurs everywhere in our use of language. This being so, a deferential operator works in many of our beliefs. And Recanati explicitly recognizes this in (2000: 262).

Recanati credits Sperber for pioneering serious work on in quasi-belief. In Recanati (2000: 261 ff.) there is an extensive treatment of deferentialism as a phenomenon in which a context-shift is involved. All throughout the book Recanati has explicitly endorsed Kaplan's view that there is no context-shift operator in natural languages. According to the view described in (2000), literally speaking it is true that there is no context-shift operator, although the stress here is on 'operator'. Natural languages are fraught with context-shifts, but they are not governed by any particular operator (not even quotation marks, which also appear in cases of cumulative mention). A context-shift is most of the time understood as one in which a word, which already possesses a character, acquires a content that depends not on the context of the utterance, but on the context to which we have shifted, which can be different. There are other cases though, as Recanati explains. A translinguistic context-shift is present when we use phrases with a deviant character. A change occurs from one language to another, paradigmatically an idiolect, and there are the 'rules' of the latter that account for the abnormal character. In translinguistic context-shifts the deferential operator guarantees grammaticality. This is the way Recanati deals with utterances that contain words apparently devoid of meaning.

The core of the dispute between Recanati and Sperber on deferential beliefs can be illustrated by the following example. In a case such as (1) Recanati detects three levels: the metarepresentation itself:

(1) the teacher says that Cicero's prose is full of 'synecdoches'

the normal object-belief:

(2) Cicero's prose is full of synecdoches

and the deferential object-belief,

(3) Cicero's prose is full of 'synecdoches'.

(2) cannot belong to the speaker's belief box because it does not express a proposition, having one of its terms uninterpreted, but (1) does, and at this point Recanati agrees with Sperber, and according to Recanati so does (3), and here the disagreement appears.

According to Sperber, who only admits two levels, (1) and (2), the latter is semantically incomplete. The speaker does not understand the word 'synecdoches' and this being so there is no proposition that she can believe using (3) as a representation of it. This is the reason that prevents (3) being considered plain belief.

Recanati has a different view. He accepts (3) as full belief, although a deferential one. His main thesis on this issue is that quasi-beliefs are genuine beliefs, i.e., they go into the belief box and interact there with other beliefs.

It is precisely this interaction which permits them to eventually become full belief, and this process is gradual. If this were not so, it would be impossible to explain the process that goes from deferential belief to full belief, a transition that takes place in the context of language acquisition and generally in education. Recanati considers that the kind of device that is at work in language acquisition and in other kinds of deferential belief is the same as the one which takes place in the pervasive phenomenon of imperfect mastery of a concept, a phenomenon pushed to the fore by Externalism. It is precisely the fact that the process that begins with a deferential belief and culminates with full belief is gradual that leads Woodfield to reject the identification of the two issues involved: deferential belief and imperfect mastery.

Recanati's explanation goes as follows. Deferential beliefs are plain beliefs because they have neither syntactical nor semantic gaps. The deferential operator turns object beliefs into completely interpreted sentences in which the character of the unknown phrase is provided by the deferential operator and the content is the content it would have had, had it been uttered in this context by the person to whom the speaker defers meaning.

Our intuition, stressed by Sperber, that there is something incomplete in deferential belief, is explained by Recanati locating this incompleteness not at the semantic but at the epistemological level.

Three levels therefore need to be distinguished: (i) the character level, whose completeness is granted, in deferential beliefs, by the deferential operator, which can even convert non-words into words; (ii) the content level, in which we place the proposition expressed, i.e., what is said; and (iii) the epistemological level, in which there is some indeterminate element because both in deferential belief and in imperfect mastery the subject is unaware of the proposition she is expressing by her utterance.

In the belief box there are representations, but these representations mean propositions which are outside our control. To be stored in the belief box a representation must express a proposition. Being deferential beliefs semantically 'saturated', nothing prevents them from going into the belief box. Recanati and Sperber agree in distinguishing two different relations that take place between the believer and her belief. First, a relation of acceptance between the subject and a representation, and second a relation of belief between the agent and the proposition intended by the representation.

Belief, according to this representationalist view, is a relation between an agent and a proposition expressed by a representation that the agent accepts. Thus, deferential belief is plain belief because the agent accepts a representation that is both syntactically and semantically complete, and thus it expresses a proposition. This proposition is believed without being fully understood. And this follows from Externalism and is accepted by Recanati, as he makes clear in (2000: 275).

So the explanation goes. A natural question now is to ask whether the content level and the epistemological level contain different things. And as I see it the answer must be negative. The 'epistemological level' is not a place or a container, not even metaphorically. What is said – the content, the proposition expressed – does not suffer any enrichment, completion or modification of any kind when the speaker finally realizes it. It is the very same content that is expressed by the utterance, what the believer believes, and what she ignores. This is the lesson of Externalism.

But if this is so, one might wonder, how does this picture fit with the Availability Principle? Representations go to the belief box, but what we believe are propositions. What is said by my utterances are propositions not representations. According to the Availability Principle, propositions and not representations are the entities that are available to me. According to Externalism, propositions do not need to be available.

3.5 Semantics and epistemology: the question of compatibility

At this point, two main options are open to us. Either what is said is not the externalist proposition, or else either the Availability Principle or the externalist thesis must go.

If we took the first option, then we would say that the externalist proposition is none of the three kinds of content that Recanati accepts in (1993) and it still has to be characterized and its place in the overall theory argued for. Thus he would not end up with a three-component picture of content but with a four-component picture: (i) second-order narrow content; (ii) relative first-order narrow content; (iii) wide content; and (iv) extra-wide content, the first three being different versions of what is said and the fourth the possibly ignored externalist proposition. Or alternatively, (iv*) extra-narrow content. And in this case, the first three would be different versions of the externalist proposition and the fourth the level of what is said and of availability. Another possibility, the identification of what is said with some kind of representation, is not open to Recanati because what is said is content.

If we took the second option, either the Availability Principle or Externalism must be thrown away. In Recanati's work the Availability Principle is essential, not so much Externalism. Giving up Externalism would not be dramatically damaging to Recanati's own semantic theory – even if Externalism currently attracts the support of many philosophers of language. Some kind of Externalism is almost universally accepted among philosophers. Giving up the Availability Principle would be a very different matter. This move would seriously affect the whole system of Recanati's semantics. It is the essential point of dispute between semantic Minimalism and pragmatic maximalism. Without it, no definitive argument is left to reject the implicature theory. If the Availability Principle is false, Recanati loses his best weapon against the application of Substitutivity to belief contexts and there would then be no need to characterize them as unstable. His other main argument against Minimalism and the implicature theory was that the pragmatically enriched proposition fell under the scope of logical constants. Now I think that this argument is not unsurmountable, and again his point loses much of its weight, once the Availability Principle has been dispensed with. TCP has obliged us to rethink the history of the philosophy of language of the last century, as Recanati says at the beginning of (2003). So, there is in principle no difficulty in also rethinking the role of logic. As I see it now, the only unavoidable constraint on an entity being the argument of a logical constant is to belong to the appropriate logical category. Then, for connectives the only constraint would be for the entity in question being propositional (or being a predicable, if we take the alternative view). But that its propositional status is acquired through primary or secondary pragmatic processes does not strike me now as essential. Carston's examples of optional free enrichment can be seen as particularized implicatures, and also Wilson's logical examples. For Bach's cases with quantifiers Recanati accepts the existence of a semantic marker restricting their scope. In this situation, rejecting Minimalism will need much more debate to disexpel the air of *petitio principii*. Against Minimalism still remains the thesis that the so-called 'minimal proposition' is not even a proposition but a propositional radical and also the thesis that the 'minimal proposition' does not play any theoretical role in a semantic theory. But without the Availability Principle these arguments are far from conclusive.

Recanati fights on different fronts at the same time, and in all of them the Availability Principle is his best ally. Against Indexicalism it is also needed. It is true that indexicalists hold an Availability Principle but the use performed by it in this theory is not the same as in Recanati's. For an indexicalist the components of what is said are fixed by the sentence somehow and although the speaker is aware of the proposition expressed, it does not depend on the speaker's meaning. In Recanati the import of the principle is bigger: it is the speaker's meaning what determines what is said. Then, Indexicalism might, if necessary, do without availability. Recanati's Contextualism cannot.

An alternative way out might be to bite the bullet and accept that for deferential beliefs availability does not apply. Nevertheless this move would be difficult at his present theory stands. Recanati maintains that deferential belief and imperfect mastery are the same kind of phenomenon. In (2000: 262), he says: 'the speaker in Burge's example mimics the use of those who, unlike her, do master the concept. Despite the differences, I take it as intuitively evident that the same sort of context-shift is involved in both cases.' In imperfect mastery a deferential operator appears as an unarticulated constituent. And Externalism implies that imperfect mastery can be found all throughout language, a conclusion that Recanati himself accepts. He acknowledges that 'many of our *beliefs* are deferential' (*ibid.*). Then, to bite the bullet it would be required to treat separately deferentiality and imperfect mastery. Or, to accept that the Availability Principle fails for the most part of our use of language. Let me state the tension I see once again. According to the Availability Principle, speakers are aware of what is said by their utterances, and what is said, the expressed proposition, are the truth-conditions as the speakers would gloss them (although in 2003 this has changed a bit). Recanati rejects that what is said is character and he also rejects as incoherent any kind of nonrelational narrow content. Thus, speakers have access to the (relational) content of the utterance. At the same time, we accept the lesson of Externalism: we might believe propositions that we do not fully understand. And these propositions, granted their completeness by the deferential operator, are expressed by representations that are in the belief box.

One might say that a defender of the two-component view, unlike the one-component view, has an obvious way out. There is a part of the content which is individualistically individuated by each individual speaker and to which the speaker has direct access. This seems to be the way in which Kaplan, for instance, makes compatible our logical intuitions with our common intuitions as ordinary language-users, i.e., the difference between logical truths and necessary truths. But is the character what is said, as opposed to what is implicated, and are both available to the speaker? The answer to this question is negative. In (1993: 215) Recanati recognizes that his two-component view is inspired by Kaplan's account of indexicals. Nevertheless he argues that content cannot be schematic and that character is not what is said. Kaplan's is not Recanati's option. There is no part of the content, according to Recanati, that is individualistically individuated. So, his alleged two-component picture cannot help here.

The difficulty lies in making TCP compatible with Externalism. Some versions of the Availability Principle can be made compatible with versions of two-component theories of meaning, *à la* Kaplan, or the principle can be reserved to some specific kinds of sentences, i.e., first-person present sentences as in Burge's view. But it requires much more debate to show that a principle such as the one we are analysing can be applied to a general notion of 'what is said' together with an externalist view of content. All utterances uttered in appropriate contexts, i.e., in which the felicity conditions hold, say something. Thus, the notion of what is said applies generally. And since meaning is an essentially relational notion, another lesson from Externalism, speakers might not know the content of their speech acts.

But not everything is lost. Compatibility can be reached at the price of weakening the Availability Principle and coming back to Earth once we have learnt the lesson of Externalism. This might be what the latest version of the Availability Principle hints at in (2003: 20) where availability is formulated as follows: 'What is said must be intuitively accessible to the conversational participants (unless something goes wrong and they do not count as "normal interpreters" '. Twin Earth situations are ones in which something goes wrong. The Twin Earth experiment is designed to show that meanings are not in the head and that definitionism, as a theory of concepts, is false. Externalism amounts to saying that meanings and concepts have an indexical component: they are related to *this world*. Therefore speakers and thinkers intend to refer to this world through their utterances. Are they aware of the content of what they say, of the propositions expressed by their utterances? It depends, but when they are it is mostly as a matter of good luck. It does not follow from the theory.

Availability is introduced to incorporate unarticulated constituents into what is said, and these unarticulated constituents modify the logical form that is the level of semantic interpretation. This explanation might seem to offer a way out from the compatibility problem, if logical form were the level of availability and semantics the level of externalist proposition. But I am not sure that this offers a solution either because thoughts cannot be schematic. In any case, I think that some modifications are called for.

These pages have not been written as a criticism of the TCP from outside, but rather as an attempt to show that this position still has puzzles that should be worked out during a period of 'normal science', to use Kuhn's successful expression, seeking to enhance Recanati's already suggestive and promising picture on content.

Notes

1. I would like to thank here Neftalí Villanueva for many illuminating discussions on this and related topics over the last months. I am also grateful to Juan J. Acero, Manuel de Pinedo, Esther Romero and Andrew Woodfield for helpful comments on an earlier draft of this chapter.
2. In *Oratio Obliqua*, the Availability Principle seems to have lost some of its weight. In fact, it is mentioned only twice. In one of them, he appeals to his doctrine of the availability of what is said to ground his preference for a particular analysis of mixed quotations. The second is in an endnote in the last page of the book, where he admits that the Availability Principle is controversial (2000: 336, n. 20).

References

Bach, K. (1987) *Thought and Reference*. Oxford: Clarendon Press
Carston, R. (1988) 'Implicature, Explicature, and Truth-theoretic Semantics'. In Ruth M. Kempson (ed.), *Mental Representations: The Interface between Language and Reality*. Cambridge: Cambridge University Press, pp. 155–81.
Kripke, S. (1980) *Naming and Necessity*. Oxford: Oxford University Press.
Putnam, H. (1970), 'Is Semantics Possible?'. In Stephen P. Schwartz (1977), pp. 10–118.
Putnam, H. (1973), 'Meaning and Reference'. In Stephen P. Schwartz (1977), pp. 119–32.
Recanati, F. (1993) *Direct Reference: From Language to Thought*. Oxford: Blackwell.
Recanati, F. (1994) 'Contextualism and Anti-Contextualism in the Philosophy of Language'. In Savas Tsohatzidis (ed.), *Foundations of Speech Act Theory: Philosopjical and Linguistic Perspectives*. Oxford: Routledge, pp. 156–66.

Recanati, F. (1996) 'Domains of Discourse'. *Linguistic and Philosophy* 19 (5): 445–75.

Recanati, F. (1995) 'The Alleged Priority of Literal Interpretation'. *Cognitive Science* 19: 207–32.

Recanati, F (2000) *Oratio Obliqua. Oratio Recta. An Essay on Metarepresentation.* Cambridge, MA: The MIT Press

Recanati, F. (2001), 'What is Said'. *Synthese* 128: 75–91.

Recanati, F. (2002a), 'Does Linguistic Communication Rest on Inference?' *Mind and Language* 17(1–2): 105–26.

Recanati, F. (2002b) 'Literal/nonliteral'. *Midwest Studies in Philosophy* 25: 264–74.

Recanati, F. (2002c) 'Pragmatics and Semantics'. In Larry Horn and Gregory Ward (eds), *Handbook of Pragmatics*. Oxford: Blackwell, pp. 442–62.

Recanati, F. (2002d) 'The Fodorian Fallacy'. *Analysis*, 64 (4): 285–9.

Recanati, F. (2002e), 'The Limits of Expressibility'. In Barry Smith (ed.), *John Searle*. Cambridge: Cambridge University Press, pp. 189–213.

Recanati, F. (2002f) 'Unarticulated Constituents'. *Linguistics and Philosophy* 25: 299–345.

Recanati, F. (2004) *Literal Meaning*. Cambridge: Cambridge University Press.

Schwartz, S.P. (1977) *Naming, Necessity and Natural Kinds*. Ithaca and London: Cornell University Press.

Recanati's Reply to Frápolli

I

When someone says something, he or she expresses a certain content, and knows which content it is that he or she expresses. That is the substance of my 'Availability Principle'. I use it in support of a broadly contextualist approach to linguistic content; for the content that is delivered compositionally through the semantics of the language, irrespective of pragmatic considerations, is either too incomplete to count as content (in the genuine, truth-evaluable sense), or, if complete, lies at a level of abstraction that makes it unavailable to the users of the language.

As Frápolli notes, four (related) phenomena, or rather, four distinct facets of a single phenomenon – a phenomenon that plays quite a central role in my philosophy of language – seem to give the lie to the Availability Principle:

- According to Externalism (a view which I accept) the content of our thoughts depends upon the external environment and not merely upon what's 'in the head' of the thinker; it follows that subjects 'do not, in general, "know" the propositional contents of the representations which they accept' (Recanati 2000: 275). This apparently contradicts the Availability Principle.
- Indexicality is a pervasive feature of both thought and speech, in virtue of which the content of our words and mental representations depends upon the context in which they are tokened. It follows that one may be unaware of what one says or thinks, insofar as the content of one's speech or thought depends upon contextual factors of which one may be unaware.
- Through quotational deference, it is possible to use words with the content they have for someone else, even if one does not know what that content is. Thus I may believe what the teacher tells me, namely, that Cicero's prose is full of 'synecdoches', even if I haven't quite understood what synecdoches are.
- Sometimes we speak as if we possessed concepts which we do not actually master but which are part of the intellectual endowment of the

community to which we belong. This is the phenomenon known as imperfect mastery. Thanks to the social nature of language, we help ourselves to conceptual resources that are beyond our individual ken.

In *Oratio Obliqua, Oratio Recta* and elsewhere I pointed out that there is a close connection between quotational deference and incomplete mastery. In both cases, arguably, we defer to other members of the linguistic community. But in quotational deference we defer deliberately and consciously; not so in the other type of case. In incomplete mastery the subject need not be aware of his or her predicament. The type of deference at issue is more surreptitious and automatic than quotational deference.

There is also a close connection between indexicality and Externalism; a connection emphasized by Putnam in his pioneering papers on the topic. Like Putnam, I think that Externalism can be construed as the thesis that our concepts have a demonstrative component. 'Water' refers to that stuff to be found in lakes and rivers around us (etc.), hence the reference of our water-concept depends upon the environment, much as the reference of a demonstrative does. The stereotype associated with a natural kind term, or whatever fixes the reference of the term for us, does not do so by providing necessary and sufficient conditions but by enabling us, in context, to identify local paradigms whose real nature is what ultimately determines the extension of the term.

Finally, I hold that deference itself (in its two forms: quotational deference and incomplete mastery) can be viewed as a form of indexicality, broadly construed. When deferentially used, an expression acquires a specific, deferential 'character', in virtue of which it expresses the same 'content', in context, as the content the expression has for the person or persons to whom the speaker defers, given the character that expression has for the person or persons in question. The Kaplanian framework, with its distinction between character and content, can be used to deal with the facts of deference in a straightforward manner, and it is that indexical treatment which I advocate in my critical discussion of Sperber's views.

The indexical theory of deference enables us to achieve the unification of the four phenomena listed above. As I said at the beginning, they are best construed as facets of a single phenomenon. Yet there are differences between the facets, and they loom large when it comes to evaluating the alleged inconsistency between (due recognition of) the multi-faceted phenomenon of context-dependence and the Availability Principle.

II

Regarding the connection between Externalism and indexicality, Frápolli sides with Burge who, in 'Other Bodies', downplays the connection emphasized by Putnam. Although I side with Putnam in this debate, I concede that there is an important difference between, say, natural kind or substance concepts ('water', 'tiger') and ordinary demonstrative concepts ('that water', 'that tiger'). This difference I have tried to cash out in terms of the distinction between the normal context in which a concept acquires its content and the actual context in which the concept is used and applied. The reference of a natural kind or substance concept depends upon the normal context (so 'water' does not refer to the same thing for us and for the inhabitants of Twin Earth), while the reference of an ordinary demonstrative concept depends upon the actual context (so 'that tiger' refers to different tigers in different contexts). The actual context is much more local than the normal context. The normal context is the world in which we live and with which we causally interact; while the actual context is the local situation (a small chunk of the world) in which the concept happens to be tokened.

This difference in locality matters greatly to the issue at hand. For us, the normal context is given: we live on Earth (where H_2O is what descends from the sky as rain, etc.), hence our concepts have whatever content they have, in a more or less stable manner. The environment-dependence of content has no practical consequence for us because the external factors upon which content depends do not change (except in the counterfactual circumstances imagined by the philosophers). Only their actual variation would be a threat to Availability, because it would entail that a change of content might not be detected by the subject. Since the external factors do not actually vary, there is no undetected variability of content, hence no threat to Availability.

To be sure, there is a sense in which subjects can be said not to 'know' the propositional contents of the representations that they accept, since those contents depend upon environmental factors of which they need not be aware; but there is also a clear sense in which they do know the contents of their beliefs. Contextualists in epistemology have emphasized how variable the conditions of satisfaction of 'know' are according to the changing stand-ards which happen to be set in context. Just as there is no real contradiction between Everyman's claim to knowledge and the philosopher's scepticism, there is no contradiction between the externalist's claim that subjects do not know the contents of the representations they accept, and the Availability Principle, according to which they know the contents of the beliefs they express by their assertions.

III

The relative stability of content that makes Externalism consistent with Availability is due to the non-local character of the normal context on which content externalistically depends. This is in contrast to the actual context of tokening, on which the content of ordinary demonstrative thoughts depends; for that context is local and eminently variable. I say 'That tiger is tamed' but unbeknown to be, the context has changed: the tiger I was looking at and thought I was pointing to (Marius, say) has been replaced by another, untamed one (Totor). Unwittingly, I say that Totor is tamed. In this case I am mistaken as to the content expressed by my own words. (I think I am referring to Marius, while I am referring to Totor.) Because the context upon which the content of our ordinary indexical thoughts depends is a local context, there is a real possibility of being mistaken as to the content of our own thoughts; hence there is a stronger sense in which we do not know the contents of our thoughts, than the sense in which that is so simply in virtue of Externalism.

Ordinary indexicality, therefore, poses a genuine threat to Availability. With deference the situation is even worse. Whenever the speaker defers to someone else in her use of a term, what content she turns out to express depends upon what is in the head of those people to whom she defers. The deferrer herself is not in control, by definition: only the deferee, or someone who can read the deferee's mind, knows what is being said. Deference and Availability therefore stand in sharp conflict, as Frápolli points out.

To get out of the contradiction spotted by Frápolli, what can I do or say? As Frápolli herself suggests, I can appeal to an innovation introduced in *Literal Meaning* in order to qualify the Availability Principle and make it more accurate. The alleged counterexamples to Availability are cases in which, admittedly, the subject does not quite know the content of what s/he is saying; yet they are not really counterexamples to the Availability Principle, as it is formulated in *Literal Meaning*. There I say that the content of our utterances is fixed by the intuitions of *normal interpreters*. The speaker's intentions etc. fix the content of his or her utterance – a content that must therefore be available to him or her – only insofar as the speaker, in the context, counts as a 'normal interpreter'. This proviso is sufficient to dispose of the counterexamples to Availability based on deference or indexicality. Normal interpreters are, by definition, people who know the language (they understand the words that are used) and the relevant contextual facts (e.g. they do not commit indexical errors such as mistaking the person or thing pointed to for someone or something else). By thus restricting Availability to normal interpreters, we get rid of the alleged counterexamples:

> Ordinary users of the language are normal interpreters, in most situations. They know the relevant facts and have the relevant abilities. But there are situations... where the actual users make mistakes and are not normal interpreters. In such situations their interpretations do not fix what is said. To determine what is said, we need to look at the interpretation which a normal interpreter would give. (*Literal Meaning*, p. 20)

After considering this way out, Frápolli notes that my framework, as it stands, cannot accommodate it. According to Externalism, imperfect mastery permeates language and thought. That is something I accept. Now I hold that imperfect mastery is a form of deference. If, therefore, I assume that deferrers are not normal interpreters, so that Availability fails for them, then I am bound to accept that 'the availability principle fails for the most part of our use of language' – hardly a welcome consequence! In order to avoid that consequence, Frápolli says, I must change the framework and 'treat separately deferentiality and imperfect mastery'.

Frápolli's objection is well-taken; there is a problem indeed. But the problem has a solution (close to what she herself suggests). Remember the distinction between the normal context, whose stability makes Externalism compatible with Availability, and the local context upon which the content of indexical thoughts (or utterances) depends. That distinction applies within the realm of deference. For we may consider, with Putnam and Burge, that the normal context (the environment) upon which content external-istically depends has a social dimension. The content of the word 'arthritis', whoever uses it, depends upon the linguistic practice of the community: that practice is an aspect of the normal context upon which the content of the word 'arthritis' depends. Insofar as the normal context (with its social dimen-sion) is stable, that form of deference – the form which permeates language and thought – does not threaten Availability. The only genuine threat to Availability comes from the cases in which the target of the speaker's act of deference is local and variable, namely the cases of quotational defer-ence. In quotational deference, as opposed to incomplete mastery, the actual context of the tokening determines who, in particular, the speaker is defer-ring to (e.g. the teacher, in the synecdoche example). Now those cases are sufficiently marginal to be excluded from the application of the Availability Principle, without making it vacuous. In contrast, we should not exclude cases of incomplete mastery from its application. When I say that speakers normally know what it is that they are saying, I mean that they know it in a sense that is compatible with the fact that, because of social externalism and imperfect mastery, virtually no one really 'knows' what he is talking about. Again there are different standards for knowledge, hence there is no real incompatibility between imperfect mastery and Availability, appearances notwithstanding.

4
Metalinguistic Demonstrations and Reference

Philippe De Brabanter

> In signing one's name, does one *refer* to oneself? Do tensed verbs *refer*
> to the time of their utterance? . . . A common mistake in philosophy
> is to suppose there must be a right and unequivocal answer to such
> questions, or worse yet, to suppose that unless there is a right and
> unequivocal answer, the concept of referring is a worthless concept.
> (Searle 1969: 28)

François Recanati has been preoccupied with mention and quotation for
more than two decades. He initially turned his attention to the subject as
part of an attempt to show just how pervasive linguistic reflexivity was, and,
accordingly, just how untenable the myth of the transparency of linguistic
signs (Recanati 1979). Though I understand his original position to have
been very much an 'identity theory' *à la* Searle (1969), Recanati has proved
receptive to the many merits of the 'demonstrative theory' (Davidson 1979).
Amongst other things, he has now fully endorsed the fundamental assumption that quotation is an act of metalinguistic demonstration. This insight
has been incorporated into what must be regarded as the most sophisticated theory of quotation (or, more broadly, of 'metalinguistic demonstration') currently available (Recanati 2000, and especially 2001). His central
move has consisted in abandoning the assumption that all quotations are
referential NPs: some are ('closed quotations'), some are not ('open quotations'). Coupled with the development of a complex explanatory apparatus,
this distinction enables him to account for a wider body of data than any
previous writer, from straightforward cases of 'flat mention' (*'Boston' is a
name*) to highly complex cases of 'simultaneous use and mention' (such
mixed cases as *If you were a French academic, you might say that the parrot was
'un symbole du Logos'*, where the sequence between quotation marks is used
and quoted at the same time). Furthermore, Recanati's theory also throws

light on most of the central properties of metalinguistic demonstrations, namely the conventional value of markers of quotation, productivity, iconicity, opacity, hybridity. There are, however, two more, albeit conjectural, properties which I regard as potentially important in the case of closed quotations, and which, I believe, do not receive a clear explanation in Recanati's framework. These properties are *referential diversity* and *recursiveness*, and they will be my central concern in this chapter.

As I have just said, the two properties that I wish to argue for can only be displayed by (some instances of) closed quotation. I cannot afford here to dwell on Recanati's distinction between closed and open quotations; suffice it to say that I fully agree with him that only closed quotations, that is quotations that occur as singular terms in a sentence, have reference. These are necessarily (sequences of) words that are mentioned but not used simultaneously. Thus, the quotations in:

(1) He said it was all a 'pile of roobish'.
(2) What does one more lie matter anyway? Politicians 'misspeak' and are forgiven by their followers. (*Time*, 03/06/91: 64),

are not referential. Indeed, they are not 'recruited' as NPs; they are *used as well as mentioned*, as evidenced by the fact that the sentences that contain them do not break down as soon as the quotation marks are removed: *He said it was all a pile of roobish* is an English sentence regardless of the presence of a metalinguistic demonstration (and so is *Politicians misspeak and are forgiven by their followers*). I shall not discuss the distinction any further in the rest of this chapter.

4.1   The various positions in the literature

The question of what a quotation refers to has been around for a very long time. I now offer a very short summary of the various positions that have been defended in the dominant theories of quotation developed in the twentieth century.

- Formal logicians (Tarski, Carnap, Quine) originally supported what has been termed a '(proper) name theory' of quotation. If quotations are names, this should presumably mean that they massively refer to individuals, since that is what proper names canonically do. Somewhat curiously, formal logicians have often claimed that quotations referred to types (or, more broadly, abstract objects) rather than tokens (individuals), a claim found in e.g. Carnap (1937: 17) or Tarski (1956: 370fn). The only conclusion that can be drawn from this observation is that these scholars did not use the word *name* in any strict sense, as they sometimes admitted themselves.

- Identity theorists take it that a quotation mentions itself. For some, this is interpreted as meaning that a quotation does not refer (reference is suspended by mention; e.g. Searle 1969: 76). For others, however, this seems to mean that a quotation refers to itself. Washington, for instance, writes that a word in quotation is 'used and mentioned in the same breath' (1992: 582). Since Washington appears to treat mention as a synonym of reference (though he does not make the claim explicitly), one is entitled to understand his position to be that quotations are self-referential. This raises an interesting issue: as reference can only be performed as part of an utterance-act (cf. Searle 1969; Recanati 2001: 648), and as only tokens are produced as the result of an utterance-act, this would seem to mean that a quoted token can only refer to the very token that it is. This is quite dubious (one need only think of direct speech, where the quoted sequence, if it refers at all, will refer to something else than the spoken or written token that is presented; otherwise, it would not be a speech *report*). To make matters worse, it would seem, some identity theorists suggest that a quotation usually refers to a type (Washington 1998: 550), which somehow implies that a referential quoting sequence in an utterance-token is a *type*. Clearly, there is a problem with the notion of identity.
- Demonstrative theorists widely hold that quotations refer to types (Davidson, Bennett, Reimer, Recanati) or classes of tokens (Cappelen and Lepore). Still, some of them are willing to qualify this assumption. Thus, Davidson (1999: 716–17) offers this corrective: 'Typically, *though by no means always*, what we want to pick out [by pointing to a token, an inscription] is an expression, and expressions are abstract entities we cannot directly pick out by pointing' (my emphasis). Similar qualifications can be found in Bennett (1988: 400) and Reimer (1996: 136fn). Other writers, Recanati among them, take up a more radical stance: for them, the referents of quotations are always of the same sort.
- Less frequently, there have been scholars who have acknowledged the existence of a variety of potential referents for quotations. This position can be found in Carnap (1937: 154–6; in apparent contradiction to the statement made on page 17 of the same book), and especially in Saka (1998: 133).

One of my main goals in the following pages will be to determine who is right. In particular, I will focus my attention on Recanati's views, especially the way that he tries to accommodate the idea that a quotation refers to a type even when it is used to 'talk about' a particular token. But, in order to be able to complete that task, I shall first have to give an outline of Recanati's theory of quotation.

4.2 Recanati on quotation

I repeat examples (1) and (2):

(1) He said it was all a 'pile of roobish'.

(2) What does one more lie matter anyway? Politicians 'misspeak' and are forgiven by their followers.

Recanati assumes all metalinguistic demonstrations to be complex acts involving a number of 'smaller' actions: in a metalinguistic demonstration, a linguistic token is *displayed* for the purpose of *demonstrating* one or more properties that are made available by the token (e.g. its form, pronunciation, sense, 'connotations'). Moreover, the 'quoter' seeks to *depict a target*; in other words, the display of the token serves to 'talk about' or 'evoke' something (e.g. a linguistic string, someone's personal manner of speaking, a particular language variety). I propose the following Recanati-like analyses for the examples above: the utterer of (1) wishes to direct the hearers' attention to an earlier utterance made by Mr Vic Wilcox (= target), inasmuch as it is pronounced with a Midlands accent (= demonstratum), a property that is made accessible by the (truncated) token displayed. The utterer of (2) wishes to evoke a particular sociolect (= target) as being typified by the use of euphemism (= demonstratum), a property made available by the display of the token of *misspeak*.

The quotations in examples (1) and (2) did not display the extra property of referentiality. Let us now look at an example in which the quoted sequence does:

(3) [. . .] he says to the passenger, 'You can't smoke in this compartment, Sir.' (Toulmin 1958: 28)

In (1) and (2), the demonstration did not play a syntactic role – it came as a pictorial 'supplement' to a sentence that was already semantically complete and interpretable without it (cf. my earlier discussion): the metalinguistic demonstration makes a contribution entirely at the pragmatic level of 'what is meant', not at the semantic level of 'what is said'. The situation is different in the case of (3), where the metalinguistic demonstration performs a syntactic function at the level of the embedding sentence (direct object of *says*): were there no demonstration, the utterance would not be an English sentence. In other words, some of the contribution of the demonstration in (3) is already encoded as part of the proposition expressed ('what is said') by an utterance of the sentence. In a case like this (but not in (1) or (2)), we have a closed quotation, and it refers. The utterer of (3) presumably wants to depict an utterance made by a guard on a train (= target). What then is the property made manifest in order for this target to be identifiable? Two main cases should be distinguished. On the one hand, an utterance of (3), especially a spoken one, might involve mimicry of a special pronunciation (that of the guard). On the other hand, especially in writing, it might well involve no such mimicry. In a case like this, the demonstratum may well turn out to be the very expression *You can't smoke in this compartment, Sir.*

If I understand him well, Recanati would say that the quotation in (3) does not have a target that is different from the demonstratum; which means that the quotation is an instance of so-called 'flat mention'. Since Recanati seeks – with reason, I believe – to avoid having to concede that some instances of quotation are deprived of a target, he chooses to call the demonstratum a 'proximal' target. As a consequence, even when a quotation does not have what Recanati now calls a 'distal' target, it will still have a proximal target. Let us see how this applies to the two possible readings of (3) laid out above: on the first, there are both a demonstrated property (the special pronunciation mimicked by the quoter, for instance) and a distal target (the words used by the guard); on the second there is no distal target: the only target is the demonstrated property, namely the quoted linguistic expression.

As regards the nature of the referent, Recanati (2001) has this to say: (i) the referent of a closed quotation is the same as its 'proximal target', (ii) this proximal target is a 'demonstrated property', (iii) demonstrated properties are always types (cf. 2001: 645, 655, 656). For reasons of internal consistency, Recanati's theory must assume that referential metalinguistic demonstrations have a single, homogeneous, kind of referent. One of my questions in the present chapter is whether this view, which is necessary for the consistency of the framework, is ultimately correct.

4.3   An 'intuitive' approach

The first few remarks that I wish to make are meant to approach our problem in a fairly intuitive manner. Intuitive comments of this sort are not, of themselves, enough to win an argument that centres on a technical notion like reference, but they help explain where my own preferred position comes from and they may also show that the 'burden of proof' is on the shoulders of those who claim that reference is systematically to a type.

Let me begin by pointing out that metalinguistic demonstrations would be peculiar demonstrations indeed if their reference was thus restricted to types. Other kinds of demonstrations, notably acts of pointing, accompanied or not by a linguistic demonstrative, routinely pick out tokens as their referents. Of course, it is possible to reply that quotations actually are demonstrations of a very special kind. Moreover, Recanati could add that, unlike some other proponents of referential homogeneity, he is fully aware of the possibility for a quotation to pick out a token located in space and time. This is no problem for his theory, he might say, as depicted targets can be tokens just as well as types (2001: 642, 644). In other words, when a speaker uses a referential quotation to 'talk about' a specific token, the quotation produced depicts that token but simultaneously refers to a type.

Let us now examine a couple of examples where appearances suggest that the quotations are used for picking out tokens:

(4) The presidential candidate exclaimed, 'There will be no new taxes'.

(5) Sue replied, 'I ain't EVER gonna tell ya'.

In (4), the direct speech report, as it purportedly reproduces the very words (the locutionary act) uttered by the candidate on a given occasion, picks out an utterance-token. The same impression is gained from considering example (5). Moreover, the degree of mimicry displayed by (5) reinforces this impression: the capitals and the choice of the non-standard *ain't, gonna* and *ya* make it clear that what the quotation reproduces is Sue's particular instantiation of an utterance-type, with its special pronunciation and intonation, both of which are features of objects located in time and space, not of abstractions.

Some writers would infer from the above that the quotations in (4) and (5) refer to tokens. Such is the opinion of the French linguist Josette Rey-Debove, who regards all instances of direct speech as token-referential (1978: 235–7), or of Leonard Linsky, who writes, 'if I say, "He said 'the cat is on the mat' ", my words have as their reference the words of the person whose speech is reported' (Edwards 1967, vol. 7: 95). This, I interpret as meaning that the quotation refers to the particular sequence uttered by the initial speaker on a particular occasion.

However, as I have indicated above, Recanati's framework allows him to maintain that the spatiotemporally located tokens are *depicted (distal) targets*, and that the referents are still types, as in all other instances of closed quotation.

I have tried several ways of settling this tricky issue. First, I have availed myself of the distinction between 'autonymous' and 'heteronymous' mention. Autonymous mention occurs when a sequence is, broadly speaking, used to 'mention itself', as is the case in all the examples so far. By contrast, heteronymous mention occurs when a description or a non-iconic name is used to mention a linguistic expression. Examples of such descriptions are easy to find, as when *Caesar's remark on crossing the Rubicon* is used to mention *Alea iacta est* (cf Carnap 1937: 154). Heteronymously mentioning names, as Carnap remarks, are much rarer. Carnap offers *The Sermon on the Mount*, though he concedes that this could also be regarded as a description. I am not sure that such names actually occur in everyday use, but some philosophers, usually while making fun of the proper name theory of quotation, have come up with a few fancy ones: for instance, Searle (1969: 74) made the tongue-in-cheek suggestion that one could use *John* as a name for the word *Socrates*. And Recanati (2000: 137) uses *Wychnevetsky* as a name of the word *cat* in order to illustrate the notion of heteronymous mention.

Originally, I thought that the parallel with heteronymous mention would be grist to the mill of those who uphold reference to tokens. Indeed, hardly anyone denies that proper names (always) and definite descriptions (often) refer to individuals. Therefore, if *Wychnevetsky* or *The last headword on page 236 of the 1979 edition of the Collins Dictionary of the English Language* are logically equivalent to the autonym *'cat'*, then it would only be natural to acknowledge, at the very least, that an autonym *can* refer to an individual, i.e. a token. There is a problem, however, with this reasoning. If, for example, I say:

(6) Wychnevetsky is a three-letter word (Recanati 2000: 137),

I do not wish to imply that *Wychnevetsky* refers to a particular instantiation of *cat*. Rather, I suppose everyone would agree that the name here refers to a type: it is as a type that *cat* has three letters. This situation is perhaps puzzling, given the existing consensus on the referents of names. Where does the paradox originate? I am not sure I can answer that question, and will venture only a few remarks. It may be that one and the same object can be viewed either as an individual (token) or as an abstraction (type). Perhaps that is precisely what happens with words: the word *cat* can be regarded as a type, i.e. as an abstraction subsuming the common features shared by all its occurrences. At the same time, however, the same word is also an individual if I consider it as being different from other elements of the set of English words (all of them 'tokens' in that sense). If I combine these two points of view, I believe it fair to suggest that *Wychnevetsky* refers to something that, although being a type, is also an individual separate from other 'individual types'. I am forced to conclude that the distinction between autonymous and heteronymous mention does not help here.

I had also thought that paraphrases or other substitutions might help strengthen the case for reference to tokens. Here is how I thought such a case could be built: an example like (3) can be rephrased as:

(3′) [. . .] he says *those words* to the passenger.
(3″) [. . .] he says to the passenger . . . [the quotation is replaced by an act of pointing at words scribbled somewhere].

As I said earlier, demonstrations that are not quotations usually pick out individuals. But (i) that is not systematically the case: demonstratives and acts of pointing can actually serve to pick out abstractions; and (ii) given the inherent ambiguity of metalinguistic predicates between 'word-type' and 'word-token', any recourse to a demonstration of words is bound to remain unenlightening. So much for that 'solution'.

So far, I have been unable to decide which of the two relevant accounts is superior. However, I have somehow put the burden of proof on those who argue against the possibility of reference to tokens. Would it not be fair, in the light of my first 'intuitive remark' above, to ask that the advocate of referential homogeneity should prove the usefulness of an account in terms of depicted targets rather than referents?

So, is Recanati justified in maintaining a distinction between target and referent in cases like (3), (4) and (5)? It would be easier to settle this issue if depiction and, especially, the much more common notion of reference could simply be equated with intuitive, 'commonsense' acts. Such, however, is not the case.

Depiction is characterized – perhaps rather than *defined* – by Recanati. As far as I am aware, Recanati does not use the terms *target* and *depiction* in *Oratio Obliqua, Oratio Recta*, and elsewhere he does not provide a more precise description than that the target is 'something which one attempts to depict through the demonstration' (2001: 642), something which, as I have pointed out before, can be either a type or a token. Depiction is further characterized as subsuming mimicry, simulation, iconic representation. There is no doubt that depiction and reference are not the same thing: as we have seen in the case of open quotation, there are many metalinguistic demonstrations which depict without referring. Besides, when a closed quotation involves mimicry, the mimicked target is clearly different from the referent. The tricky cases remain those closed quotations that involve no mimicry, as in the second interpretation I offered for (3) above. I will return to those in a moment, but in the meantime, I would like to say a word about reference.

At bottom, reference remains a technical notion, however painstaking the attempts to root it in actual experience or tangible reality. Therefore, it is highly unlikely to lend itself to an intuitive grasp by language users, including specialists. This is a point that has been made by a variety of authors, notably Noam Chomsky (cf. 2000: 148–50, and *passim*). In other words, as long as I have not defined precisely what I mean by *reference*, I can make no definite claims about the referent of any given expression in an utterance. This may seem to go without saying, but it is none the less the case that quite a bit of scholarship in linguistics and some of the philosophical literature avails itself of the term *reference* rather loosely (i.e. as if the term captured an unproblematic, straightforward notion).

How do philosophers define *reference*? As far as I can see, there is wide agreement that referring is an act that is 'ancillary' to an utterance-act. In other words, there is no reference if there is no speaker doing the referring as part of a speech act. There is less of a consensus when it comes to the nature of referents. Some writers adopt the view that reference holds between linguistic expressions and *mental representations* of objects in the 'world', others that it captures a relation between linguistic expressions and *actual objects* in the 'world'. Although I do not feel competent to sort out this question one way or another, I will opt for the second conception, for the following two reasons. First, reference is widely understood to be a central means for language to 'connect' with the 'world'. Perhaps speakers are deluded when they imagine that they have access to external reality – though I am not even sure that this question can ultimately be settled. Still, I think it sensible to focus on the fact that, when referring, speakers often *intend* to speak about extralinguistic, extramental entities rather than about concepts of these. For instance, when I say, *Samuel is getting married*, I mean to say something about a person named *Samuel*, not my concept of him. My second reason is much more practical: as I see it, Recanati understands reference to obtain between language and the world. It is therefore easier to discuss his positions on the reference of quotations within a shared framework. Otherwise, the discussion is in danger of boiling down to a definitional divergence, a situation that I wish to avoid.

All in all, my definition of reference is close to that given by Searle in *Speech Acts* (1969: 28). Reference is the relation that holds between a linguistic expression and the object a speaker intends to pick out by using it, namely the referent. When this referent is combined with a predicate within a statement, the statement can be judged to be true or false. Many other definitions (e.g. in textbooks and encyclopaedic articles) adopt this Fregean picture and emphasize the contribution of referents to the truth-condition of an assertion, and I too shall regard it as a central feature of referents.

Let me now return to examples (3), (4) and (5). What does it take for an utterance of one of these to be a true assertion? Consider (4): for an utterance of (4) to be true, it must be the case that the presidential candidate actually exclaimed the very words *There will be no new taxes*. Because of the inherent ambiguity of the word *word*, the question must be rephrased as 'What does it take for an act of exclaiming to take place, other than an agent?' In other words, what is the product of an exclamation, is it a type or a token?

A type being an abstract object, it seems difficult to assume that it could ever be produced by an exclamation. Yet I must acknowledge the possibility of mounting a defence along the following lines: there are uses of verbs of saying for which it seems fair to assume that they take a *type* as their second argument; such is arguably the case when such a verb selects an indirect speech report as its complement. It is theoretically possible to extend this analysis to cases where the complement is a direct speech report. One might then claim that *say + direct speech* is close to *say + indirect speech*. In the former construction, the verb could be defined as meaning 'to utter tokens of (the following type)', and in the second as 'to utter tokens which mean the same as (the following sentence-type)'. In other words, the verb could, in both cases, be defined as taking an abstract object as its second argument.

Since definitions are not naturally given to speakers – they are constructions – it is impossible to state positively which definition is more correct than the other. In other words, it is impossible to decide whether a predicate denoting an act of saying (exclaiming, replying) requires a second argument that is an actual token or one that is an abstract type. As a result, we are still none the wiser as to what is the better account.

Before losing heart completely, I wish to take another look at example (3) (and perhaps at (4) too, if *exclaimed* was turned into *said*). Near the end of section 4.2, I suggested that, on one interpretation, (3) could be taken to involve a case of flat mention. In other words, (3) could have been uttered without mimicry, and the quotation would then be devoid of a distal target (Recanati 2001: 644–5 makes these two notions interdependent). Now consider the following problem. If *You can't smoke in this compartment, Sir* is an instance of flat mention, then it has no other target than its demonstrated property (namely the class of tokens relevantly similar to the displayed token), and this demonstrated property is also the referent of the quotation. Still, even in the absence of mimicry, I would still wish to say that the reporting speaker intended to talk about (depict) the unique token uttered by *that* guard on *that* train on *that* day. Unfortunately, this intention can no longer be accounted for in terms of a distal target, since there is no distal target left. I see only one way out of Recanati's quandary, but it is a dubious move: it consists in renouncing the second interpretation (flat mention) and conclude that any depiction of a token involves mimicry. Then there is room again for a distal target distinct from the demonstrated property. But, as I said, this move does not strike me as very convincing.

A related difficulty for the internal consistency of Recanati's account is the following: granting again that the two readings offered for (3) are acceptable, this would mean that each reading determines a different referent (because each selects a different demonstratum): a special pronunciation (when there is mimicry), and the utterance-type of which the guard's utterance is a token (in the absence of mimicry). This oddity is not addressed anywhere in Recanati (2000, 2001), as far as I am aware.

4.4   A theoretical argument

Although I believe that section 4.3 may have strengthened the case for referential diversity somewhat, I am aware that I have not been able to demonstrate the *necessity* of recognizing a quotation's ability to refer to tokens. That is why I now wish to bring up a theoretical argument that may go some way towards buttressing my claim. This argument depends on what I regard as another useful feature of (some) closed quotations, namely *recursiveness*. This is a property whose validity is widely debated in scholarship on mention, quotation, etc., with opposing views being championed by e.g. Paul Saka (1998: 119–20) in the 'pro' camp and Cappelen and Lepore (1997: 439–40) in the 'contra' camp. As far as I can see, one of the reasons behind the controversy is the failure to separate out various forms of recursiveness. In my view, one should distinguish between '*typographical*' recursiveness (the mechanical iteration of markers of quotation, esp. quote marks, as in ' *"Boston"* ' *is a quotation*), '*compositional*' recursiveness, where a quoted sequence embedded within a wider quotation retains its ability to mean something (to have compositional meaning, as in *Then the Lord said unto Moses: 'Go in unto Pharaoh, and tell him: "Thus saith the Lord, the God of the Hebrews: 'Let my people go, that they may serve me.' " '*; Nunberg 1990: 46), and '*referential recursiveness*', namely the ability for a quotation to refer to another quotation which itself refers. I shall focus on this last form of recursiveness, because it is the one that provides, I believe, strong evidence in favour of the referential diversity of closed quotations.

To begin with, I take it that referential recursiveness has an analogue in nonlinguistic 'semiotic' situations. Let us assume that Bart and Homer are hiking through the woods. The hike is signposted with arrows, but Homer has lost track of them and thinks he and his son are lost. 'How do you know we're going in the right direction?', he whines. To which Bart responds by pointing at an arrow fifty yards ahead that itself points forward.

In this case, I believe that the first demonstration (Bart's act of pointing) goes together with a second one (the arrow that is found to be pointing forward). In other words, the object pointed at by Bart is a 'sign' that does not cease to function demonstratively. As a matter of fact, its ability to signify is reactivated by Bart's pointing. The arrow lay inert as long as no one was there to point at it and thereby, so to speak, turn it into a token involved in a particular ostensive act.

There exist other such cases of demonstrated signs that are in turn made to demonstrate something else. Let us picture two oral examiners waiting for their next student. One of them asks who the following 'victim' will be. The other responds by pointing at a student number on their list. This number stands for Jane Brown, the student in question, the one who was 'intended' by the initial question. Clearly, in this case too the demonstrated object does not cease to indexically signify something beyond itself.

This, I take it, establishes the iterability of acts of pointing. But, given that I wish to reserve the property of reference for linguistic expressions, proving the existence of referential recursiveness proper requires finding examples of recursiveness that are quotational. Here is one that should do the trick:

(7) In each utterance of the previous sentence (*'Boston' is a six-letter word*), ' "Boston" ' refers to an orthographic form.

I assume that any instantiation of (7) can be regarded as a true assertion. If such is the case, then the subject of (7) – a name plus two pairs of quote marks – has reference (to a given instantiation of *Boston* enclosed in a single pair of quote marks). Moreover, since the property validly predicated of the subject's referent is that of *referring* to a further entity, we have a situation in which the subject of (7) refers to a quotation which itself refers to an orthographic form. In other words, we have a case of iterated reference.

How this point relates to the issue of referential diversity is as follows: as I explained earlier, I regard reference as a discourse phenomenon, and hold that it can only be accomplished as part of a specific utterance-act. Each utterance-act produces an utterance-token made up of smaller tokens. For the subject of *'Boston' is a six-letter word* to be able to refer to an orthographic form, it must be a token. Therefore, if an utterance of (7) is true, its own subject (' "*Boston*" ') refers to an entity that has reference, namely a token. This I take to be a demonstration that not all closed quotations should be understood to refer to abstract objects (types, classes of tokens): some must be held to refer to specific tokens.

4.5 Tentative conclusion

Having reached the end of this chapter, I believe that I have been able to build a case for the possibility of a quotation's referring to a token. If the idea of referential recursiveness is correct, it is difficult to maintain that quotations cannot refer to tokens (but I am aware that my argument rests on a made-up example). Besides, the postulate of referential homogeneity raises issues concerning the internal consistency of Recanati's scheme, and – less significantly, perhaps – it clashes with some speakers' intuitions (but what are intuitions worth in the face of technical, theoretical, questions?).

Some of the inconclusiveness of my results is perhaps inherent in the kind of investigation undertaken in this chapter: appeal to linguistic proof is not something straightforward. We have seen that the imprecision of such notions as reference and depiction got in the way of positive theoretical decisions. We have also seen that the way predicates (e.g. verbs of saying) are defined affects our perception of the truth-condition of a sentence. And I have even been led to suggest that objects that are types from one point of view can perhaps be regarded as tokens from another. These definitional and ontological issues may seem a bit worrying, but I suggest that linguists and philosophers take some solace from the Searle quotation that I put in as an epigraph to this chapter.

References

Bennett, J. (1988) 'Quotation'. *Noûs* 22: 399–418.
Cappelen, H. and Lepore, E. (1997) 'Varieties of Quotation'. *Mind* 106: 429–50.
Cappelen, H. and Lepore, E. (1999) 'Using, Mentioning and Quoting: a Reply to Saka'. *Mind* 108: 741–50.
Carnap, R. (1937) *The Logical Syntax of Language*, trans. from the German by Amethe Smeaton. London: Kegan Paul, Trench, Trübner & Co.
Chomsky, N. (2000) *New Horizons in the Study of Language and Mind*. Cambridge: Cambridge University Press.

Craig, E. (general ed.) (1998) *Routledge Encyclopedia of Philosophy*, 10 vols. London and New York: Routledge.

Davidson, D. (1979) 'Quotation'. *Theory and Decision* 11: 27–40.

Davidson, D. (1999) 'Reply to Ernie Lepore'. In Lewis Edwin Hahn (ed.), *The Philosophy of Donald Davidson*. Chicago/La Salle: Open Court, pp. 715–17.

Edwards, P. (ed. in chief) (1967) *The Encyclopedia of Philosophy*, 7 vols., New York: Macmillan and The Free Press; London: Collier-Macmillan.

Nunberg, G. (1990) *The Linguistics of Punctuation*. Stanford, CSLI lecture notes, 18.

Recanati, F. (1979) *La transparence et l'énonciation. Pour introduire à la pragmatique*. Paris: Seuil, coll. L'ordre philosophique.

Recanati, F. (2000) *Oratio Obliqua, Oratio Recta: An Essay on Metarepresentation*. Cambridge, MA: MIT Press, Bradford Books.

Recanati, F. (2001) 'Open Quotation'. *Mind* 110, 637–87.

Reimer, M. (1996) 'Quotation Marks: Demonstratives or Demonstrations?' *Analysis*, 56: 131–41.

Rey-Debove, J. (1978) *Le Métalangage. Etude linguistique du discours sur le langage*. Paris: Le Robert, coll. L'ordre des mots.

Saka, P. (1998) 'Quotation and the Use-Mention Distinction'. *Mind*, 107: 113–35.

Searle, J.R. (1969) *Speech Acts: An Essay in the Philosophy of Language*. Cambridge and New York: Cambridge University Press.

Tarski, A. (1956) *Logic, Semantics, Metamathematics. Papers from 1923 to 1938*, transl. by J.H. Woodger. 2nd edition 1983 edited and introduced by John Corcoran. Indianapolis: Hackett Publishing Company.

Toulmin, S.E. (1958) *The Uses of Argument*. Cambridge: Cambridge University Press.

Washington, C. (1992) 'Identity Theory of Quotation'. *Journal of Philosophy*, 89: 582–605.

Washington, C. (1998) 'Use/Mention Distinction and Quotation'. In E. Craig (ed.), *Routledge Encyclopedia of Philosophy* vol. 9, pp. 548–51.

Recanati's Reply to De Brabanter

Philippe De Brabanter notes that paradigmatic singular terms, namely proper names, 'canonically' refer to individuals; he therefore finds it strange that quotations, insofar as they act as singular terms, should always refer to types, i.e. to abstract objects or classes of individuals, as most theorists of quotation think they do. There is, he points out, no a priori reason why closed quotations should have a single, homogenous kind of reference. He therefore tentatively endorses the 'referential diversity' thesis.

On this issue I am quite open-minded. I hold that closed quotations refer to the type they demonstrate, but that view, which I maintain, is not 'necessary for the consistency of [my] framework', contrary to what De Brabanter says. I would be happy to accept the thesis of 'referential diversity' if sufficient evidence was adduced in its favour. Does Philippe De Brabanter provide such evidence in his paper? I do not think so.

Let us start by laying out my framework, within which Philippe De Brabanter sets up his own discussion. I distinguish three sorts of thing one does in quoting: one displays a token, one demonstrates a type, and one (optionally) depicts a target. Token-display is something that takes place in all instances of quotation (whether open or closed), but also in many forms of language use that are not quotational. A token is displayed when the speaker who produces it specifically draws the hearer's attention to it, and that is something that also happens whenever one stresses a particular word or phrase. What is distinctive of quotation is the fact that the token is displayed not, for example, in order to contrast it with some other expression which might have been used in its place (contrastive stress), but in order to demonstrate – illustrate by exemplification – some property or complex of properties which it instantiates. This property or complex of properties is the 'demonstrated type'. So what distinguishes quotational displays from other linguistic displays is the speaker's demonstrative intention.

The demonstration itself has a (higher-level) purpose. Sometimes, one demonstrates a type in order to picture (or, as I say, 'depict') something that is of that type, through some form of mimicry. In other cases ('flat mention') one demonstrates a type in order to communicate something directly about that type, without attempting to depict a particular token – or anything else – as being of that type. Whenever there is an attempt at depicting something through the demonstration, I call the object of the depiction the 'target' of the quotation. (See below for qualifications.)

The distinction between the three components is common to open and closed quotation. What distinguishes closed from open quotation is the fact that, in closed quotation, something additional happens: the demonstration is recruited as a singular term and endowed with a linguistic reference. In open quotation, one displays a token and thereby demonstrates a type, without referring to either the token or the type (let alone to whatever one is attempting to depict through the demonstration). Thus when, in *Hôtel du Nord*, the character played by Arletty says

- 'Atmosphère', 'atmosphère' . . . Est-ce que j'ai une gueule d'atmosphère ?

she mimics her interlocutor's use of the word 'atmosphère' (target) by producing two tokens of the same type, but she refers neither to the tokens which she herself produces, nor to the token which her interlocutor has just produced and which she imitates, nor to the type which all these tokens instantiate. In contrast, if I say

- 'Atmosphère' is a word which has been made famous by Arletty

then my demonstration of the word 'atmosphère' (a token of which I display) is recruited as a singular term referring to that word, and filling the role of subject in the sentence.

So far, so good. Now the question arises: what exactly does the closed quotation refer to? Does it refer to the displayed token, to the demonstrated type, to the target (if there is one), or to anything else? Does it always refer to the same sort of thing, or is its reference variable, as De Brabanter claims?

Before answering these questions, I should say something more about the notion of depicted target. De Brabanter rightly notes that, for me, the notions of target and of mimicry are interdependent, and I must explain why that is so.

Imagine that the speaker is reporting Arletty's speech. He says:

(1) And then she uttered the famous sentence 'Est-ce que j'ai une gueule d'atmosphère'.

It is pretty clear that the speaker is talking about Arletty's utterance and conveying information about it. So Arletty's utterance is the speaker's target, as it were. But it is not – or not necessarily – the 'target' of the quotation in the technical sense in which I use the term. For a quotation to have a target in this narrow sense, it must have mimetic properties in virtue of which it evokes something, namely, that thing which it pictures or depicts. If the speaker pronounces the quoted words 'Est-ce que j'ai une gueule d'atmosphère' with Arletty's accent, for example, the quotation will be understood as mimicking Arletty's utterance, and the latter will acquire the status of target. But if there is no mimicry – and, like De Brabanter, 'I do not see why it should be impossible to simply report someone's words without the slightest amount of mimicry' – then it is unclear that my restricted notion of target applies, even though the speaker talks about Arletty's utterance and attempts to characterize it.

To see why that is so, consider a negative variant of the example:

(a) But she did not actually utter the sentence 'Est-ce que j'ai une gueule d'atmosphère'

Here it is obvious that the quotation is not offered as a picture of Arletty's utterance: on the contrary the speaker asserts that her utterance was not of the demonstrated type, and it would be contradictory simultaneously to offer a type as picturing the target while denying that the target is of that type. Still, the speaker is talking about Arletty's utterance and attempts to provide information regarding it. It follows that what the speaker is talking about (the speaker's target, as it were) is not necessarily the target of the quotation in my sense. The relation of a quotation to its target does not depend upon the rest of the sentence. The quotation itself, in virtue of its mimetic properties, is offered as a picture of the target, and whenever that is so it would be contradictory to deny that the target in question is of the demonstrated type. A good example is provided by the parenthetical 'he said' which, as Cornulier pointed out, can only be appended to a linguistic demonstration endowed with mimetic properties. In the schema

(b) p, he said

the quotation which the letter 'p' stands for is bound to be mimetic, so that negation is impossible:

(c) * p, he did not say

I admit that this is a rather complex and controversial story. For my present purposes, it suffices to point out that there is a distinction between what the speaker is talking about and the target of the quotation (in the restricted sense in which I use that term). For this distinction is enough to invalidate one of De Brabanter's two arguments in favour of his view that quotations sometimes refer to a particular token.

De Brabanter's argument runs like this. In many cases, like (1) above, it is clear that the speaker is talking about a particular token (e.g. Arletty's utterance). Yet I hold that the quotation refers to the demonstrated type. In my framework, De Brabanter says, the distinction between target and demonstratum provides a way out: one may say that what is demonstrated is a type, while the target is a token. But this solution, De Brabanter argues, is not available in a case like (1), for the following reason: since we assume that the report has no mimetic properties, the quotation can be ascribed no target. Hence the intuition that the speaker somehow 'refers' to Arletty's particular utterance is not accounted for. To account for it, he says, we must either give up the view that the quotation refers to the type (and admits that in that sort of case it refers to a token), or, in order to make a 'target' available, implausibly maintain that some form of mimicry is involved in all cases in which, intuitively, the quoter talks about a particular token.

In my view this argument bears no force. The intuition that the speaker somehow 'refers' to Arletty's utterance can be accounted for quite easily, simply by saying that the speaker is reporting Arletty's utterance and providing a characterization of it. Beside the displayed token, the demonstrated type, and the depicted target, a fourth notion is available: what the speaker is talking about (what earlier I called the speaker's target). That is all we need to take care of De Brabanter's examples.

De Brabanter's second argument in favour of the thesis of referential diversity appeals to the phenomenon of iterated quotation, illustrated by the following example:

(2) In each utterance of the previous sentence ['Boston' is a six-letter word], ' "Boston" ' refers to an orthographic form.

De Brabanter argues that, 'for the subject of "Boston" is a six-letter word to be able to refer to an orthographic form, it must be a token". Let us assume that he is right and that only tokens can refer. Does it not follow that the iterated quotation ' "Boston" ' in (2) refers to a token? Well, not necessarily. A token may be represented as a pair consisting of (i) a type and (ii) a context in which the type is tokened. Let us now assume that the iterated quotation ' "Boston" ' in (2) refers to a type, in accordance with my view. Sentence (2) says that in each utterance of the previous sentence, this type refers to an orthographic form. Now the words 'in each utterance of the previous sentence' provide a context for the type; and once the type is paired with an appropriate context, it becomes a token and can refer. To sum up: we can accept that 'only tokens refer', while maintaining that in (2) the quotation refers to a type; for the type in question is said to refer not by itself (qua type), but insofar as it occurs in a certain context (qua token).

I conclude that De Brabanter has failed to establish the referential diversity thesis. This is not to deny that, in some (rather exceptional) cases, a quotation may perhaps refer to a token. Manuel Garcia-Carpintero described one such case during the Granada workshop. But such cases arguably involve a metonymy, similar to that in virtue of which one can refer to, say, a person by means of a quotation. (Thus, François Mitterrand's son Christophe was referred to in Africa as 'Papa m'a dit'.)

5

On Rigidity, Direct Reference and Natural Kind Terms

Luis Fernández Moreno

5.1 Introduction

In the first chapter of his book *Direct Reference* – and also in his paper 'Rigidity and Direct Reference' – François Recanati's main intention is to advance a definition of pure or direct referentiality in language. To this purpose he takes into account three different notions of rigidity 'all stemming from Kripke's characterization of a rigid designator as a designator that denotes the same object in all possible worlds. The three different notions are: rigidity as a matter of scope, rigidity as a matter of truth-conditions, and rigidity as (pure or direct) referentiality' (Recanati 1993: 7). The latter notion of rigidity is that which Recanati aims to characterize in a precise way.

Recanati's remarks on the notions of rigidity and direct referentiality only concern singular terms, mainly proper names and indexicals; they do not concern natural kind terms, which some authors, like Kripke and Putnam, have included into the category of rigid designators. Kripke has regarded natural kind terms explicitly as rigid designators, and so has Putnam, who asserts: '[i]f we extend the notion of rigidity to substance names, then we may express Kripke's theory and mine by saying that the term "water" is *rigid*' (Putnam 1975c: 231; this assertion concerning 'substance names' is intended to apply to all sorts of natural kind terms).

It is noteworthy that, though Kripke and Putnam regard natural kind terms explicitly as a sort of *general terms* (see, for example, Kripke 1980: 134 and Putnam 1975b: 139), both of them claim that natural kind terms have affinities with some sorts of singular terms which are rigid designators; in the case of Kripke with proper names, in Putnam's case with indexicals. Kripke asserts that 'terms for natural kinds are much closer to proper names than is ordinarily supposed' (Kripke 1980: 127), while Putnam alludes to his theory on natural kind terms as '[t]he theory that natural-kind words like 'water' are indexical' (Putnam 1975c: 234).

The aim of this chapter is to examine some of Recanati's remarks on the notions of rigidity and direct reference in language in order to extend them to natural kind terms. In pursuing this objective we will pay attention to the theories on natural kind terms put forward by Kripke and Putnam

5.2 Kripke on natural kind terms and natural kinds

The justification of the assertion that natural kind terms are rigid designators depends on how the notion of rigid designator is understood and how natural kinds, which are generally regarded as the referents of natural kind terms, are conceived, since not every view about natural kinds allows for natural kind terms to be rigid designators.

Concerning the first question, it is appropriate to introduce Kripke's definition of rigid designator. Kripke's most detailed characterization of the notion of rigid designator is contained in a letter to D. Kaplan quoted in Kaplan (1989):

> A designator d of an object x is *rigid*, if it designates x with respect to all possible worlds where x exists, and *never designates an object other than x with respect to any possible world.* (Kaplan 1989: 569; emphasis in the original)

Kripke's definition is neutral concerning the question of whether a rigid designator denotes the object x even with respect to worlds in which x does not exist or whether it does not denote anything with respect to those worlds. We will take into account as a definition of rigid designator a simplified form of this definition, according to which a rigid designator is a designator which denotes the same object with respect to *all* possible worlds – this is the Kripkean notion of rigid designator which Recanati takes into account in the above-quoted text – although later we will also pay brief attention to the other alternative – to wit, that a rigid designator does not denote anything with respect to worlds in which its referent does not exist. In any event, Kripke characterizes the notion of rigid designation only concerning singular terms, but in order to extend this definition to natural kind terms we will have to answer the question about what sort of entity is the referent of a natural kind term.

In this regard it is relevant to pay attention to Kripke's conception of natural kinds, since, as has already been stated, natural kinds are usually regarded as the referents of natural kind terms.

Kripke's conception of natural kinds is that they are abstract entities instantiated in concrete entities. This is the view put forward in the following passage:

I believe that, in general, terms for natural kinds (e.g., animal, vegetable, and chemical kinds) get their reference fixed in this way; the substance is defined as the kind instantiated by (almost all of) a given sample. (Kripke 1980: 135–136)[1]

However, Kripke fails to state more precisely the conception of natural kinds he is appealing to. In some passages, as in the aforementioned one, he uses the terms 'substance' and 'kind' interchangeably – see also Kripke (1980: 119) – and the same applies occasionally to the terms 'species' and 'kind' – see (1980: 121 f.), but since he does not provide an explication of the notions of substance and species, that interchangeable usage throws no light on the notion of natural kind. A proposal about the place to look for a clarification of this notion would consist in taking into account Kripke's claim that natural kind terms give rise to identity statements that, if true, are necessarily true, but necessary *a posteriori*, not *a priori*. Kripke considers that the sort of identity statements, which he refers to as 'theoretical identifications' or 'theoretical identities', express an identity of properties – see Kripke (1980: 138 f. and 140, n. 7) – which leads to the conception of natural kinds as a sort of property. But Kripke does not explain his conception of properties; so he asserts that '[the term – L.F.M.] "[p]roperties" is used here in a broad sense, and may include larger kinds: for example animality and felinity, for tigers' (1980: 137).

Nevertheless, according to a view on properties which can be attributed to Kripke properties are components of the (actual) world and discoverable through *empirical* research. Properties are conceived as abstract entities, although they are instantiated in concrete entities, and have causal efficacy. We shall call this sort of properties 'empirical properties'.[2] In this sense the statement 'Water is H_2O' can be understood as expressing the identity of two properties, namely that of being water and that of being (composed of molecules of) H_2O. If natural kinds are conceived as such sorts of properties, then natural kind terms can be rigid designators, since they will designate the same property with respect to all possible worlds – though in some of them that property might not be instantiated and hence not exist. Thus, the most plausible interpretation of Kripke's assertions that natural kind terms are general terms, rigid designators, and give rise to identity statements that, if true, are necessarily true, but necessary *a posteriori*, not *a priori*, is to attribute to him the view according to which the referents of natural kind terms, that is, natural kinds, are properties conceived in that way – to wit, empirical properties.

Although, as has already been said, Kripke defined the notion of rigid designation only in the context of singular terms, we can extend Kripkes's above-quoted characterization of rigid designation to natural kind terms by substituting in it the word 'object' by the word 'entity' – objects or individuals as well as properties are sorts of entities. Henceforth I shall assume this extension of Kripke's characterization of rigid designator to natural kind terms; yet I shall not usually make such substitution explicit.

Thus provided with a conception of the referents of natural kind terms that allows that natural kind terms be rigid designators we can proceed to examine some of Recanati's remarks on the notions of rigidity and direct reference. We will begin by paying attention to Recanati's remarks on the first two notions of rigidity – that is, rigidity as (i) a matter of scope and as (ii) a matter of truth-conditions. Afterwards we will look into the third notion of rigidity, i.e. rigidity as direct referentiality.

5.3 Natural kind terms and the first two notions of rigidity

Let us begin with Recanati's remarks concerning the first notion of 'rigidity', that is, rigidity as a matter of scope. Kripke claims that proper names and natural kind terms are rigid designators, while most definite descriptions are non-rigid ones. This contrast clashes with the descriptivist theory, according to which proper names – and also natural kind terms – are semantically and hence referentially equivalent to definite descriptions. One sort of objection against this supposed equivalence lies on the different logical behaviour in modal contexts of proper names and definite descriptions. This sort of objection would also be applicable to the relations between natural kind terms and definite descriptions; for brevity's sake, I shall only take into account the issue concerning the equivalence of proper names and definite descriptions. However, the conclusion to be obtained will apply to the claim concerning the equivalence of natural kind terms and definite descriptions.

According to one sort of descriptivist reply to that objection, the difference between proper names and definite descriptions consists in the fact that proper names always take the wide scope in modal contexts, while descriptions may take either a wide or a narrow scope; thus, a proper name will not be equivalent to a definite description, but only to a definite description which (always) takes wide scope in modal contexts. This is the notion of rigidity as a matter of scope: a rigid designator is simply a designator that (always) takes wide scope in modal contexts. I agree with Recanati that this view of rigidity is *misguided*, since if a rigid designator were merely an expression which (always) takes wide scope in modal contexts, then that notion would only be relevant to modal contexts. But the notion of rigid designation has a wider application. As Kripke says, rigidity is 'a doctrine about the truth conditions, with respect to counterfactual situations, of . . . *all* sentences, including *simple* sentences' (Kripke 1980: 12). Now the distinction of wide/narrow scope concerning descriptions does not have any application in the case of simple sentences; therefore, rigidity is not, and cannot be reduced to, a matter of scope.

Nevertheless, Recanati adds a further objection against the descriptivist's characterization of rigid designation in terms of scope; Recanati argues that a definite description designates non-rigidly not only when it takes narrow scope, but *also* when it takes wide scope. As I understand the objection, this lies on the indexicality of the expression 'actual', from which it follows that 'with respect to any world w, "the actual world" will be that very world w' (Recanati 1993: 9). The objection is presented as follows:

> [T]he description's taking wide scope means that its reference should be picked out in this 'actual' world, notwithstanding the fact that the sentence ['The president of France might have been tall' – L.F.M.] is used to describe another possible world. But this is not enough to make the designation rigid; for every world is the actual world with respect to itself, so that it will still be possible to change the description's reference simply by changing the world with respect to which the sentence is evaluated. It follows that, even if it was stipulated that a certain definite description always takes maximal scope in modal contexts, this description would still not count as a rigid designator. (Recanati 1993: 10)

I find this objection well made although, as Recanati concedes, it rests on a 'not very Kripkean' (1993: 23, n. 4) view. In this regard I would like to mention that besides this relative, indexical notion of actuality, there is an absolute notion, and this is Kripke's one of actuality or rather of actual world, which is a component of this view on regidity.

As Kripke points out: 'When I say that a designator is rigid, and designates the same thing in all possible worlds, I mean that, as used in *our* language, it stands for that thing, when *we* talk about counterfactual situations' (Kripke 1980: 77). A term can only be a rigid designator if it has a fixed interpretation and this is the interpretation given to the term by us here in the actual world. Kripke's view is that there is a unique actual world – 'the real world' (1980: 132) – the other possible worlds or counterfactual situations being merely stipulated. Thus, the referent of a rigid designator is the same object in all possible worlds, but there is a unique world relevant to the fixing of the reference of a rigid designator, and this is the actual world. In this way Kripke's notion of rigid designation presupposes a non-relative conception of the actual world. Recanati's objection could be countered by a descriptivist on the basis of that conception, since, even accepting that 'the description's taking wide scope means that its reference should be picked out in this "actual" world' (Recanati 1993: 10), the descriptivist may claim that in this assertion the notion of actual world has to be understood in a non-relative sense and that, in any case, the world of the context he is taking into account is just the actual world in that sense. Thus, it may be questioned that it is 'possible to change the description's reference simply by changing the world with respect to which the sentence is evaluated' (*ibid.*). Nevertheless, as Recanati emphasizes, the notion of 'rigidity' as scope is misguided as it cannot explain rigid designation in the framework of contexts where the distinction of wide/narrow scope concerning descriptions does not apply, for example, in the case of simple sentences.

One reason to bear in mind Kripke's notion of actual world is that it allows the introduction of a descriptivist proposal concerning rigid designation that Recanati does not take into account explicitly. According to that proposal, proper names are semantically and hence referentially equivalent not to any sort of descriptions, but only to one sort of them, i.e. to rigidified descriptions. In this regard it is appropriate to put forward two proposals – among others contained in the literature – which may be regarded as equivalent. In accordance with the first one, descriptions will turn into rigid ones by adding to them the clause 'at the actual world' or 'in the actual world', in the non-relative sense of the expression 'actual world'. According to the second proposal, descriptions can be turned into rigid descriptions by means of the actuality operator. This operator may be conceived as an operator that is applied to an open or closed sentence to form a more complex sentence. Now, given the indexicality of 'actually' we will have to specify in which world the descriptions constructed with the actuality operator would be being used. But since the reference of rigid designators is fixed in the actual world, we will consider that the descriptions rigidified by means of the actuality operator would be being used in the actual world, in the non-relative sense of 'actual world'. (Thus, we assume that the formula 'actually Fx' is satisfied by an object in a possible world w if and only if in the actual world that object has the property expressed by the predicate 'F'.) Following either of these procedures, which may be considered as equivalent, we are provided with one sort of rigid descriptions, i.e. rigidified descriptions.

Once we have presented rigidified descriptions, let us consider the second notion of rigidity, i.e. the notion of rigidity as a matter or truth-conditions – see the aforementioned passage from Kripke. According to this notion, a designator is rigid if there is an entity such that, with respect to every counterfactual situation or possible world, the truth-condition of every sentence containing the designator involves the entity in question. In this way the contribution of a rigid designator to the truth-conditions of the sentences in which it appears is its referent. Recanati accepts that this conception of rigid designation may be subscribed by a descriptivist who maintains the referential equivalence between proper names and rigid descriptions. And this claim applies, of course, to that special sort of rigid descriptions which are rigidified descriptions.

Now it could be objected that the truth-conditions or, at least, the truth-values of sentences containing proper names and those of the sentences containing rigidified descriptions may be different. As has already been said, Kripke's most precise characterization of rigid designator is neutral concerning the question of whether a rigid designator denotes the same object with respect to worlds in which the object does not exist or does not denote anything with respect to those worlds. In this respect, it is relevant to introduce the distinction drawn by some authors – for example, by Nathan Salmon in (1981) – between persistently and obstinately rigid designators or, in short, between persistent and obstinate designators. A persistent designator denotes the same object with respect to every world in which the object exists, and denotes nothing with respect to worlds in which the object does not exist. By contrast, an obstinate designator denotes the same object with respect to every world whatsoever. Now, in their usual interpretation, rigid descriptions – of contingently existing objects – even rigidified descriptions, are persistent designators, while it is held generally that proper names are obstinate designators, and this is the conception of proper names which corresponds to the characterization of rigid designator employed by Recanati. So it could be claimed that proper names are not referentially equivalent to rigidified descriptions. Nevertheless, this conclusion may be a little hasty, since there are procedures to turn rigidified descriptions into obstinate designators, for example, by allowing that the domain over which individual variables range with respect to a world *w* consists not only of the objects existing in that world but also of other objects that are merely possible relative to it – see Soames (2002: 325 f., n. 31).

In any event, it is noteworthy that not only descriptivists have resorted to rigidified descriptions. These sorts of descriptions are implicit in some of Kripke's claims concerning the fixing of the reference of proper names or of natural kind terms by means of a description,[3] and are more explicit in some of Putnam's (1975c) statements concerning the rigidity of natural kind terms. Putnam claims that there are two ways of explaining what one means by a natural kind term – to wit, by means of an ostensive definition or of a description (Putnam 1975c: 229). He explicitly uses the clause 'in the actual world' in regard to the fixing of the reference of natural kind terms by means of an ostensive definition (see 1975c: 231 f.), but the descriptions which may play the same role of reference fixing are being regarded – although sometimes Putnam does not say it clearly – as rigidified ones.

Concerning that sort of description he asserts that it 'typically consists of one or more markers together with a *stereotype* – a standardized description of features of the kind that are typical, or "normal", or at any rate stereotypical' (1975c: 230), but since such sorts of descriptions are being understood as rigidified ones, the description in question concerning the natural kind term 'water' may be the following one: the colourless, tasteless, thirst-quenching liquid that fills the oceans, falls from the sky, and so on, in the actual world.

In this regard it is appropriate to make two remarks. Firstly, the force of the reference fixing of the term 'water' by means of that description is that water is the liquid in any possible world which is in the relation of being the same liquid as the colourless, tasteless, thirst-quenching liquid that fills the oceans, falls from the sky, and so on, in the actual world. Secondly, we could ask how to justify Putnam's claim that his theory on natural kind terms is a theory according to which 'natural-kind words like "water" are indexical' (Putnam 1975c: 234). And the answer is that in a strict sense Putnam's thesis is not that natural kind terms are indexicals, but rather that natural kind terms 'like "water" have an unnoticed indexical component' (*ibid.*), and we can agree with this claim, since in the mentioned description which fixes the reference of the term 'water' it appears an indexical expression, such as 'actual' as part of the expression 'in the actual world'[4] – the indexicals that Putnam uses in the context of that claim are 'here' in the expression 'the water *around here'* and 'our' as part of the expression '*our* "water" ' (*ibid.*). Anyway a descriptivist could resort to such sort of rigidified descriptions to claim that according to descriptivism natural kind terms are rigid designators, since they are referentially equivalent to rigid descriptions.

Nevertheless, Putnam claims that 'Kripke's doctrine that natural-kind words are rigid designators and our doctrine that they are indexical are but two ways of making the same point' (*ibid.*). And part of the point in question is that natural kind terms are *non-descriptional* (or non-connotative), i.e. on the one hand, even if the reference of a natural kind term is fixed by a description which expresses the stereotype associated with the term, the stereotype provides neither necessary nor sufficient conditions for the membership in the extension of the term, and, on the other hand, the natural kind term is not synonymous with that description.[5] In this last sense it may be claimed that rigidified descriptions, even if they may be used to fix the reference of natural kind terms and are referentially equivalent to natural kind terms, have not the same meaning as natural kind terms.

5.4 Direct reference and natural kind terms

Recanati, restricting his considerations to singular terms, accepts the notion of rigidity in terms of truth-conditions, which he reformulates by means of the notion of *singular truth-condition*. A rigid designator is an expression such that the truth-condition of any utterance (of a sentence) where it occurs is singular, and the truth-condition of an utterance is singular if there is a certain object such that the utterance is true if and only if the object satisfies the open sentence which results from the elimination of the term (Recanati 1993: 16). Nevertheless, since it could be claimed that the truth-condition of utterances containing rigid definite descriptions of objects is also singular, Recanati aims to make precise a feature which allows a distinction to be made between proper names from definite descriptions, even from rigid descriptions, at least in their non-referential uses; this feature is direct referentiality – henceforth we will follow Recanati's use of 'referential' and 'referentiality' as short for 'directly referential' and 'direct referentiality'.

The notion of referentiality has been usually characterized only in a rather metaphorical way, for example, by claiming that the link between a proper name and its referent is purely stipulative while that between a definite description and its referent is qualitative or by asserting that proper names are rigid *de jure*, while rigid definite descriptions are rigid *de facto*. Recanati aims to characterize the notion of referentiality in a less metaphorical way. Now since Recanati only takes into account singular terms his definition of (type-)referentiality only concerns such terms.[6] Recanati claims that type-referentiality is a feature of the *linguistic meaning* of the referential terms which he defines as follows:

> A term is (type-)referential if and only if its linguistic meaning includes a feature, call it 'REF', by virtue of which it indicates that the truth-condition (or, more generally, satisfaction-condition) of the utterance where it occurs is singular. (1993: 17)

Recanati accepts the thesis that the meaning of referential terms contains a mode of presentation of their referent, but the characteristic property of a referential term is that its meaning includes a feature, the feature REF, which presents the truth-conditions of the utterances where the term occurs as singular – hence as excluding the mode of presentation of its referent – and so makes the contribution of a referential term to the proposition expressed by the utterance – the content of the term – to be its referent.

Before paying attention to the way in which natural kind terms could be regarded as referential terms, it is relevant to take into account the terms considered by Recanati as paradigmatic examples of referential terms, namely proper names and indexicals. On the one hand, both of them are referential terms – they convey the feature REF –, on account of which their unique contribution to the propositions expressed by the utterances containing them are their referents. On the other hand, their meaning includes, in addition to the feature REF, a mode of presentation of their referent. Nevertheless, this mode of presentation is not the same in the case of proper names as in the case of indexicals. *Each indexical* contains as a part of its meaning a particular linguistic mode of presentation, namely, its character; for example, the pronoun 'I' presents its referent as being the speaker by virtue of the linguistic convention that 'I' refers to the speaker. While *all names* present their referent in the *same* way – to wit, as the bearer of the name by virtue of the linguistic convention that a proper name refers to its bearer; however, this linguistic convention, which is general, involves a specific social convention which links *each* proper name to its bearer. Which object or individual is the bearer of a proper name is a matter of social convention, and hence a contextual matter, since the social convention in question is determined by the context. In this sense Recanati claims that '[t]he reference of the name thus depends on a contextual factor, as the reference of an indexical expression does' (1993: 140). This sort of metalinguistic view of proper names, which includes the claim that name-conventions which pair each name with its bearer are not linguistic but social conventions, is the view on proper names maintained by Recanati, to which he refers as 'the indexical view'.

But Recanati's conception of proper names is different from his view concerning general terms and hence concerning natural kind terms, a sort of general terms. In this regard it is appropriate to pay attention to two different sorts of contrasts that Recanati draws between proper names and general terms.

On the one hand, in paragraph 9.4 he contrasts proper names with general terms – he says 'ordinary words' (1993: 163 f.) – by comparing the proper name 'Socrates' with the general terms 'red' and 'alienist'. Recanati puts forward three conventions concerning these expressions: 'This man [pointing to Socrates] is called "Socrates" ', 'This colour [pointing to a sample of red] is called "red" ' and 'Psychiatrists are called "alienists" '. Recanati makes some remarks on these conventions. Firstly, in these conventions linguistic expressions are related to something else – 'the relatum' – so that in these conventions it can be distinguished between the relatum and the relation between a word and the relatum. Secondly, the first convention, i.e. the convention concerning the proper name 'Socrates', in contrast to the other ones, is not a linguistic convention; for that reason that convention does not constitute the meaning of the name 'Socrates', although a component of that convention – the relation contained in it, i.e. the relation 'being so-called' or 'bearer of the name' – is part of the meaning of the name 'Socrates'. As Recanati (1993: 164) says: "it is the relation, not the relatum, which constitutes the meaning of a proper name.' But he adds that 'it is the relatum, not the relation, which constitutes the meaning of words such as "red" or "alienist" ' (*ibid.*). In this regard I suppose that the relatum of the word 'red', i.e. the colour red, is the referent of the word 'red', and that the relatum of the word 'alienist' is constituted by the psychiatrists, who, according to that convention, will be the members of the extension of 'alienist'.[7] So it seems that if the semantic conventions for general terms are like those for 'red' and 'alienist', then the meaning of a general term would be its referent or extension. In this case we would have to conclude that general terms, and hence natural kind terms, are semantically very different from referential terms, since according to Recanati the meaning of referential terms is not their referent or extension.

Nevertheless, on the other hand, Recanati puts forward in paragraph 8.5 a different contrast between proper names and general terms – he says 'other names' (1993: 147) – taking into account explicitly natural kind terms, which conflicts with the view that the meaning of a natural kind term is its reference or its extension. There he agrees with the following passage from Putnam:

> [I]t is instructive to observe that nouns like 'tiger' or 'water' are very different from proper names. One can use the proper name 'Sanders' correctly without knowing anything about the referent except that he is called 'Sanders' [. . .] But one cannot use the word 'tiger' correctly, save *per accidens*, without knowing a good deal about tigers, or at least about a certain conception of tigers. (Putnam 1975c: 247)

Recanati agrees with Putnam that in order to be a competent speaker concerning a natural kind term one has to know the stereotype of the (extension of the) natural kind term, whereas in order to be a competent speaker concerning a proper name one only needs to know about the referent of a proper name that it is the bearer of the name. He also agrees with Putnam's thesis that the stereotype associated with a word can be more or less extensive. In regard to this thesis Recanati characterizes a word as 'local' when its stereotype contains few features and claims that the characteristic of proper names lies in their *local* character – the 'stereotype' of proper names only contains the trait according to which a proper name refers to its bearer. But in this way Recanati seems to accept that the meaning of a natural kind term contains the stereotype associated with the term. So we have a component of the meaning of a natural kind term, the *stereotype*, which can be regarded as a linguistic mode of presentation of the reference (or extension) of the term. In order to consider natural kind terms as referential terms we have to add the claim that a natural kind term contains as a part of their meaning also the feature REF, a feature which prevents the stereotype from going into the truth-conditions of utterances containing the natural kind term and so makes the contribution of a natural kind term to the propositions expressed by utterances containing the term to be not its stereotype, but its referent – as it was said, an empirical property.

The definition of (type-)referentiality for natural kind terms would be as follows: a natural kind term T is (type)-referential if and only if its linguistic meaning includes a feature, the feature REF, by virtue of which it indicates that there is a property P such that an utterance of Ta is true – or, more generally, satisfied – if and only if the object a is an instance of P, i.e. if only if the object a possesses the property P.

In this way Recanati's characterization of direct reference could be extended with certain modifications to natural kind terms. The referent of a natural kind term is an (empirical) property, whereas the linguistic meaning of a natural kind term has two ingredients, its stereotype and the feature REF.[8]

Notes

1. We shall over look the qualification 'almost all of', since its justification is rather obvious. The sample on the basis of which the reference of a natural kind term is fixed may contain a small number of entities of a distinct kind; if the number is not a small one so that most of the sample does not instantiate one uniform kind, distinct reactions are possible; see Kripke (1980: 136).

2. This view on properties agrees with the conception held by Putnam in (1970), for which he has used the term 'physical properties' in a wide sense of the word 'physical' – I prefer the broader term 'empirical properties'. Some of Putnam's claims could be interpreted as pointing to the conception of natural kinds, and thus of the referents of natural kind terms, as this sort of properties. Nevertheless, the most explicitly formulated view on natural kinds put forward by Putnam is that they are the extensions of natural kind terms – see (1975b: 139) – but the conception of the referents of natural kind terms as their extensions is incompatible with the thesis that natural kind terms are rigid designators.

3. Sometimes this sort of description appears in an explicit way in Kripke's writings: 'I imagined a hypothetical formal language in which a rigid designator "a" is introduced with the ceremony, "Let 'a' (rigidly) denote the unique object that actually has property F, when talking about any situation, actual or counterfactual" ' Kripke (1980: 14).

4. In the famous thought experiment concerning Twin Earth, this planet is sometimes imagined as belonging to the actual world, but situated very far from Earth; nevertheless, Putnam's assertions – especially those in which he explicitly uses the clause 'in the actual world' – are better interpreted as supposing that Twin Earth is in another possible world. We have been also adopting this last assumption. In the first case, it would be appropriate to replace in the description above mentioned the clause 'in the actual world' by some other, for instance, by 'in our environment', with the indexical 'our'.

5. It could be claimed that not only natural kind terms but all general terms can be regarded as rigid designators in a trivial sense, if we consider that their referent is a property conceived merely as an abstract entity (whose existence does not depend on its being instantiated). Nevertheless, it can be pointed out that there are at least two differences between the general terms considered by both, Kripke and Putnam, as rigid designators – which include especially natural kind terms, but also some adjectives such as 'red' – and other general terms. On the one hand, the referent of the first class of general terms is a specific sort of property, an empirical property – see section 5.2. On the other hand, general terms of the first class are, like proper names, non-descriptional in the above-mentioned sense, while the other general terms lack this feature.

6. I will only deal with direct reference considered as a linguistic phenomenon, i.e. with type-referentiality, that is, referentiality *qua* semantic property of expression types.

7. Though Recanati will probably not agree with this reading of the conventions for 'red' and 'alienist', I think that he has to concede that this reading is possible.

8. I am grateful to Isabel Ferrari and Lorenzo Peña for their comments on a preliminary version of this chapter. I would like to thank the Spanish Ministry of Education for finantial support through the Project UM2005–03439 and to the Madrid Community Educational Council and to the Comphetense University of Madrid for the finantial support given to the Research Group 930174 ("Philosophy of language, of nature and of Science").

References

Kaplan, D. (1989) 'Afterthoughts'. In J. Almog, J. Perry, and H. Wettstein (eds), *Themes from Kaplan*. Oxford: Oxford University Press, pp. 565–614.

Kripke, S. (1980) *Naming and Necessity*. Oxford: Basil Blackwell.

Putnam, H. (1970) 'On Properties'. In N. Rescher *et al.* (eds), *Essays in Honor of Carl G. Hempel*, Dordrecht, Holland. Reprinted in H. Putnam, *Mathematics, Matter and Method: Philosophical Papers*, vol. I, Cambridge, Cambridge University Press, 1975, pp. 305–22.

Putnam, H. (1975a) *Mind, Language and Reality: Philosophical Papers*, vol. 2. Cambridge: Cambridge University Press.

Putnam, H. (1975b) 'Is Semantics Possible?'. In Putnam (1975a), pp. 139–52.

Putnam, H. (1975c) 'The Meaning of "Meaning"'. In Putnam (1975a), pp. 215–71.

Recanati, F. (1988) 'Rigidity and Direct Reference'. *Philosophical Studies*, 53: 103–17.

Recanati, F. (1993) *Direct Reference: From Language to Thought*. Oxford: Blackwell.

Salmon, N. (1981) *Reference and Essence*. Princeton: Princeton University Press.

Soames, S. (2002) *Beyond Rigidity*. Oxford: Oxford University Press.

Recanati's Reply to Fernández Moreno

I

There are, I maintain, three distinct notions of rigidity in the literature:

- The strongest notion is that in terms of which proper names (and indexicals) can be squarely contrasted with definite descriptions. Proper names are rigid in the sense of 'directly referential' (Kaplan 1989); definite descriptions are not.
- Kripke's official notion of rigidity is weaker, and it is not sufficient to distinguish referential terms from definite descriptions. Certain descriptions – namely, those where the property that is the content of the description is necessary rather than contingent – are rigid in Kripke's official sense: they denote the same object in every possible world in which that object exists.
- The weakest notion of rigidity also applies to some descriptions which exploit contingent properties of the denotatum. Such a description is rigid (in the weakest sense) if and only if, in a modal context, it takes wide scope.

The weaker the notion of rigidity one assumes for proper names, the less sharp the contrast one gets between names and descriptions. This gives rise to various descriptivist strategies, i.e. strategies for reducing names (and other referential expressions) to descriptions.

A common descriptivist strategy is based upon the idea that rigidity is a matter of scope. It says that the only difference between a name and a description is that a name always (or, perhaps, usually) takes wide scope, while a description may take either wide scope or narrow scope. This view raises an obvious objection: if rigidity was merely a matter of scope, the notion would not apply to referential expressions as they occur in simple sentences. But it does. As Kripke says, rigidity is a matter of truth-conditions, and it concerns simple sentences as well as complex sentences.

In *Direct Reference* I advanced another argument against that descriptivist strategy. A wide scope description, I claimed, is not rigid, appearances notwithstanding. Consider 'The French president might have been a philosopher'. On the wide scope reading, it says of the president that he might have been a philosopher (had his life been different); on the narrow scope reading it says that a philosopher might have been president. Let us focus on the wide scope reading. The description, on that reading, refers to whoever is the president in the circumstance relative to which the complex sentence is evaluated. But that need not be the same person in all circumstances of evaluation. It follows that even a wide scope description is not rigid in Kripke's official sense.[1]

Fernández Moreno claims that the descriptivist has a way out. To say that a description takes wide scope is to say that its reference is picked out in the actual world rather than in the world or worlds introduced by the modal operator. If we opt for a relative, indexical view of actuality, according to which every world is actual with respect to itself, then the reference of a wide scope description will be seen as nonrigidly shifting as we shift the world of evaluation for the complex sentence. But if we opt for an absolute, Kripkean notion of actuality, then, Fernández Moreno says, we can maintain that a wide scope description is rigid: its reference is picked out in the actual world, and 'there is a unique actual world': so the reference of the description is not liable to vary, even if we vary the world of evaluation.

I agree with Fernández Moreno that there is an 'absolute' notion of actuality alongside the relative, indexical notion. But I maintain that a wide scope description is not a description that is evaluated with respect to the actual world in that absolute sense. A wide scope description is a description whose denotation is picked out in the world of evaluation for the complex sentence, rather than in the world(s) introduced by the modal operator for the evaluation of the simple sentence in its scope. Any world can serve as the world of evaluation for the complex sentence, and there is no guarantee that the description's denotation will not shift as we shift the world of evaluation.

Can we not introduce, besides wide scope descriptions, another sort of description, namely *rigidified* descriptions, by stipulating that such a description picks out its reference in the actual world understood in the absolute sense? Indeed we can. This, Fernández Moreno says, suggests another way of implementing the descriptivist strategy: a proper name (or a referential term more generally) can be equated to a rigidified description 'the x such that x is actually F'. Such a description will be rigid in Kripke's official sense, even if the property F is contingent; for the property of being actually F is necessary: the object (if any) which is actually F is the same with respect to every world w, on the absolute understanding of 'actually'.

Fernández Moreno notes that I do not discuss this proposal. (He also notes that both Kripke and Putnam have implicitly appealed to rigidified descriptions to handle cases in which the reference of a referential term is fixed by a definite description.) I am grateful to him for providing me with an opportunity to say something about it.

To put it bluntly: I have no objection whatever to the claim that referential terms, or at least some of them, can be construed as rigidified descriptions. Indeed that is very close to what I myself propose for indexicals. Indexicals have a descriptive content ; thus an occurrence of 'I' presents its reference as the speaker of that occurrence. That mode of presentation is truth-conditionally irrelevant, and its truth-conditional irrelevance is imposed at the lexical level by the feature REF. As I say in *Direct Reference*, 'REF does exactly the same job as [Kaplan's] DTHAT; the difference between them is simply that I take REF to be a semantic feature of natural language, while DTHAT is an operator in an artificial language' (p. 31). Now DTHAT is a rigidifying operator. As Stalnaker puts it, it 'turns any singular term into a rigid designator for the thing that is the actual referent of that term' (Stalnaker 2003: 197). It follows that on my analysis, an indexical is like a rigidified description since its meaning consists of: (i) a descriptive content or mode of presentation, and (ii) the rigidifying operator carried by the feature REF. The same analysis applies to proper names insofar as, in my framework, they are treated as a special sort of indexical.

Does this mean that I am a descriptivist? Not at all! I maintain that there is a sharp contrast between directly referential terms (proper names and indexicals) and definite descriptions. Directly referential terms are rigid in virtue of their linguistic meaning (*viz.* in virtue of the feature REF); descriptions are not. If a description is rigid, it is so only 'de facto', either because the property in terms of which the denotation is described happens to be necessary, or because the speaker uses the description referentially. In the latter type of case, the description is rigidified, but the rigidifying operator that is contributed in virtue of the speaker's intention is not linguistically articulated; it is not part of the lexical meaning of the description.

II

What about natural kind terms, the focus of Fernández Moreno's enquiry? Before answering this question, I must first say something more about names and indexicals. It is possible to treat names as indexicals, as I do; but there is an alternative treatment which construes them as Millian tags. Consider, for example, a descriptive name such as Evans's 'Julius'. Even though the reference of the name is fixed via the description 'the inventor of the zip', still, on the Millian view, that description is not part of the meaning of the name. Instead of construing the meaning of the name as consisting of a description ('the inventor of the zip') and a rigidifying operator, the Millian view takes the reference-fixing description to play a *presemantic* role: it fixes the meaning of the name, which meaning is its reference – period. On this view, the difference between names and indexicals is that indexicals have a two-dimensional semantics, while names (like descriptions) have a one-dimensional semantics (Stalnaker 2003: chapter 10). Indexicals have both a 'character' and a 'content'. Their character is a mode of presentation which, evaluated in the context, yields an object as value, which object goes into the content to be evaluated with respect to a circumstance. The rigidifying operator is there to guarantee that the object, not the mode of presentation, goes into the truth-conditional content of the utterance. With descriptions, the mode of presentation goes into the truth-conditional content (unless the description is used referentially); with proper names, on the Millian view, the meaning is, from the very start, an object, and that object is the name's contribution to truth-conditional content. It is only in the case of indexicals that we have two distinct levels: a meaning that is, in part, descriptive, and a content that results from evaluating the descriptive meaning in the context, with the rigidifying operator constraining the content to be the object resulting from the prior evaluation of the descriptive meaning in context and not the descriptive meaning itself.

The reason why I have just introduced the Millian option for proper names, even though I myself favour a unified, two-dimensional approach to referential terms, is that the same two options (the indexical view, and the Millian view) are available for natural kind terms. Either we say that the meaning of a natural kind term is the natural kind it names, period; or we say that a natural kind term is like an indexical: it has a first level meaning which consists of a superficial property or complex of properties (the stereotype), and a second level meaning (the content) which is the 'deep' natural kind rather than the superficial property serving as its 'mode of presentation'. I take it that Kripke and Burge advocate the Millian view, while Putnam and Donnellan favour the indexical view. I myself, unsurprisingly, favour the indexical view.

How can the indexical view be implemented, in the case of natural kind terms? A first difficulty is that, when we evaluate the stereotypical property (or complex of properties) in context, i.e. when we look for something that satisfies the property, what we get is an ordinary object or, rather, a set of such objects. Evaluating the stereotype of tigers in context gives us the set of objects that, in the context, look or behave like stereotypical tigers. Those objects which actually satisfy the stereotype are not the objects we want to get into the content of natural kind terms; for we want the content to be the kind or the deep property, not the objects which satisfy the superficial property! So applying a rigidifying operator to the stereotype construed as mode of presentation does not yield the right results. A second difficulty is due to the fact that we want to contrast natural kind terms with other general terms such as 'rectangle'; but all general terms rigidly contribute the 'property' that is their semantic value. How, then, can rigidity be the distinguishing characteristics of natural kind terms, which makes them similar to referential terms in the singular domain?

The solution consists in making the picture slightly more complex than for indexicals. Like indexicals, natural kind terms are evaluated in two stages: they are associated with a stereotype which is evaluated in context, and which is distinct from their content (the natural kind); but their content is not the contextual value of the stereotype. The value of the stereotype is a set of objects, which is mapped to the natural kind by an abstractive function.

I think an analogy can be useful here. Sometimes we express a property through an act of demonstrative reference to an instance of the property. So we can say: 'The wall is that colour', where 'that colour' (i) demonstrates a particular colour sample, and (ii) semantically contributes the colour property which that sample instantiates. In such a case, a function abs_{colour} takes us from the instance to the colour property it instantiates. I suggest that some such abstractive function is operative in the case of natural kind terms. The stereotype associated with the term is evaluated in context, yielding the local exemplars that satisfy the stereotype; those exemplars serve as argument to a function abs_{nk} whose value is the natural kind which the exemplars instantiate. A natural kind term, therefore, involves (i) a rigidified description denoting the exemplars which satisfy the stereotype in the local context, and (ii) a function abs_{nk} taking us from those exemplars to the kind they instantiate. On this view what distinguishes natural kind terms from other general terms is not the fact that they rigidly contribute a property (all general terms do), but the fact that that property is reached via a form of indexical reference to the local exemplars.

Note

1. This argument was anticipated by Stephen Schiffer (1977: 31).

References

Burge, T. (1982) 'Other Bodies'. In A. Woodfield (ed.), *Thought and Object*. Oxford: Clarendon Press, pp. 97–120.
Donnellan, K. (1993) 'There is a Word for That Kind of Thing: An Investigation of Two Thought Experiments'. *Philosophical Perspectives* 7: 155–71.
Kaplan, D. (1989) 'Demonstratives'. In J. Almog, H. Wettstein and J. Perry (eds), *Themes from Kaplan*. New York: Oxford University Press, pp. 481–563.
Kripke, S. (1980) *Naming and Necessity*. Oxford: Blackwell.
Putnam, H. (1975) 'The Meaning of Meaning'. In H. Putnam, *Philosophical Papers 2: Mind, Language and Reality*. Cambridge: Cambridge University Press, pp. 215–71.
Recanati, F. (1993) *Direct Reference: From Language to Thought*. Oxford: Blackwell.
Schiffer, S. (1977) 'Naming and Knowing'. *Midwest Studies in Philosophy* 2: 28–41.
Stalnaker, R. (2003) *Ways a World Might Be*. Oxford: Oxford University Press.

6
Meaning 'Literal'

Manuel Hernández Iglesias

6.1 Introduction

The notion of literality is central to all metalinguistic studies and, in particular, to the philosophical analysis of the concept of meaning. The standard view of linguistic communication is, roughly, something along the following lines. Knowledge of the meanings of words, of the compositional semantic rules and of the relevant aspects of context allows the interpreter to understand the literal meaning of any utterance of the language in question. Very often, what the speaker wants to communicate is different from this literal meaning. In these cases, the interpreter must find out what this nonliteral meaning is, typically by appeal to conversational maxims. The input of this second step of interpretation is the literal (or primary) meaning of the utterance (what the speaker says) and the output is the nonliteral (or secondary) meaning of the utterance (what the speaker means). Even if it is assumed that speaker's meaning always departs more or less dramatically from utterance meaning, that is, even if we always or almost always mean something more, something less or something different from what we say, the grasping of the literal meaning of the utterance is a necessary first step in any interpretation. Any theory of meaning must then, according to this standard view, explain how the literal meanings of utterances are generated.

The same holds for everyday talk about language. 'Literality' is not like 'indexicality', 'truth-functionality' or 'implicature'. Ordinary speakers do talk of literal or nonliteral meanings of words, readings of sentences and laws, translations, etc. The literal/nonliteral distinction is as central to folk linguistics as to technical studies on language. This ubiquity of the notion of literality both in technical linguistics and folk linguistics gives rise to very different and often-conflicting senses. We talk of literal reports or quotations, as opposed to paraphrases; of literal meanings of utterances, as opposed to elaborated meanings; of literal meanings of words, as opposed to figurative or extended meanings; of what is literally said, as opposed to what is conveyed or suggested, etc. This variety of senses in which an utterance, an expression or an interpretation can be said to be literal or nonliteral raises reasonable doubts about the usefulness of the distinction. It is tempting to get rid of the very notion of literal meaning or, at least, to take it as a folk linguistics term useless for the scientific or philosophical analysis of meaning.[1]

In his paper 'Literal/nonliteral' (2002) and in chapter 5 of his recent book *Literal Meaning: The Very Idea* (2004), François Recanati tries to vindicate and clarify the notion of literality. The problem, he claims, is not the notion itself, but the failure of language theorists to distinguish between its different senses, and, particularly, between the semantic and the ordinary sense. The literal meaning of an expression in the semantic sense is the meaning assigned to it by linguistic conventions (relativized to context if they are indexical). The literal meaning in the ordinary sense is normal meaning, as opposed to deviant or special meanings that depart from the norm.

Language theorists use the same terms for both distinctions, Recanati claims, and in doing so confuse them. And this confusion comes from the widespread tacit assumption that the literal meaning in the semantic sense (the conventional meaning) is also the literal meaning in the ordinary sense (the normal meaning). But this assumption is, as Recanati holds, mistaken, for words used literally in the ordinary sense usually express meanings different from those dictated by linguistic conventions. Take the sentence 'The policeman raised his hand and stopped the car'. We naturally understand utterances of this sentence as meaning that the policeman stopped the car by raising his hand. Since the temporal ordering and the causal connection are not part of the conventionally encoded meaning of the sentence, the meaning of the utterance is not literal in the semantic sense. But it is literal in the ordinary sense, for no special or deviant meaning is involved. Most (if not all) expressions used nonliterally in the semantic sense are used literally in the ordinary sense.

Recanati's analysis successfully removes widespread confusions. Nevertheless, I think his definition of literality fails to capture the ordinary sense of this notion. This chapter is an attempt to clarify and develop Recanati's classification of the different kinds of literality in order to give and vindicate a more realistic characterization of the common use of 'literal'.[2]

6.2   Recanati's classification

Recanati makes the classification of meanings shown in Figure 6.1.

T-literal (= type literal) meanings are those determined exclusively by linguistic conventions regardless of context. M-literal (= minimally literal) are the meanings determined by t-literal meanings and aspects of context encoded by conventions (e.g. indexical sentences). P-literal (= primary literal) meanings are determined by the adjustment of m-literal meanings to the situation. This adjustment takes two forms: sense elaboration and sense extension. The latter, above some threshold, gives rise to figurative meanings. P-nonliteral meanings are secondary meanings. In these cases,

T-literal

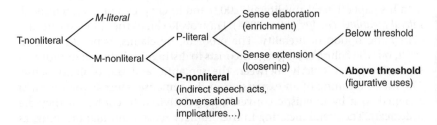

Figure 6.1   Classification of meanings

speakers mean something different from what they say or pretend to say. This includes conversational implicatures, indirect speech acts and 'staged' acts like irony, overstatement, rhetorical questions, sarcasm, etc.

I will illustrate these different meanings with the following example (I exclude sense extension for the sake of clarity). Let's imagine a conversation between A and B on sexual equality. The discussion takes place outdoors in the city of Murcia, at noon in a sunny day, say, 7th July 2003. A says:

(1) Men and women are different.

What is the meaning of (1)? Semantic conventions tell us that the utterance means that there are some differences between men and women. This, obviously, needs elaboration. Without elaboration, it is impossible to make sense of it, for the word 'different' is used to say many very different things. We say, for instance, that Clark Kent is different from Superman, that I am different than when I was young, that all humans are different from each other, that Spaniards are different from Portuguese, that humans are different from gorillas, that animals are different from plants, gases from liquids, planets from stars, numbers from stones, etc. We would clearly misunderstand A if we interpreted (1) as meaning that men and women are different in the sense in which all persons are different from each other, or in the sense in which humans are different from gorillas. And this is clearly not a matter of disambiguation between a series of conventional meanings of 'different', but of meaning enrichment. In this case, part of the enriched meaning of (1) would be that men and women differ in a sense stronger than the sense in which all humans differ from each other, but weaker than the sense in which humans are different from gorillas.[3]

Let's suppose now that, annoyed by A's insistence on the fact that men and women are different, B replies:

(2) Men and women are different, and it is daytime here now,

conversationally implying that the statement that women and men are different is a triviality from which nothing interesting relevant to the issues under discussion can be deduced. The different literal meanings of (2) would then be:

> *T-literal meaning*: Men and women are different and it is daytime in the place of the utterance at the moment of the utterance.
>
> *M-literal meaning*: Men and women are different and it is daytime in Murcia the 7th July 2003 at noon.
>
> *P-literal meaning*: Men and women differ in a sense stronger than the sense in which all humans differ from each other but weaker than the sense in which humans are different from gorillas, and it is daytime in Murcia the 7th July 2003 at noon.
>
> *P-nonliteral meaning*: Men and women differ in a sense stronger than the sense in which all humans differ from each other but weaker than the sense in which humans are different from gorillas, it is daytime in Murcia the 7th July 2003 at noon, and nothing interesting relevant to the issues under discussion can be deduced from this.

These concepts of literality allow Recanati to distinguish between the semantic and the ordinary sense of 'literal'. T-literal and m-literal meanings are literal in the semantic sense, while all m-nonliteral meanings are nonliteral in this semantic sense. But not every nonliteral meaning in this semantic sense is nonliteral in the ordinary sense, for elaborated and below threshold extended meanings are literal in the ordinary sense. For a meaning to be nonliteral in the ordinary sense, there must be a two-step process transparent to normal speakers. This transparency condition is met only by utterances involving above threshold extended meanings (figurative meanings) and p-nonliteral utterances (those with a secondary meaning). In Figure 6.1 above, italicized categories are literal in the semantic and the ordinary sense; unemphasized categories are nonliteral in the semantic sense and literal in the ordinary sense; categories in bold are nonliteral in both senses.

6.3 Elaborating Recanati's classification

Although Recanati talks of p-nonliteral and literal utterances, Recanati (2004: 74 and 81–2) (and also of literal and nonliteral propositions), it is clear enough that his classification is a classification of meanings, not of expressions or utterances. Nevertheless, it is interesting to explore whether it could be used to classify utterances according to their literality. First, because we do as normal speakers talk of literal or nonliteral expressions, utterances or uses of them; second, and more importantly, because I think this exploration will cast light on our ordinary notion of literality.

A straightforward way of using Recanati's schema to classify utterances would be something like the following. We find different degrees of literality. In one extreme we have t-literal utterances (those whose meaning coincide with sentence meaning). Then come m-literal utterances (utterances of indexical sentences), p-literal non-figurative utterances (utterances with enriched or below threshold extended meanings), p-literal figurative utterances and, finally, p-nonliteral utterances:

But this obviously does not work. Let's go back to the example of the discussion on sexual equality and suppose that, instead of (2), B says:

(3) Men and women are different, and $2 + 2 = 4$.

There is an important difference between (2) and (3): (2) is indexical and (3) is not. If we applied Recanati's scheme to the classification of these utterances, (3) would count as t-literal and (2) as t-nonliteral, but m-literal. But B's utterance of (3) is obviously p-nonliteral, and for the same reasons as (2). The question then is: is it also t-literal? If the answer is yes, we face a paradoxical result: (3) is at the same time t-literal and p-nonliteral and, therefore, following Recanati's classification, t-nonliteral. The right answer must then be that, in this conversational context, (3) is not t-literal. The problem now is that an important difference between (2) and (3) is lost: the fact that, only in the first case, the hearer can understand the utterance only if he has the relevant information about the context of utterance (that it is daytime where and when the conversation takes place).

It is then clear that, as it stands, Recanati's scheme cannot be straightforwardly used to classify utterances. A possible rejoinder is that the apparent paradox derives from the duality of meanings. In the story, utterances of (2) and (3) have both a primary and a secondary meaning. We could then say that they are respectively m-literal and t-literal regarding their primary meaning, while they are both p-nonliteral regarding their secondary meaning. But, even if we can make sense of that, it doesn't solve the problem, for a similar difficulty can be raised in cases where no secondary meaning is involved.

Take for instance the following sentences:

(4) Yesterday, a policeman raised his hand and stopped my car.
(5) Yesterday, a policeman stopped my car by raising his hand.

Imagine I utter (4) the 8th July 2003 to mean (5) without intending to convey anything else. My utterance would be t-nonliteral, for it contains the indexical expression 'yesterday'. It is also m-nonliteral: its meaning is an enriched meaning, for it requires background assumptions and world knowledge. The conventional meanings and the assignments of values to the indexical variables do not suffice to determine that it is part of what the speaker says that there is a causal connection between the raising of the hand and the stopping of the car. Finally, it is also p-literal, for there is no

Table 6.1   The layers of meaning

Layer of meaning	Meaning determined by	Process
1. Type meaning	Semantic conventions	Decodification
2. Minimal meaning	Type meaning + encoded aspects of context	Saturation
3. Primary meaning	Minimal meaning + background and context	Adjustment (enrichment and loosening)
4. Secondary meaning	Primary meaning + conversational maxims	Secondary pragmatic processes

inference from a primary meaning to a secondary meaning: the meaning is grasped directly at the subpersonal level.

Let's suppose now that, instead of (4), I utter:

(6) On 7th July 2003, a policeman raised his hand and stopped Manuel's car.

Like (4), (6) is m-nonliteral and p-literal, for the same reasons. The question is, again, whether it is t-literal. A positive answer leads to contradiction, for the utterance would then be both t-literal and m-nonliteral (and hence t-nonliteral). A negative answer eliminates the important difference between (4) and (6), that is, that (4) is indexical while (6) is not.

In this case distinguishing between two meanings and relativizing literality to them cannot neutralize paradox, for the utterance has no secondary meaning. This suggests that we must relativize literality, not to meanings, but to levels of meaning analysis (I will call these levels of analysis layers of meaning):

The way of classifying things shown in Table 6.1 does not contradict Recanati's views. It is only a clarification of his scheme. I believe, however, that this reformulation makes it more obvious that what is being classified are layers of meaning, helps to prevent paradoxical moves and avoids apparent commitment with highly problematic entities like t-literal (or even m-literal) utterances. We can now go a step forward and classify utterances according to their literality.

6.4   Extending Recanati's classification

Although it is not its author's intention, Recanati's classification (Figure 6.1) might suggest that there is a continuum of kinds of meaning, ordered from the bottom to the top according to their degree of literality; or, better, a continuum of nested senses of literality ranging from the widest sense to the narrowest. The widest would include all meanings except P-nonliteral meanings. The narrowest would coincide with t-literal meaning. In between we find what Recanati calls the semantic sense (= M-literality) and the ordinary sense (= elaborated and below threshold extended P-literality). This in turn suggests that the scheme can be used to order utterances according to their degree of literality. But, as we have just seen, the attempt to use Recanati's classification to classify utterances leads to contradictions.

There are two reasons why Recanati's scheme cannot do the job of classifying utterances. The first is that it is not homogeneous, for it appeals to three different basic conceptual distinctions. The second is that these distinctions cannot be nested.

The three basic distinctions are the following:[4]

D1) Nonindexical *vs* indexical
D2) Crude *vs* adjusted
D3) Primary *vs* secondary

We can improve clarity by using the scheme in Table 6.1 to classify utterances according to these three basic distinctions. An utterance is nonindexical if its type meaning and its minimal meanings coincide, and indexical otherwise. It is crude if its minimal meaning and its primary meaning coincide, and adjusted otherwise. It is primary if its primary meaning (what the speaker says) coincides with its secondary meaning (what the speaker means), and secondary otherwise. The result is the classification shown in Table 6.2. The table shows the correspondence between dichotomies D1, D2 and D3, the layers of meaning (Table 6.1) and Recanati's different senses of literality and nonliterality (Figure 6.1).

Table 6.2 Recanati's classification of categories

Layer	Recanati's category	'Translation'	Definition
2	t-literal	nonindexical	minimal meaning = type meaning
	t-nonliteral	indexical	minimal meaning ≠ type meaning
3	m-literal	crude	primary meaning = minimal meaning
	m-nonliteral	adjusted	primary meaning ≠ minimal meaning
4	p-literal	primary	primary meaning = secondary meaning
	p-nonliteral	secondary	primary meaning ≠ secondary meaning

It is now obvious that these dichotomies, contrary to what Figure 6.1 above might suggest, cannot be nested. Let's take the term on the left-hand side of each dichotomy as its 'literal pole' and the one on the right-hand side as its 'nonliteral pole'. We find that utterances (or meanings or interpretations) can be simultaneously nonliteral in any of the three senses and literal in the others, and vice versa, as the examples in sections 6.2 and 6.3 illustrate.

Therefore, there is no hierarchy of degrees of kinds of literality. There are different levels of analysis of meaning, each with its own internal literal/nonliteral dichotomy. A follower of the standard view (not Recanati) would see these layers of meaning as hierarchical in the sense that the grasping of the secondary meaning of an utterance presupposes the understanding of the primary meaning, which in turn presupposes the understanding of the minimal meaning, which in turn presupposes the understanding of the type meaning. This view would entail that there is a hierarchy within each layer, for the understanding of the x-nonliteral meaning of any utterance presupposes the understanding of its x-literal meaning. And this can produce the misleading illusion that the different senses of literality corresponding to each layer are also hierarchized. But they are not. Although there are degrees of literality within each of the layers, there is no bottom-up nested hierarchy of senses of literality. Utterances literal at, say, the minimal meaning level are neither more nor less literal than those literal at the secondary meaning level: they are simply literal in a different sense. And an utterance being literal or nonliteral in one sense does not entail the utterance being literal or nonliteral in any of the others.

In addition to the three basic dichotomies above, Recanati appeals to two other distinctions:

D4) Raw *vs* enriched.
D5) Strict *vs* loose.

These dichotomies are related to the basic ones in the following way. All crude utterances are raw and strict, while all enriched and loose utterances are adjusted. Therefore, pairs D3 and D4 are nested in pair D2 and are mutually independent.

Finally, we find a sixth dichotomy:

D6) Nonfigurative *vs* figurative.

All figurative utterances are (if we follow Recanati's analysis) loose. So pair D6 is nested in pair D4. The result is the classification of utterances according to their m-literality shown in Table 6.3.

Table 6.3 The classification of utterances according to their m-literality

ADJUSTMENT	——EXTENSION——⟶ *threshold*		
| ELABORATION ↓	crude (raw and strict)	loose (and raw) nonfigurative	loose (and raw) figurative
	enriched (and strict)	enriched and loose nonfigurative	enriched and loose figurative

6.5 Disseminating literality

The conclusion of Recanati's analysis of literality is that

[. . .] the literal/nonliteral distinction covers two quite different things:

- For the semanticist, the literal meaning of an expression is the semantic value which the conventions of the language assign to that expression ('with respect to context' if the expression is indexical). [. . .]
- In the ordinary sense of the term, nonliteral meaning contrasts with normal meaning. Nonliteral meaning is special, it involves a form of deviance of departure from the norm; a form of deviance or departure which must be transparent to language users (2004: 81).

In the previous section we encountered six possible senses in which an utterance can be said to be literal:

S1) The strictly semantic sense: unsaturated
S2) The semantic sense: crude
    S2a) The strictly pragmatic sense: raw
    S2b) The widely rhetoric (etymological?) sense: strict
    S2b*) The rhetoric sense: nonfigurative
S3) The pragmatic sense: primary

What Recanati calls the semanticist sense of literality corresponds to S2 above (the semantic sense). What he calls the ordinary sense includes both senses S2b* and S3 above: an utterance is nonliteral in the ordinary sense if and only if it has a figurative meaning or it has a secondary meaning.[5]

As Recanati claims, both distinctions are legitimate, for we need both, but it is important to keep them separate, for they are easily confused. I fully agree with these remarks, but I think they apply to all possible senses the dichotomy literal/nonliteral may have. We also need the unsaturated/saturated, strict/loose and raw/enriched distinctions. It is important to keep them separate, but this holds also for the rhetorical and the pragmatic senses. My position is then that the literal/nonliteral distinction does not cover two, but, at least, six different things, all the six necessary and all the six distinct.

Why does Recanati reduce the legitimate meanings of literality to these two? This question involves two separate issues. The first is why senses S1, S2a and S2b are excluded. The second is why senses S2b* and S3 are put together. The plausible answer to the first issue is that, as a matter of fact, not even language theorists use 'literal' to mean unsaturated, raw or strict. The answer to the second issue is that, in ordinary language, 'literal' means 'deviant', and this covers both figurative and secondary meanings.

But, is this so? Let's begin with the first issue. It is true that language theorists do not normally use 'literal' as opposed to 'saturated', 'enriched' or 'loosened'. But it is also true that as (I hope) the following examples illustrate, the word 'literal' can be used in some contexts to mean 't-literal', 'raw' or 'strict' without making violence to ordinary language.

Case 1: 'literal' as 't-literal'

A is in Granada sitting in front of the Alhambra and says to B:

(7) This in front of us is a marvel.

B interprets that A is talking about the Alhambra and later reports A's words to C in the following way:

(8) A said that the Alhambra is a marvel.

Then C replies that he finds this implausible, for A is particularly insensitive to this kind of architecture. In this moment B remembers that A is particularly fond of cars and that, when A uttered (7), a Rolls Royce was parked in front of them. B then says:

(9) Well, what A *literally* said is 'This in front of us is a marvel'

or:

(10) Well, what A *literally* said is that what was in front of us was a marvel.

Case 2: 'literal' as 'strict' (but not raw)

Private A survives to a serious injury and tells Private B:

(11) It's a miracle that I'm not going to die

B interprets (11) as meaning that A has been extremely lucky not to die from this injury and says: 'Yes, you really were very lucky to receive immediate good medical care'. A then replies:

(12) I *literally* mean that it's a miracle that I'm not going to die: Saint Josemaría Escrivá de Balaguer saved me.

Case 3: 'literal' as 'raw' (but not strict)

Private A has a minor injury and tells Private B:

(13) My Doctor is mad. He said that I was not going to kick the bucket.

B interprets (13) as meaning that A was not going to die from the injury and, unimpressed, says that the Doctor is right, for it is really a minor injury. A then replies:

(14) But he *literally* means that I'm not going to kick the bucket: he said that we are not humans, but immortal human-like aliens.

The important point here is that the uses of 'literal' in (9), (10), (12) and (14) are not strange or deviant at all. On the contrary, they fit ordinary use and would be perfectly understood by an average interpreter.

The second issue was why Recanati sticks together the rhetoric and the pragmatic senses of literality. His argument is:

1. In its ordinary use, nonliterality means departure from the norm.
2. Transparency is an essential property of deviant (not normal) uses of words.
3. Both figurative and secondary meanings, and only them, share the property of being transparent.

   Therefore: figurative and P-nonliteral uses (indirect speech acts, conversational implicatures, etc.) are the only nonliteral uses in the ordinary sense of 'literal'.

I have nothing to object to premise 3 (although I find it counts against Recanati's view that nonconventional metaphors are p-literal). Premise 2 is more problematic, for most of the times secondary meanings are grasped directly; more often than not, conversational implicatures work at the subpersonal level. If the transparency condition states that departure from normal meaning must be actually perceived, it is too strong, for it excludes paradigmatic cases of p-nonliteral utterances. Actually, Recanati's formulation is weaker: the uses of words are nonliteral in the ordinary sense 'only if there is something special about that use *that is, or can be, perceived by the language users themselves*'.[6] The problem with this weaker formulation of the transparency condition is that meaning enrichment and loosening can also be perceived by language users (this is particularly obvious in the case of below-threshold sense extensions, e.g. conventional metaphors). So, if we take actual transparency as a condition of nonliterality in the ordinary sense, it is too strong a requirement for Recanati's point, for it excludes many cases of p-nonliteral utterances; if we take just potential transparency, it is too weak, for it is satisfied by p-literal nonfigurative utterances.

But the weakest point of Recanati's account of the ordinary notion of literality is premise 1. Even if we accept that figurative and secondary uses of language have important and interesting features in common (for instance, transparency), it does not follow that this captures the essence of the ordinary sense of 'nonliteral'. The pragmatic sense of the literal/nonliteral distinction corresponds to what would be more naturally described by ordinary speakers as the difference between what is said and what is implied by what is said, not as the difference between standard and deviant uses of words. Normal speakers do use and understand the word 'literal' in this pragmatic sense to refer to the speaker's saying as opposed to what he implicates or conveys, but they also use it, as I have tried to show above, in the semantic and even the strict semantic sense. And none of these uses is more similar to any of them than it is to the rest.

It could perhaps be thought that the rhetoric sense is the closest to ordinary use, and that the others are extensions of this paradigmatic sense. I don't think this is even the case, as the following example illustrates. Imagine that A says to B: 'C told me that I am extremely insensitive'. Surprised, B replies: 'I can't believe A said that to you'. A then answers:

(15) Believe it: C *literally* said that I am a block of ice.

If the rhetoric use was the core meaning of 'literal', we would find (15) paradoxical or, at least, odd, for we would primarily interpret it as meaning

(16) C nonfiguratively said that I am a block of ice.

But we don't understand (15) as meaning (16) and then, finding it odd or paradoxical, look for an extended meaning of 'literally'. In this context, we directly understand 'literally' as meaning 'with this words'.

6.6 Conclusions

Although the path has been tortuous, the morals are simple, or so I hope. If the preceding analysis is right, it shows that any attempt (Recanati's included) to define the ordinary notion of literality is essentially misguided for the following reasons:

1. Literality is not a univocal concept. There is, in ordinary speech, a cluster of different uses of 'literal', all of them legitimate and perfectly normal. None of these uses can be taken as the paradigmatic one and none of the technical definitions of literality captures the ordinary sense, for there is no single or paradigmatic ordinary sense. There is no essential property of literal utterances or meanings. In particular, there are perfectly sound uses of 'nonliteral' in ordinary language that do not entail transparency.
2. Literality is not equivocal either. Its cluster of uses is not a mess. All technical notions of literality correspond to sound uses of the word 'literal' in ordinary language. The reason why the same terms are used for different distinctions is not that the distinctions themselves have been confused. The senses of 'literal' are relative to layers of analysis of meaning and interpretation processes and they are unproblematic-ally determined by context. If layers are taken to correspond (ideally) to different steps of interpretation, then, relative to each step, 'literal' refers to the input of the step of interpretation and 'nonliteral' to the output. The utterance is called 'literal' when both coincide. The different notions of literality are logically independent and do not constitute a nested hierarchy.

There is then no folk linguistics notion to repudiate, no equivocation to avoid and no univocal definition to find. The literal/nonliteral distinction is a cluster of productive analogical dichotomies, which is perfectly in order as it stands.[7]

Notes

1. See §7 of D. Wilson and D. Sperber (2002), 'Truthfulness and Relevance', *Mind*, 111: 583–632.
2. Of course, there can be deeper theoretical reasons to reject the notion of literal meaning, other than its vagueness or ambiguity. But I will not address them in this chapter. I will concentrate only in the criticisms of the literal/nonliteral distinction based on its allegedly inescapable equivocity.
3. This 'analysis', of course, deserves more elaboration, but we don't need to pursue it for our purposes.
4. The terminology for the conceptual distinctions is mine, not Recanati's. This also holds for the list of the different senses of literality below. Nevertheless, I have tried to stick as far as possible to Recanati's terminology, or to choose the terms more coherent with it.
5. The corresponding senses of nonliterality would be:

    S1) The strictly semantic sense: saturated
    S2) The semantic sense: elaborated
       S2a) The strictly pragmatic sense: enriched
       S2b) The widely rhetoric (etymological?) sense: loose
          S2b*) The rhetoric sense: figurative
    S4) The pragmatic sense: secondary.

6. *Literal Meaning*, p. 75, emphasis in the original.
7. I am grateful to the Spanish Ministry of Science and Technology for financial support (BFF2000-1073-C04-02) and to Esther Romero for very helpful comments and suggestions.

References

Recanati, F. (2002) 'Literal/nonliteral'. *Midwest Studies in Philosophy* 25: 264–74.
Recanati, F. (2004) *Literal Meaning: The Very Idea*. Cambridge: Cambridge: University Press.
Wilson, D. and Sperber, D.(2002) 'Truthfulness and Relevance' *Mind*, 111: 583–632.

Recanati's Reply to Hernández Iglesias

Manuel Hernández Iglesias is concerned with the senses (or uses) of 'literal' and 'nonliteral' in ordinary language. The cluster of uses that he finds in ordinary speech is, he says, perfectly in order as it stands. There is no need to reduce some of the senses to others, considered as more fundamental or basic. So Hernández Iglesias criticizes the contrast I draw between the technical notion of literality prominent in the philosophy of language (where 'literal' means something like 'determined by the semantic conventions of the language'), and the ordinary notion. According to Hernández Iglesias, 'all technical notions of "literal" have correlates in ordinary language', and in any case, 'there is no single or paradigmatic ordinary sense'.

I think that Hernández Iglesias and I agree on the essentials, so my discussion will be brief. We agree that there are a number of 'layers of meaning' that must be distinguished, each layer corresponding to a different step of interpretation. 'Relative to each step', Hernández Iglesias says, ' "literal" refers to the input of the step of interpretation and "nonliteral" to the output'. But not all utterances involve all the interpretive steps. For example, some utterances (those that I classify as 'p-literal') do not involve the step from a 'primary' meaning to a 'secondary' meaning derived through e.g. conversational implicature; utterances of nonindexical sentences do not involve the interpretive step which I call 'saturation', namely the assignment of contextual values to indexical variables; etc. In order to maintain a common grid of analysis (with a fixed number of interpretive steps) for every utterance, Hernández Iglesias suggests that we handle such cases by saying that the output of the (superfluous) step is the same as its input. So for nonindexical sentences the pre-saturation meaning coincides with the post-saturation meaning. In this framework Hernández Iglesias makes the following proposal: an utterance is literal (with respect to a given interpretive step) iff the output of the step coincides with its input. So there will be as many senses of 'literal' as there are interpretive steps in the grid.

I welcome the proposal; so where do Hernández Iglesias and I differ? Well, as I said, he criticizes me for attempting to reduce the plurality of uses of the literal/nonliteral distinction in ordinary speech to a basic core. With respect to the uses that do not correspond to that core, he objects to my dismissing them as technical uses of the distinction. He points out that we find such uses in ordinary speech as much as in the writings of language theorists. And he attempts to show that the alleged core that I discern in the ordinary uses of the literal/nonliteral distinction is based on a condition that is either too weak or too strong to do the work I expect it to do.

The first thing I want to say in response to that criticism is that I am not concerned with the analysis of ordinary usage, appearances notwithstanding. I know that in my paper 'Literal/nonliteral' and in the chapter of *Literal Meaning* that is based on that paper I give that impression by constantly speaking of the ordinary sense of 'literal'. I apologize for that misleading formulation. When I speak of the ordinary sense of 'literal', what I really intend to talk about is: what is literal (or nonliteral) *for the ordinary user of the language* (rather than for the language theorist). Let me elaborate.

Philosophers of language use 'literal' and 'nonliteral' in a sense that has to do with conformity to the linguistic conventions, at different levels. I hold that the literal/nonliteral distinction, thus understood, is not something which ordinary users of the language spontaneously and systematically pay attention to when they talk or when they process the speech of others. Free enrichment, for example, is pervasive but passes unnoticed most of the time. It is not perceived as nonliteral, even though technically it is. That is what I mean when I contrast the technical sense and the ordinary sense. An utterance counts as 'nonliteral in the ordinary sense' if and only if it is perceived as such by the ordinary user of the language. An utterance which does not counts as 'nonliteral in the ordinary sense' in this framework may still be classified as 'nonliteral' in ordinary speech, in an appropriate context. That is what Hernández Iglesias's examples show. But it has never been my intention to deny that the literal/nonliteral distinction which philosophers of language typically invoke can also be appealed to in ordinary speech. I agree with Hernández Iglesias that it can, but I think this is irrelevant to my point. My point is that there is a form of nonliterality that is transparent and conscious, and another form that is not. This is the contrast I have in mind, between the technical and the ordinary notion of nonliterality.

But Hernández Iglesias does not think that we can make sense of my suggestion that there is a form of nonliterality that corresponds to the users' perception of nonliterality. I draw a distinction between the cases of nonliterality that satisfy the 'transparency condition', i.e., that are perceived as nonliteral by the ordinary users of the language (implicatures, indirect speech acts, figurative uses) and the cases that count as nonliteral only by the theorist's lights (free enrichment, below-threshold loosening and transfer). Hernández Iglesias objects that the transparency condition is either too weak or too strong. It is too weak if what we're talking about is *potential* perception, because free enrichment also can be perceived as nonliteral, even though normally it is not.[1] It is too strong if what we're talking about is *actual* perception: for even implicatures, he says, are often grasped directly, at a subpersonal level, without being perceived as supplementing the literal meaning of the utterance.

Let me deal with the two sides of the objection in turn. Regarding implicatures, I have already responded to a similar charge in the published version of *Literal Meaning* (distinct from the earlier version which Hernández Iglesias used for his presentation at the Granada conference). Even if sometimes implicatures are arrived at 'directly' or (as Grice says) 'intuitively', still they count as implicatures only if the interpreter is aware of the inferential link between the implicature and the speaker's locutionary act. That means that the implicature *must* be perceived as distinct from what is said, thereby satisfying the transparency condition. To sum up: An implicature may be processed subpersonally, as Hernández Iglesias says, but even in that case the output of the process must be available to the subject as distinct from what is said (which must also be available).

As regards Hernández Iglesias's claim that 'meaning enrichment and loosening can also be perceived by language users', I think it is somewhat ambiguous. On a first reading, what is claimed is that an aspect of nonliteral meaning that is not actually perceived as such could be so perceived: it would be so perceived if e.g. the speaker had been instructed to pay attention etc. (See Kent Bach on the 'educability' of our intuitions.) On a second reading, what is claimed is that sometimes a primary pragmatic process of enrichment or below-threshold sense extension is *actually* detected by the users. Now the claim is hard to make sense of on this second reading. How could a case of below-threshold sense extension be *actually* detected by the language users, without thereby becoming a case of above-threshold sense extension? This is a difficulty for Hernández Iglesias if he wishes to maintain the objection in this form.

With respect to the first reading, I agree that we can become aware of some nonliteral aspect of the (primary) meaning of an utterance, by exercising our reflective abilities; but – this is the crucial point – this reflective ability with which we may credit the ordinary user of the language is not constitutive of the ability to communicate at the primary level. Enrichment, loosening, and transfer could still take place even if the language users were deprived of this reflective ability. In the case of implicatures and indirect speech acts, the situation is different: without a modicum of reflective ability, no implicature could ever be derived.

Note

1. A similar point has been made by Kent Bach and by Jonathan Berg (and also by Carston in her contribution to this volume).

References

Bach, K. (2002) 'Seemingly Semantic Intuitions'. In Keim Campbell, J., O'Rourke, M., and Schier, D. (eds), *Meaning and Truth*. New York: Seven Bridges Press, pp. 21–33.

Berg, J. (1998) 'In Defense of Direct Belief: Substitutivity, Availability, and Iterability'. *Lingua e Stile* 33: 461–70.

Recanati, F. (2002) 'Literal/Nonliteral'. *Midwest Studies in Philosophy* 25: 264–74.

7
A View of Novel Metaphor in the Light of Recanati's Proposals[1]

Esther Romero and Belén Soria

In *Literal Meaning* (2004), François Recanati wrote:

> I want to argue for contextualism. According to contextualism, the contrast between what the speaker means and what she literally says is illusory, and the notion of 'what a sentence says' incoherent. What is said (the truth-conditional content of the utterance) is nothing but an aspect of speaker's meaning. That is not to deny that there is a legitimate contrast to be drawn between what the speaker says and what he or she merely implies. Both, however, belong to the realm of 'speaker's meaning' and are pragmatic through and through. (2004: 4)

In the present chapter, we show our agreement with Recanati's defence of contextualism – that is, with his defence of what is said as part of speaker's meaning, and we will make it clear that we find his work an important step forward in the discussion about what is said. Indeed, we find his description of the participation of primary pragmatic processes in what is said a great improvement. In particular, we agree with his defence of metaphor as involving a primary pragmatic process.

However, Recanati deals with metaphor only in a tangential way, mentioning it only to include it in the description of what is said, without developing a full description of metaphorical phenomena. Furthermore, when he does write about metaphor, he takes different positions which are not fully consistent with each other.

In Recanati's *Literal Meaning*, metaphor involves loosening,[2] but in Recanati (1993 and 1995) metaphor involves transfer. In this chapter, we are going to side with Recanati (1993 and 1995) to argue that novel metaphor is a case of transfer, although we are not going to belittle some correct intuitions included in the idea that metaphor involves loosening. But, as Recanati's works are not very explicit about how metaphor is identified and

145

interpreted, we will detail the criteria for the identification and interpretation of metaphor. In doing this, we will argue that novel metaphor is a case of transfer of meaning that depends on a context-shift of the metaphorical utterance, prompted by the identification of a metaphorical use of language. We defend this by using an extended notion of context-shifting in order to include metaphor as one type of context-shift, in particular, a type of language-shift required by the process of transfer involved in metaphor. But before explaining this, we will expound Recanati's proposals on metaphor and state our degree of agreement with them.

7.1 Recanati's proposals on metaphor

The notion of what is said constitutes the most important contribution of Recanati's proposal about meaning. What is said has to do with the truth-conditions of an utterance, its truth-conditional content. When the sentence-meaning included in the utterance cannot determine this content, we must introduce a number of pragmatic processes which play a role in the very constitution of what is said: the primary pragmatic processes (from now on *p-processes*). P-processes operate locally and, in this respect, they contrast with the secondary pragmatic processes, which presuppose that something has been said. Not only saturation (and sense selection) but also optional processes such as free enrichment, loosening and semantic transfer are p-processes recognized by Recanati in his latest work. Optional processes take us from the *literal meaning* of some constituent (the meaning that is linguistically encoded, or that which results from saturating the linguistically encoded meaning) to a *derived meaning* which may be richer, poorer, or involve some kind of transfer. For such processes to take place, we needn't antecedently compute what is said.

Loosening and transfer are the two p-processes that Recanati uses to explain how metaphor works. These two explanations both reject the view of metaphor as implicature. When the speaker produces a metaphorical utterance he says something metaphorically. This is one of the reasons for thinking, as Recanati does, that the difference between what the speaker means and what he literally says is illusory. It is not always the case that what is said must be said literally.

7.1.1 Metaphor is not a case of conversational implicature

As we have said, among the different positions on metaphor proposed by Recanati, there is one which is retained throughout, the claim that the proposition expressed by a metaphor is only achieved when some local p-process is involved. This proposal is in opposition to the view of metaphor as requiring any kind of secondary process for its interpretation, that is, the view of metaphor as implicature (Grice 1989). Resorting to the Gricean distinction between what the speaker literally *says* and what he *implicates*, it could be said that by uttering (1)

(1) The sky is crying

the speaker literally says that the sky is crying, something he believes to be false. Thus, the speaker is flouting the first maxim of quality of the cooperative principle, 'do not say what you believe to be false', although what the speaker implicates with (1), that it is raining, re-establishes the situation and serves to show that his behaviour is cooperative. The speaker has just made as if to say that the sky is crying to convey the implicated meaning.

Recanati (1987) notes two closely related problems for this explanation. The first is how it is possible to determine what the speaker implicates, how we can derive that it is raining from an utterance of (1). For Recanati (1987: 228), the implicature made by the speaker is the one that reconciles the utterance with the apparently flouted conversational maxim. The flouting of the first maxim of quality could be made apparent by determining the implicature so that the cooperative principle would be followed. If this is so, the second problem appears: there would be no way of calculating the implicature that it is raining, since there is no proposition that when added to what is said with (1), the false proposition that the sky is crying, makes the cooperative principle be followed. To reconcile the utterance with the maxim, it must be supposed that the implicature is not added to what is said. When a trope is involved, if the hearer wants to maintain the presumption that the speaker observes the conversational maxims, he must refrain from the presumption that he observes the principle of literalness, according to which what the speaker means is in agreement with the literal meaning of the sentence uttered. In this case, since what is literally said is only evoked, the maxims are not really violated and it is not necessary to suppose that the speaker has implicated anything in order to maintain the cooperative principle. Along these lines, Recanati considers metaphor as a use of language that affects what is said, although what is said does not follow the literalness principle.[3]

This objection, however, is not conclusive. Indeed, if we bear the Gricean notion of implicature in mind, we can say that in speaking metaphorically we make *as if to say p* in order to implicate *q*. In the figurative use of language what the speaker means is exhausted by what he implicates. And what the speaker means is characterized as an implicature because when the speaker makes as if to say *p*, he says nothing and directly flouts the maxim of quantity, a maxim that is repaired by the implicature.

We do not know if Recanati is aware of this possible rejoinder of the implicature theorist. What we do know is that in 1995 he again attacks the theory of the nonliteral as implicature. Recanati (1995: 208) says that the view of metaphor as implicature is still accepted because its theorists have an a priori philosophical argument in favour of it. This goes as follows: Given the asymmetric dependence of nonliteral meaning on literal meaning, the meaning conveyed by an expression is 'nonliteral' only if it is derived from some literal meaning which must be processed for the former to be accessed. Cases in which the alleged nonliteral meaning can be accessed directly are cases where the nonliteral meaning has become conventionalized.

But this argument is not conclusive for Recanati because the asymmetric dependence that nonliteral meaning has on literal meaning can not only be explained by resorting to the asymmetric dependence of an implicature with respect to what is literally said, but the asymmetric dependence can also be explained at a subpropositional level. Indeed, Recanati argues that his subpropositional interpretation of asymmetric dependence is the right one because without it we cannot account for some types of examples, examples in which we must compute the nonliteral interpretation in order to compute the proposition literally said. Let's consider (2)

(2) [A is at home. Her only daughter, who is a two-year-old girl, is playing with a woollen ball on the mat. B, a good friend of A, enters the room, asks A where her daughter is, and, A answers:] My cat is on the mat.

In (2), part of 'My cat' is used nonliterally. If we understand that in this expression there is a relation between the cat and the speaker, we must determine what the relation is. But, to do this, we have first to determine the reference of these descriptions. To know what 'the cat' refers to, we have to construct its nonliteral meaning and then it is possible to saturate the relation between the metaphorical cat and the speaker. The optional process of metaphor is prior to the mandatory one of saturation.

This argument would not be conclusive for the implicature theorist because he could explain example (2), arguing that what the speaker makes as if to say is that the only cat of the speaker is on the only mat of his house, and he makes as if to say this because it is obvious by the context that he does not have any cat. What causes the requirement of the nonliteral interpretation to be prior to saturation is the referential use of the definite description included in (2), but this referential use must be understood as a case of implicature. Recanati's argument depends on the defence of the referential use of the definite description in what is said to which the theoreticians of metaphor as implicature do not have to commit themselves.

By contrast, in our opinion, the argument against the theory of metaphor as implicature becomes really conclusive when we point out that the speaker cannot make as if to say something literally in all nonliteral utterances. Can we make as if to say something literally by uttering (1)? As far as the notion of trope as implicature is concerned, a speaker implicates q when he makes as if to say p. But we could argue that literally the speaker has not made as if to say any proposition at all with a normal (in the absence of special circumstances) utterance of (1) because the normal utterance of (1) cannot be interpreted literally, as far as our linguistic competence is concerned. It shows that 'to cry' is the type of action that requires, for example, eyes, which the sky lacks. The normal utterance of (1) cannot fix literally expressed truth-conditions. Since (1) cannot fix a literal content, it cannot be a literally false utterance. There is no situation literally represented by a metaphorical utterance of (1) and, if there is no situation literally represented, there is nothing that can be true and nothing that can be false. As there is no truth-conditional content literally expressed, nothing is said and, thus, it will be difficult for us to explain the asymmetric dependence of metaphorical meaning as an asymmetry between the implicature and what is literally said by a metaphor.

7.1.2 The primary pragmatic process involved in what is metaphorically said: loosening or transfer

Accepting that what is said by metaphorical utterances is metaphorically said and that a p-process is involved in metaphorical interpretation, we will consider Recanati's characterization of what type of p-process is involved in metaphorical interpretation. In this respect two p-processes are relevant: transfer and loosening. Although the former is prior, we will expound first his most recent position because we will partially depart from his view of metaphor as loosening and we will back the less recent one, that of metaphor as transfer.

In his *Literal Meaning*, we read

> Through the interaction between the context-independent meanings of our words and the particulars of the situation talked about, contextual-ised, modulated senses emerge, appropriate to the situation at hand. The meaning of a word can thus be made contextually more specific, or it may, on the contrary, be loosened and suitably extended, as in metaphor. It may also undergo 'semantic transfer', etc. (Recanati 2004: 131)

Metaphorical interpretation is explained by means of one type of modulation: it requires the p-process of loosening.

Loosening is the converse of enrichment and there is loosening whenever a condition of application packed into the concept literally expressed by a predicate is contextually dropped so that the application of the predicate is widened. Thus, as far as Recanati (2004) is concerned, in (3):

(3) The ATM swallowed my credit card

we relax the conditions of application for 'swallow' and construct an *ad hoc* concept with wider application. In this way, not only living organisms but also ATMs can swallow. Knowing the linguistic meaning of 'swallow', and knowing what sometimes happens with ATMs, the hearer unreflectively constructs the sense in which the ATM can be said to 'swallow' the card by adjusting the meaning of the word to the situation talked about.

This way of explaining how a metaphor works is inappropriate for several reasons. The most important reason is that if (3) is a metaphor, it is a conventional metaphor, and if a conventional metaphor requires some p-process in order to be interpreted, the p-process involved is not loosening but just sense selection (Romero and Soria 1998). As far as we are concerned, 'swallow' is a polysemous word, there is an array of senses of the expression 'swallow' which 'reflects conventionalised patterns of modulation' (Recanati 2004: 135) and one of them is selected for the occasion. It might have gone under a process of metaphorical modulation some time ago, but now we do not have to apply a process of loosening every time we have to interpret an utterance of (3), we just have to select one of the normal modulated meanings stored (by previous experience and world knowledge) in our conceptual system, one of 'the conventionalised patterns of modulation'. But if it is normal now for ATMs to 'swallow', then when we interpret (3) we do not have to drop part of the meaning of this word. Even if some metaphors are interpreted resorting to loosening, conventional metaphor is not the sort of candidate requiring this interpretation process. The idea of loosening, if it is right, could only explain how the figurative meaning of 'swallow' that intervenes in (3) was originally modulated.

Not all the examples of metaphor are cases of the so-called 'conventional metaphor'. An example of genuine metaphor, of a special use of language that, as Recanati (2004: 77) would say, goes beyond the threshold and whose nonliteral character cannot be ignored[4] is (4)

(4) [A and B are at the seaside talking about the deceptive appearance of the sea as imperturbable and even if looked at from a distance, when in fact there are so many living creatures inside. A, who is reading *Hamlet*, says:] That apparently imperturbable sea is the English character and English literature is a flying fish.

We can say that (4) is a case of novel metaphor. In this example, we note that, as English literature is not the sort of thing that can be included in the semantic potential of 'flying fish', the overall interpretation of (4) is likely to involve some process of nonliteral interpretation for 'flying fish' if 'English literature' literally applies to a type of literature (Recanati 1995, 2004: 34). A process of loosening, typical of metaphor, is involved in the interpretation of (4). From Recanati's line of reasoning, we learn that there is a criterion of identification of metaphor reflected in the claim that English literature is not the sort of thing that can be included in the semantic combinatorial potential of 'flying fish'; we detect an abnormality. The problem with this criterion is that we detect that 'the ham sandwich' is not the sort of thing that can leave without paying in 'The ham sandwich left without paying' and a normal utterance of this sentence is not identified as a metaphor but as a metonymy.[5]

Let us continue with (4) which is identified as a metaphor and is an example very different from (3), in that it does not seem to be a case of conventional metaphor. But, how do we interpret (4)? As a metaphor, the p-process needed is loosening, Recanati would say. So, we merely have to drop the conditions of application packed into the concept literally expressed by 'flying fish' so that this application should be widened. We construct an *ad hoc* concept with wider application, and less information. But, if loosening produces the *ad hoc* concept, at what point do we have to stop loosening? We can say that by this task one selects only the properties that are literally applied to the target, to the English literature. 'Flying fish' can be interpreted metaphorically in the sense of 'something that rises over something else'. But can we understand this property literally in order to say something about English literature? It is likely that the task of reducing the concept to properties that are applied literally to the target leads us to a loss of the whole concept.

We believe that when we interpret a metaphor we construct, at least, an *ad hoc* concept for the metaphorical vehicle, for the terms metaphorically attributed to what we are talking about. It is true that we select some properties of the normal concept and forget others and, in this sense, we can admit loosening. But this process of loosening cannot be done by selecting the properties of the concept related to the metaphorical vehicle that can be attributed literally to the target because there are no such literal properties which can be applied to the target. We decide what part of the concept can be attributed to the target of the utterance, because this part will be able to change its meaning and be applied to the target. Metaphor not only reduces the information of the concept represented by the metaphorical vehicle; it also changes the information associated with the remaining part so that it will fit with the target. Thus, we construct an *ad hoc* concept with a different application and not with a wider application.

When we use 'flying fish' metaphorically in (4) we are not interested in applying this predicate to the thing that it is usually applied to. In its metaphorical sense, this predicate is not applied to animate beings that live in water. The normal meaning of 'flying fish' is substituted by another meaning which involves not only the loss of part of the meaning of the expression 'flying fish', but also the change of the remaining meaning of this expression, this change is produced as a result of the reconceptualization of the concept we are talking about, English character.[6]

There are some weaknesses in Recanati's proposal of metaphor as loosening. Among them, we can note the following: (i) How do we know that the metaphorical *ad hoc* concept is constructed metaphorically and not metonymically if, in Recanati's writings, these mechanisms are applied to utterances that are identified in the same way? (ii) If we construct an *ad hoc* concept for the term used metaphorically in a metaphorical utterance reducing its conditions of applicability, how do we know what conditions may be lost if the remaining conditions cannot be literally applied to the target concept anyway? English literature cannot literally rise over something. The solution of the last problem entails, as we indicated at the beginning, the understanding of metaphor as a case of transfer.

In Recanati (1993: 263), metaphor is considered, like metonymy, as a case of transfer. This proposal seems to be kept in 1995, though not explicitly stated in any of the two works. In 1995, Recanati refers to metaphorical and metonymic interpretations as cases of contextual nonliteral processes.[7] The contextual nonliteral interpretation refers to the process whereby a semantic value distinct from the literal one is contextually assigned to an expression or a constituent of the uttered sentence, that is, refers to transfer. Transfer in (1993) is characterized as an interpretation process by which we can map an already available constituent into another one which replaces it (Recanati 1993: 263).

What triggers the local process of metaphorical transfer, for Recanati, is a change of accessibility produced by the interpretation of the constituents that are around the transferred term. Thus, in (5),

(5) The city is asleep

the activation of the literal interpretation of the noun phrase 'the city' triggers the local process of the metaphorical transfer of 'is asleep'. The literal interpretation of 'is asleep' was more accessible than that of its metaphorical interpretation ('quiet and showing little activity'); but the metaphorical interpretation becomes more accessible as a result of interpreting the noun phrase literally. Yet how do we know that 'quiet and showing little activity' is the transferred meaning of 'is asleep'? How do we determine its correct interpretation, the transferred meaning to which we magically have access? The description of metaphorical interpretation should include the specification of how a metaphorical transferred meaning is produced, and his approach also lacks such an explanation.

7.2 Context-shifting and what is said in metaphorical utterances

The solution to one of the problems of the proposal of metaphor as loosening, as we indicated at the beginning, entails the understanding of metaphor as a case of transfer. Nevertheless, Recanati's proposal on transfer is not completely articulated. We would need a criterion that permits us to distinguish metaphor from other uses of language in which a contextual abnormality is involved, and afterwards we would also need to specify how the metaphorical transfer is produced. In this respect, we will argue that the key to metaphorical interpretation can be explained resorting to another proposal by Recanati, to wit, that of context-shifting.

7.2.1   A brief account of context-shifting

We normally interpret utterances with respect to the context, *k*, in which they take place. But it is not always appropriate for us to interpret them with respect to that context; on certain occasions we have to interpret them with respect to a context *k'* distinct from the context in which it is actually uttered. Context-shifting, from *k* to *k'*, is a p-process and can be produced in several different ways, according to what aspect of context is shifted (Recanati 2001). If we represent a context, following Lewis (1980), as consisting of three parameters, a language, a situation, and a circumstance of evaluation, a context can be shifted by modifying one of these parameters. A context *k* is therefore analysed as a triple $< L, s, c >$ where *L* is a language, *s* is a situation of utterance comprising a number of parameters corresponding to the situation of utterance (speaker, hearer, time, place, etc.), and *c* a circumstance of evaluation or a possible world.

There are examples of context-shifting which involve a situation-shift, a world-shift, or a language-shift, but we are going to concentrate only on a case of language-shift such as (6)

(6) [It is mutually known to the speaker and his addressee that Paul is wrong about the use of 'paper session' that he understands with the meaning of 'poster session'. The speaker says:] Paul says he's due to present his work in the 'paper session'.

In (6), the context-shift can be described by a language-shift because the speaker of (6) does not use the expression 'paper session' in its normal sense, but in the sense that the expression has in Paul's idiolect, where it means the same as 'poster session' in its normal sense. Paul's is a deviant use of the phrase 'paper session'. The expression within the quotation marks, in this example, is not used with its standard meaning and so (6) has truth-conditions that differ completely from the truth-conditions of the utterance of the sentence when it does not include a quoted expression. In this sense, (6) is a non-cumulative case of literal meaning.

7.2.2   Metaphorical interpretation and language-shifting

A type of transfer of meaning that depends on a context-shift is induced by the metaphor itself. In arguing for this position, we will resort to our previous proposals, that a metaphor is identified when the hearer perceives a contextual abnormality and a conceptual contrast, and that, once the utterance is identified as metaphorical, the hearer applies, among other things, the metaphorical mechanism for its interpretation.[8]

This mechanism involves a special type of human ability which is not found in other processes – that is, it involves the analogical ability by which the interlocutors make a coherent partial mapping of a set of features from source domain to target domain in order to obtain a metaphorically restructured target domain. This mechanism affects the context from which we must interpret the utterance; in particular, it generates a new context of interpretation. This new context can be seen as a result of changing the parameter of language included in the actual context of utterance. When we identify a metaphorical use of language,[9] we are prompted to change the meaning of some constituents of the sentence metaphorically used. But this is possible only if we also change the target concept from which we interpret the constituents of the sentence used.

Let us consider again the sentence included in the utterance (4), but now in the linguistic context where it is used by Forster. We reproduce it in (7).

(7) We know what the sea looks like from a distance: it is of one color, and level, and obviously cannot contain such creatures as fish. But if we look into the sea over the edge of a boat, we see a dozen colors, and depth below depth, and fish swimming in them. That sea is the English character – apparently imperturbable and even. The depths and the colors are the English romanticism and the English sensitiveness – we do not expect to find such things, but they exist. And – to continue my metaphor – the fish are the English emotions, which are always trying to get to the surface, but don't quite know how. For the most part we see them moving far below, distorted and obscure. Now and then they succeed and we exclaim, 'Why, the Englishman has emotions! He actually can feel!' And occasionally we see that beautiful creature the flying fish, which rises out of the water altogether into the air and the sunlight. English literature is a flying fish. It is a sample of the life that goes on day after day beneath the surface; it is a proof that beauty and emotion exist in the salt, inhospitable sea. (Example taken from Forster's *Abinger Harvest* and quoted in Helen Monfries, 1970: 1)

In this example we detect a metaphorical use of language. We identify (7) as metaphorical because it is abnormal to talk about the English character as the sort of thing that can be considered as the sea (in the normal sense of the term 'sea') and because there is a conceptual contrast between the concept ENGLISH CHARACTER, the target concept of this utterance, and the concept SEA, the source concept. The conceptual contrast permits us to distinguish metaphor from other uses of language such as metonymy.

Once the speaker has recognized that (7), in its actual extralinguistic and linguistic context, is a case of metaphor, he interprets it and, doing so, is but applying the mechanism that characterizes this phenomenon, the mechanism that entails the production of a new meaning at least for its metaphorical vehicles, if we want to represent some propositional content. In (7), the vehicles are the terms that are involved in the description of SEA, the meaning of 'sea' or of 'flying fish' must be modified in order to fit the topics English character and English literature respectively. We are not talking about a sea or about a fish in any of the normal senses of these terms.

The application of the metaphorical mechanism results in the elaboration of these new senses. The metaphorical mechanism consists in linking two separate cognitive domains, the source and the target domains, by using the language appropriate to the first as a lens through which to observe the second (Black 1954; Indurkhya 1992). When a metaphorical use of language is identified, we must establish the metaphorical restructuring or recategorization that is made by a partial mapping from source domain to target domain.

If we want to interpret (7), we have to restructure the concept ENGLISH CHARACTER through the concept SEA. The result of the metaphorical restructuring, the restructured target domain, provides us with a context of interpretation of the metaphorical utterance provisionally restructured for that occasion. The context of interpretation of (7), the metaphorical context, shows our conception of the English character provisionally modified by those aspects of the concept SEA that intervene in its restructuring. The English character has the features of an apparently imperturbable and even sea which are analogically transferable to the English character. As the context of interpretation from which the terms that are involved in a metaphorical utterance changes, the meanings associated with these terms change too. Some terms acquire a metaphorical provisional meaning. The relation between the terms and the originated metaphorical meanings is not established or conventionalized.

The English character seen provisionally from the sea-life world provides a context of interpretation for a selected part of (7), (7a)

(7a) English literature is a flying fish

from which the term 'flying fish' changes its meaning and gets a provisional one that depends on the new relations that it establishes with other terms in the characterization of English literature as a feature of the English character. The concept ENGLISH LITERATURE is partially shaped by the concept FLYING FISH. The metaphorical utterance of (7a) is dependent on the wider conceptual metaphor THE ENGLISH CHARACTER IS THE SEA.

(7) is interpreted as a result of a context-shift by which the expression 'sea' is not used in its normal sense; it is used abnormally to describe the metaphorical sea-like English character. The language-shift allows us to interpret the terms belonging to the source domain SEA as referring to concepts of the target domain. For example, when it is said that 'beauty and emotion exist in the salt, inhospitable sea' the expression 'sea' must be interpreted from the shifted context not as a mass of salt water but as the metaphorical English character.

Similarly, the speaker of (7a) does not use the word 'flying fish' in its normal sense because he is not speaking about a fish that has enlarged pectoral fins used for gliding above the surface of the salt water. He is talking about English literature and so in (7a) 'flying fish' stands for a metaphorical flying fish-like literature. We might think that this is a case of loosening because 'flying fish' has now relaxed its conditions of application and has lost part of its meaning to arrive at the following abridged literal semantic value: 'something that rises over something else'. But we find this rather objectionable because 'rise over' means something very different when it is attributed to a sea creature than when it is attributed to a manifestation of the English character. In addition, the expression 'English literature' also changes its meaning.

By the metaphorical interpretation, we achieve a propositional content which is yielded by subpropositional metaphorical provisional meanings not available in the linguistic competence of a linguistic community (understanding by linguistic competence the kind of implicit knowledge that a normal speaker of that language has about the normal semantic potential of linguistic expressions when uttered).

In the interpretation of (7a), we go from the primary semantic value of 'flying fish' to a transferred value interpreted from the shifted metaphorical context and which, for explanatory reasons, we can verbalize as: 'the only aspect of the apparently imperturbable English character that rises over the rest and glides showing a beauty and dynamism incomparable to any other', and it is only the latter which forms a part of the global interpretation of the utterance. Indeed, what is said in an utterance of (7b),

(7b) English literature is something that rises over something else

if taken out of its metaphorical context, would not coincide with what is said in (7a).

(7a) would not be relevant if we had to apply a process to loose meaning and obtain (7b). By contrast, it is quite revealing and economic to use (7a) to convey the metaphorical value. The semantic value achieved in metaphorical interpretation is by no means a case of loosening. The application of the p-process involved in metaphorical interpretation does not consist in using just the core meaning of the expression 'flying fish' that can be literally applied to both English literature and flying fish. What this process achieves is an analogical transfer of meaning since the output is 'a different concept all together, bearing a systematic relation to it' (Recanati 2004: 26).

Going back to our consideration of Recanati's example of context-shifting, example (6), we are now ready to indicate the parallelism and also the difference between cases such as (6) and cases of novel metaphor such as (7a). In our opinion, (6) and (7a) can both be explained as cases whose correct interpretation requires a p-process of context-shift. Nevertheless, there is an important difference between them with respect to their truth-conditions. The sentence uttered in (6), if taken out of the quotation, has truth-conditions (although different from the truth-conditions of this sentence when quoted). By contrast, in metaphor, if the sentence is uttered out of the metaphorical context, it might not have truth-conditions at all, as is the case in (7a). The context-shift involved in metaphor shows that all metaphorical utterances are cases of non-cumulative uses of the literal meaning of constituents. Indeed, with respect to the metaphorical context, (7a) expresses the proposition that English literature is a flying fish. If the context-shift is not produced, (7a) expresses no proposition at all.

Here arises a new difference with respect to Recanati's view. If we understand that a p-process is mandatory when it is necessary for a propositional content to be present in the interpretation of an utterance (2004: 62), then the metaphorical transfer achieved by a language-shift is not an optional p-process, it is but a mandatory one.[10] But this consequence, surely, is worse for the minimalist. If metaphorical transfer is a mandatory p-process, the minimal proposition expressed by a metaphorical utterance must be nonliteral. Thus, we have to dismiss the notion of what is literally said as the point of departure of what is implicated in every utterance.

Notes

1. Financial support for this research, which has been carried out in the project 'El significado y los procesos pragmáticos primaries y secundarios', has been provided by Spanish DEICYT and FEDER BFF 2003-07141.
2. Recanati follows relevance theory (Sperber and Wilson 1986).
3. The literalness principle is not mentioned in his subsequent works, but it is implicitly included in the acceptance of p-processes such as transfer, processes that do not allow what is said to be exactly what the sentence conventionally means.
4. 'The paradigm case of nonliteral meaning is metaphor. Now metaphor, in its most central variety, counts as *p*-literal' (Recanati 2004: 76). This we find quite an astonishing remark: some metaphors have a nonliteral character but are interpreted p-literally. The nonliteral character of metaphor depends on the perception of the speaker but this does not have any consequence at the interpretative level.
5. The abnormality as a criterion of identification can be applied both to metaphor and to metonymy (Romero and Soria 2002).
6. As loosening is not the p-process that can explain how we interpret metaphor, it cannot explain the metaphorical origin of the figurative meaning of 'swallow' in (2). The conventional figurative meaning of 'swallow' in (2) is not merely a loss of meaning with respect to the original meaning of this term. This can be seen in (2) because, on the one hand, the meaning of 'swallow' is not only reduced, the change also affects the quality of the part of the meaning of this term that can be attributed to ATMs, and, on the other, this change also involves a change in the semantic potential of ATMs, the concept of ATM has changed as well since they can now swallow. In the metaphorical interpretation process we change the target schema, and so we do not construct an *ad hoc* concept with wider application, and less information, but we construct *ad hoc* concepts with different applications that replace the already available semantic values of the constituents of the metaphorical utterance.
7. The linguistic resource used by Recanati to exemplify the contextual process of transfer is metonymy. This does not mean that we consider both metaphor and

metonymy as phenomena whose interpretation requires a process of transfer. Metonymy or 'metonymical transfer', as we have argued (Romero and Soria, 2002), is not really a case of transfer; metonymy does not exploit a transferred meaning. Metonymy is a non-textual use of language in which there is at least one unarticulated sub-phrasal constituent. We would only consider metonymy as a case of transfer if we took the term 'transfer' in a different sense from its normal one to mean apparent transfer of syntactic function. We cannot see in what sense 'ham sandwich' in 'The ham sandwich left without paying' denotes, through transfer, the derived property 'hand sandwich orderer' instead of its linguistically encoded property. The expression 'the ham sandwich' keeps its ordinary meaning and refers to a sandwich. The metonymic use makes the hearer recover some non-explicit but required subpropositional and sub-phrasal element in order to have an accessible proposition, but once we recover what is unarticulated ('orderer') both terms ('orderer' and 'ham sandwich') refer to their respective normal meanings. We agree with the most recent Recanati when he considers that both metaphor and metonymy are different phenomena whose interpretations depend on different processes, although we do not agree with him in what type of processes are involved in each case.

8. The metaphorical identification does not have to be conscious and neither does metaphorical interpretation. For a detailed argument on this see Romero and Soria (1997–98).

9. If metaphor is a case of context-shift, it is not normally controlled by any representational operator, even though it coincides with the language-shift effected through the expression 'metaphorically'. The context-shift produced by the metaphoric interpretation is activated by the metaphorical identification: from the appreciation of an abnormality and a conceptual contrast one may conclude that the context from which we determine what is said is different from the normal one. The context-shift at issue is of the *free* variety because it is not controlled by any linguistic operator but by the conditions of metaphorical identification of that specific use of language.

10. Recanati does not always understand by 'mandatory' what is indicated in the text. In fact, in 2004 (p. 98) he also points out that a process is mandatory when it is required in virtue of a linguistic convention governing the use of a particular construction (or class of constructions). Obviously, following this definition, metaphorical transfer would not be mandatory since there is no need to consider lexical items as requiring a transferred meaning. This makes it manifest that Recanati has several criteria for 'mandatory' and that if some of his proposals change, his criteria would lead us to say that a pragmatic process is at the same time mandatory and not mandatory.

References

Black, M. (1954) 'Metaphor'. *Proceedings of the Aristotelian Society* 55: 273–94.

Grice, H.P. (1989) *Studies in the Way of Words*. Cambridge, MA: Harvard University Press.

Indurkhya, B. (1992) *Metaphor and Cognition: an Interactionist Approach*. Dordrecht: Kluwer Academic Publishers.

Lewis, D. (1980) 'Index, Context, and Content'. In Kanger and Öhman (eds), *Philosophy and Grammar*. Dordrecht: Reidel, pp. 79–100.

Recanati, F. (1987) *Meaning and Force: The Pragmatics of Performative Utterances.* Cambridge: Cambridge University Press.

Recanati, F. (1993) *Direct Reference: From Language to Thought.* Oxford: Blackwell.

Recanati, F. (1995) 'The Alleged Priority of Literal Interpretation'. *Cognitive Science,* 19: 207–32.

Recanati, F. (2001) 'Open Quotation'. *Mind* 110 (439): 637–87.

Recanati, F. (2004) *Literal Meaning.* Cambridge: Cambridge University Press.

Romero, E. and Soria, B. (1997/1998) 'Stylistic Analysis and Novel Metaphor'. *Pragmalingüística* 5(6): 373–89.

Romero, E. and Soria, B. (1998) 'Convention, Metaphor and Discourse'. *Atlantis* 20(1): 145–59.

Romero, E. and Soria, B. (2002) 'La metonimia referencial'. *Theoria* 17(3): 435–55.

Sperber, D. and Wilson, D. (1986) 'Loose talk'. In Davies (1991) *Pragmatics: A Reader.* Oxford: Oxford University Press: 540–9. First published in *Proceedings of the Aristotelian Society* 86: 540–9.

Recanati's Reply to Romero and Soria

I think the notions of 'context-shift' and 'language-shift' (a special case of context-shift) can be used to account for a wide array of semantic phenomena. Thus, I once suggested to Robyn Carston that standard instances of metalinguistic negation such as Larry Horn's example, 'I did not buy to<u>mé</u>toes, I bought to<u>ma</u>toes', could perhaps be handled by viewing the speaker as pretending that those are two different words with different meanings (rather than two different pronunciations of the same word). This would be a case of shift to an imaginary context – a context in which there are two distinct things: tomatoes and tométoes, and two different words for them.

Romero and Soria think *metaphor* can be handled by appealing to context-shift. According to them, the metaphorical vehicles are given new senses – senses which make them applicable to the metaphorical targets. Those senses are the senses that the words have in the context to which we shift, when we interpret a metaphor. Such senses are not arrived at by loosening the literal meaning of the words. 'Metaphoric interpretation', they write, 'is by no means a case of loosening.' It is a case of transfer: we go from the literal meaning of the words to some other meaning that is systematically related to it, namely the meaning the words have in the shifted context.

More specifically, Romero and Soria write that metaphorical interpretation

> involves the analogical ability by which the interlocutors make a coherent partial mapping of a set of features from source domain to target domain to obtain a metaphorically restructured target domain. This mechanism affects the context from which we must interpret the utterance; in particular, it generates a new context of interpretation. This new context can be seen as a result of changing the parameter of language included in the actual context of utterance. When we identify a metaphorical use of language, we are prompted to change the meaning of some constituents of the sentence metaphorically used.

In Forster's flying fish example, which they discuss at length, the apparently imperturbable English character is compared to the sea, which presents an even, uniform and opaque surface when seen from a distance, but reveals an internal life full of colour and dynamism when one looks beneath the surface. Seen from a distance, the sea 'is of one color, and level, and obviously cannot contain such creatures as fish. But if we look into the sea over the edge of a boat, we see a dozen colors, and depth below depth, and fish swimming in them'. Similarly, the English character reveals unexpected features when one looks closer: 'The depths and the colours are the English romanticism and the English sensitiveness – we do not expect to find such things, but they exist.' This mapping from the source domain (the sea) to the target domain (the English character) is completed by equating the fish swimming below the surface to the English emotions, 'which are always trying to get to the surface, but don't quite know how'. Thus completed, the mapping provides the metaphorical context in which, Romero and Soria argue, we are to interpret the metaphorical sentences at the end of Forster's passage:

> For the most part we see them [the emotions] moving far below, distorted and obscure. Now and then they succeed and we exclaim, 'Why, the Englishman has emotions! He actually can feel!' And occasionally we see that beautiful creature the flying fish, which rises out of the water altogether into the air and the sunlight. English literature is a flying fish. It is a sample of the life that goes on day after day beneath the surface; it is a proof that beauty and emotion exist in the salt, inhospitable sea.

In this passage, elements of the target domain (the English character) are systematically described in terms of the source domain. For an emotion to be overtly expressed is for it to 'get to the surface'. Since the English emotions typically do not get expressed, we can only 'see them moving far below, distorted and obscure'. And so on and so forth.

According to Romero and Soria, metaphor starts with a conceptual conflict, due to the fact that vocabulary appropriate to one domain (the source) is used in talking about some other domain (the target). This conflict triggers a specific process of metaphorical interpretation. The first phase of metaphorical interpretation consists in setting up a mapping from source domain to target domain, which leads us to view the target domain through the lenses provided by the structure of the source domain. Once the mapping is in place, each relevant element in the source domain is associated with a corresponding element in the restructured target domain. This association creates a new, metaphorical context. In that context, each expression designating a relevant element in the source domain acquires a new semantic value, in virtue of which it refers to the corresponding element in the target domain. Thus, Romero and Soria tell us that 'flying fish', in the sentence 'English literature is a flying fish', refers to 'the only aspect of the apparently imperturbable English character that rises over the rest and glides showing a beauty and dynamism incomparable to any other'. Similarly, 'salt, inhospitable sea' in the sentence 'beauty and emotion exist in the salt, inhospitable sea' refers to the English character qua imperturbable and apparently unhospitable to emotions. The vehicles (expressions from the source domain) therefore convey '*ad hoc* concepts' corresponding to elements in the restructured target domain, i.e. elements of the target domain viewed through the lenses provided by the source domain.

Although I tend to agree with the overall picture, I have two objections, admittedly more technical than substantial. First, Romero and Soria's criticism of the view that metaphor proceeds through loosening seems to me exaggerated (at least when they claim that metaphor is 'by no means' a case of loosening.) Second, their appeal to the notion of context-shift seems to me insufficiently motivated.

II

According to Romero and Soria, metaphor is an imaginative exercise in which we restructure a domain via a mapping from a source domain. As a result, we see the target domain 'through the lenses' provided by the source domain. This clearly involves loosening: by using words that have their primary application in the source domain, the speaker forces the interpreter to adjust the meaning of those words in order to make them applicable to the target domain, and that involves filtering the inappropriate features so as to retain only what is common to the two domains. Romero and Soria say that, in the metaphorical context provided by Forster's analogy between the sea and the English character, 'flying fish' means something like 'the only aspect of the apparently imperturbable English character that rises over the rest and glides showing a beauty and dynamism incomparable to any other'. But in this paraphrase what 'flying fish' specifically contributes is: 'something that rises over the rest and glides showing beauty and dynamism'. *That* can be got through loosening, by abstracting from the fishy nature of the flying fish, and retaining only the properties it has in common with English literature (in the metaphorical context). The further idea that the thing in question is 'an aspect of the apparently imperturbable English character' comes from the rest of the metaphorical mapping.

Romero and Soria object that 'rise over' does not literally apply to the English character: 'English literature cannot literally rise over something'. They conclude that the loosening account is only partly right: we get rid of certain inappropriate features (having to do with the fishy nature of the flying fish), but what we retain are not abstract features common to the two domains, but something else:

> It is true that we select some properties of the normal concept and forget others and, in this sense, we can admit loosening. But this process of loosening cannot [select] the properties of the concept related to the metaphoric vehicle that can be attributed literally to the target because there are no such literal properties which can be applied to the target. We decide what part of the concept can be attributed to the target of the utterance, because this part will be able to change its meaning and be applied to the target. Metaphor does not only reduce the information of the concept represented by the metaphorical vehicle, but also changes the information associated with the remaining part so that it will fit with the target. Thus, we construct an *ad hoc* concept with a different application and not with a wider application.

I think this goes too far. I do not accept that none of the properties encoded by the source expression literally apply to the target. Analogy making proceeds by extracting commonalities – so there *must* be commonalities, and it is those commonalities that are primarily retained in the selection process.

Beside its beauty and exceptional character, the relevant property of the flying fish, Forster tells us, is that it 'rises out of the water altogether into the air and the sunlight'. This contrasts with two other sorts of fish: those that remain far below the surface and can only be seen 'distorted and obscure', and those that succeed in getting to the surface, but do not rise out of the water. The three-terms scale is preserved in the mapping: most English emotions go unexpressed, some are fugitively expressed, and English literature is a public, durable display of emotion and feeling. Even if we have trouble verbally expressing the features common to flying fish and English literature, still they are there and they justify the metaphor. They also justify talk of loosening, since through the metaphor some, though not all, of the properties of the source are ascribed to the target.

What Romero and Soria's criticism shows is not that loosening is not involved in metaphor; it is centrally involved. But it is not all there is to metaphor. As Fauconnier and Turner have argued, four mental spaces are involved in metaphorical mappings: not only the source domain and the target domain, but also a 'generic space' containing the abstract structure common to the two domains, and a 'blended space' in which features from both domains mix and emergent features show up (Fauconnier and Turner 2002). The extraction of generic structure is a form of loosening, but the apparition of emergent features is a form of enrichment, and the imaginary mixing of features from both the source and the target is the most characteristic property of metaphor. That property is, indeed, irreducible to loosening.

III

Contrary to Romero and Soria, I am not sure the notion of 'language-shift' (a species of context-shift) is appropriate in dealing with metaphor. If we use it for dealing with metaphor, what will prevent us from using it also in dealing with metonymic transfer? After all, when the waiter associates a customer with the meal he has ordered and uses the name of the meal to refer to the customer, it would be possible to describe the situation as involving a shift to a new, 'metonymic context' in which the words, say 'ham sandwich', mean something different from what they mean in a standard context. But I think the notion of language-shift is best reserved for those cases in which tacit or explicit reference is made to some speaker or language user, to whom the speaker defers in his use of the words. No such thing seems to be involved in the sort of example discussed by R&S. To be sure, this makes their use of language-shift a possibly interesting extension or broadening of the notion, but I find this extension insufficiently motivated.

Language-shifts account for some of the cases in which an expression means something different from what it means in a standard context. This is accounted for by saying that the speaker uses the expression with the sense that it has in some other context (a context in which a different language is spoken). In both metaphor and metonymy, an expression conveys something different from what it means standardly, but we do not need to postulate a language-shift to account for this. We (more or less) know how to get from the literal meaning to the conveyed meaning. In metaphor, the correspondence established between the two domains makes the expressions appropriate to the source domain applicable (via the mapping) to the target domain, modulo loosening. We do not have to imagine a context in which the metaphorical meaning would be the literal meaning of the words.

Note that the notion of language-shift is more powerful than what we need to account for metaphor. When a language-shift is involved, there need not be any semantic commonality between the literal meaning of the words and their meaning in the shifted context. But in metaphor there always is some commonality, precisely because the metaphor relies upon an analogy between the source domain and the target domain rather than upon a deferential shift of language.

References

Fauconnier, G. and Turner, M. (2002) *The Way We Think: Conceptual Blending and the Mind's Hidden Complexities.* New York: Basic Books.

8

On the 'Hyperinsulation' and 'Transparency' of Imaginary Situations

Jérôme Pelletier

According to Recanati (2000), imaginary situations may belong to at least two different realms: the realm of the fictional and the realm of the ascription of beliefs. Let's call 'fictional situations' the imaginary situations of the first realm and 'ascribed situations' the imaginary situations of the second realm. 'Fictional situations' are imaginary situations one entertains while, for instance, playing a game of make-believe, writing fiction or watching a fiction film. 'Ascribed situations' are situations one entertains while metarepresenting in thought or in language someone else's beliefs. Recanati describes 'ascribed situations' as imaginary situations since, like fictional situations, ascribed situations are representations entertained through mental simulation and 'de-coupled' from the actual world.[1] In what follows, I make a few comments concerning the way Recanati analyses imaginary situations in these two realms.

8.1 Are fictional situations 'hyperinsulated'?

8.1.1 Recanati's claim

According to Recanati, imaginary situations in the fictional realm have the property of 'hyperinsulation':

> There is (...) a general property which distinguishes imaginary from real situations (...). The property I have in mind I call *hyperinsulation*. (...) [R]eal situations are insulated from each other because the facts which hold in them need not hold outside them. Thus if a fact belongs to the nonpersistent variety, it may hold in a situation *s* without holding in a situation *s'* comprising *s*. Persistent facts which hold in *s* will necessarily hold in *s'*, however. Thus if there is a man with a hat in this room, there is a man with a hat in the building of which this room is a part.

That is because existentially quantified facts are persistent, in contrast to universally quantified facts. (If everybody is happy in this room, it does not follow that everybody is happy in the building.) Now, if we turn to imaginary situations, we see that even persistent facts holding in such situations need not hold in situations comprising them . . .

Take a book: that is a real world entity which supports a number of facts hence can (like any other entity) be construed as a situation. Among the facts in question there will be facts concerning who authored the book, when it was issued; and so forth, as well as facts about the content of the book – the situation which it describes. We can therefore distinguish a number of situations ordered by the comprise relation. First, we have, say, the reading situation s_1 in which (let us suppose) I presently find myself, with a certain book in my hands. The book in question itself is a situation s_2, supporting a number of facts (e.g., the fact that there are twelve chapters and 156 pages). The imaginary situation described in the book is a third situation s_3. Situation s_1 comprises situation s_2 which comprises situation s_3. Now suppose that, in the imaginary situation described by the book, there is a man who can fly. We have:

(2) $s_1 \models_@ << s_2 \models_@ << s_3 \models_w <<$ There is a man who can fly $>> >> >>$

In other words: it is a fact concerning my present reading situation (s_1) that it contains a book (s_2) which 'contains' a situation (s_3) in which there is a man who can fly. But it does not follow that in my present situation s_1 there is a man who can fly, even though 'There is a man who can fly' is a persistent fact. *It is because s_3 is an imaginary situation (whose factual set is relative to a world w distinct from @) that the facts it supports, whether 'persistent' or not, do not persist when we move upward from that situation to the situations comprising it.* That is the property which I call hyperinsulation (Recanati, 84; emphasis mine).[2]

8.1.2   A new name for an old fact?

One may wonder first whether 'hyperinsulation' is a new name for an old fact concerning fictional truths, i.e., the fact that fictional truths are isolated from actual truths. This fact has been put forward most notably by Lewis in 'Truth in Fiction'. In 'Truth in Fiction', Lewis suggests thinking of a fiction not in the abstract as, for instance, a string of sentences, but as a story told by a storyteller on a particular occasion. Lewis adds that, depending on the world one considers, a same story may be told either as fiction or as known fact. In our world – the actual world – storytelling is nothing but pretence. But nothing prevents us considering worlds where the same story that is told as fiction in the actual world is told as known fact. On that basis, Lewis presents the view that true statements about fiction are true in virtue of the states of affairs in a possible world where the story is told as known fact.

'A sentence of the form "In the fiction f, ϕ" is true iff ϕ is true at every world where f is told as known fact rather than fiction' (Lewis 1978/1983: 268)

Lewis is also well known for his modal realism according to which other possible worlds are just other flesh-and-blood worlds. Other possible worlds are not, for Lewis, in any way, ontologically subordinated to this world, the actual world. This is the reason why Lewis attaches great importance to the boundaries between worlds. How then are worlds to be individuated? Lewis answers that what separates worlds one from another is spatiotemporal disconnection. A world is unified, according to Lewis, by the spatiotemporal interrelation of its parts. In other words, if two things are not spatiotemporally related, they are not worldmates. All this implies that there does not exist any path – either spatiotemporal or causal – from one world to another.[3]

Two consequences of Lewis's theory of truth in fiction matter for our discussion. First consequence: there is no path from a possible world where a fiction is told as known fact to the actual world where the same story is told as fiction. Second consequence: there is no path between the many possible worlds where a fiction is told as known fact. Let's call 'fictional world' a possible world where a fiction is told as known fact rather than fiction. For Lewis, there is no path either from a fictional world to the actual world or between two different fictional worlds. In Recanati's terminology, Lewis claims that fictional worlds are twice 'hyperinsulated': they are first 'hyperinsulated' from the actual world and secondly they are 'hyperinsulated' from each other.

8.1.3 One or two Supermen?

Remember that it is a fact concerning my present reading situation (s_1) that it contains a book (s_2) which 'contains' a situation (s_3) in which there is a man who can fly. Let's add that the man who can fly is called in the story 'Superman'. The hyperinsulation of imaginary situations from the actual world entails, according to Recanati, that there *need* not be in the actual world a man who can fly called 'Superman'. On that basis, the question one wants to raise is whether there *can* be in (s_1) a man who can fly bearing the same name as the man of whom it is said in (s_3) that he can fly.

To give to this question a more dramatic turn, let's imagine that one finds in my present reading situation (s_1) a man who can fly called 'Superman' who possesses all the characteristics of the man who can fly described in the book (s_2). Does the hyperinsulation of imaginary situations from the actual world entail that, contrary to what it seems to a non-philosopher,[4] the Superman of (s_3) and the Superman of (s_1) cannot bear the same name?

A philosopher having lost his pre-Kripkean innocence would certainly claim that the Superman of (s_3) being essentially fictional cannot exist and, as a consequence, that the nonexistent Superman of (s_3) and the existent

Superman of (s_1) cannot and do not bear the same name. For the post-Kripkean philosopher, both names are nothing but homonyms.[5] On Kripke's view, the name 'Superman' of the Superman of (s_3) is a rigid nondesignator designating nothing either in a fictional world or in the actual world.[6] And the name 'Superman' of the Superman of (s_1), if it designates anything in the actual world, rigidly designates, on Kripke's view, the same individual in every possible world in which this individual exists. As a consequence, there *cannot* be in (s_1) a man who can fly bearing the same name as the man of whom it is said in (s_3) that he can fly.

Note that what has just been said is true only because the Superman of (s_3) is a native of (s_3): the Superman of (s_3) does not exist in the actual world and is not imported from the actual world into (s_3). If this were not the case, if, for instance, the author of the book I am presently reading knew about the existence of the Superman of (s_1) and intended to tell a fictional story about this individual, the Superman of (s_3) would then certainly bear the same name as the Superman of (s_1). Nothing prevents a member of the actual world – for instance, a city or a famous individual – from migrating into an imaginary situation. Imaginary situations are hyperinsulated from the real world without the real world being hyperinsulated from imaginary situations.

8.1.4   Fictions within fictions

If one is ready to admit that Recanati follows Lewis when he claims that fictional situations are 'hyperinsulated' from the real world, still, one may wonder whether Recanati would be ready to follow Lewis's claim that fictional worlds are 'hyperinsulated' one from another. In other words, is Lewis right when he claims that fictional worlds are, in Recanati's terminology, 'hyperinsulated' one from another? This last question really matters to any theory of fiction which aims to give an account of fictions within fictions. Whenever an author of fiction writes fictions within fictions, he or she is led to embed fictional situations within other fictional situations. One of the questions which matters in this context is whether the so-called property of hyperinsulation applies to embedded fictional situations or not.

To answer this question, let's construct a follow-up of Recanati's story about the man who can fly. Suppose that the author of the book I am currently reading is a postmodern writer who enjoys fictions within fictions. Suppose then that, in the imaginary situation described by the book, the man who can fly – Superman – is said to be an author of fictional stories. Suppose finally that in the course of writing a book, Superman creates a beautiful woman. We have then embedded in the imaginary situation s_3 another imaginary situation s_4 – the book written by Superman – a situation supporting[7] a number of facts (the fact that there are five chapters and 98 pages). Moreover, we have the imaginary situation s_5 described by the book written by Superman, an imaginary situation which supports among other facts the fact that there is a beautiful woman who, let's say, is called 'Sarah', the factual set of s_5, w', being different from the factual set of s_3, w. We have in Recanati's symbolism:

(3) $s_1 \models_@ << s_2 \models_@ << s_3 \models_w <<$ There is a man who can fly who is called 'Superman' and writes a $<< s_4 \models_w << s_5 \models_{w'} <<$ There is a beautiful woman who is called 'Sarah' $>> >> >> >>$

In these new circumstances, it is a fact concerning my present reading situation (s_1) that it contains a book (s_2) which 'contains' a situation (s_3) in which there is a man called 'Superman' who can fly and writes a book (s_4) which 'contains' a situation (s_5) in which there is a woman called 'Sarah' who is beautiful. Still it does not follow that there is a beautiful woman called 'Sarah' either in my present reading situation (s_1), or in the imaginary situation (s_3) described by the book I am reading, even though 'There is a beautiful woman called "Sarah"' is a persistent fact. It looks then as if imaginary situations in the fictional realm still have the property of 'hyper-insulation', even when they contain other imaginary situations embedded in themselves. Lewis's theory seems vindicated and it seems that Recanati would be justified if he followed Lewis all the way and claimed that fictional worlds are 'hyperinsulated' one from another.

8.1.5 A 'metaleptic' meeting

Still one may wonder whether it is possible to generalize what has just been said to *all* instances of fictions within fictions. Consider a fiction containing another fiction (as in the last example), but in which the author allows some of the characters belonging to the embedded fiction to meet some other characters from the embedding fiction. Actually there exist many fictions which allow the boundary between embedded and embedding fictions to dissolve.[8] It is relatively easy to construct a fiction of this kind. It suffices to continue the preceding story a little further. Suppose now that in the imaginary situation (s_5) described in the book (fictionally) written by Superman, Superman falls in love with the beautiful Sarah and conceives a child with her.[9] This is an instance of what Genette (1980) labels 'metalepsis'. Metalepsis is defined as:

[...] any intrusion by the extradiegetic narrator or narratee into the diegetic universe (or by diegetic characters into a metadiegetic universe, etc.), or the inverse (as in Cortazar)[...]. (Genette 1980: 234–5)

In our example, Superman is the (fictional) extradiegetic author of a particular fiction (s_5) in which he himself intervenes. Superman who, in the embedding fiction (s_3), is said to be the author of a story about a character called 'Sarah', is also said in an embedded fiction (s_5) to conceive a child with his own character. Let's call 'metaleptic' a fiction which has the following two characteristics:

1. It contains embedded in itself at least another fiction.
2. At least one character in the fiction is said to intervene at a particular level of the fiction of which this character is not a native.

The story (fictionally) written by Superman is an instance of a 'metaleptic' fiction. Metaleptic fictions create a problem for theories of truth fiction in the style of Lewis's theory. If the possible worlds in which a fiction is truthfully told are entirely isolated one from another or, in Recanati's terminology, entirely 'hyperinsulated' one from another, it becomes difficult, if not impossible to find a possible world in which a metaleptic fiction would be truthfully told. In fact, metaleptic fictions would require admitting an overlap of fictional worlds and, also, the existence of trans-world individuals. In order to give an analysis of the fictional truth that Superman meets Sarah and conceives a child with her, one should allow that different fictional worlds (s_3) and (s_5) have parts in common or that Superman, and maybe also Sarah, exist in (s_3) as well as in (s_5). But Lewis's modal realism is a modal realism without overlap of worlds and Lewis's counterpart theory is not a trans-world identity theory.[10] A metaleptic fiction is, for Lewis's style theories of truth in fiction and modal realism, an instance of an impossible fiction.[11]

8.1.6   Are 'metaleptic' fictions too unorthodox?

It is likely that, in order to make his case, an adept of Lewis's theory of truth in fiction and modal realism might object that metaleptic fictions are too bizarre and unorthodox to be analysed in the same way as normal fictions. According to this objection, the fact that it is impossible to find a possible world in which a metaleptic fiction would be truthfully told does not constitute a real difficulty for Lewis's possible worlds analysis of true statements about fiction. If there is a real problem here, it lies with metaleptic fictions themselves which, according to the objection, break the rules of fiction, not with Lewis's analysis of truth in fiction.

To this objection, one may reply that metaleptic fictions may also be considered as the modern follow-ups of those fictions in which a narrator enters into the narrated world. The reply, relying on Genette's definition of metalepsis, suggests that there is a continuity between metaleptic fictions in which a character intervenes into a narrated world and fictions in which the narrator enters into the narrated world, for instance to comment on it or to invite the narratee to enter himself or herself into the narrated world. Here are some examples of fictions in which a narrator enters into the narrated world:

> **Leaving it** [the coach] to pursue its journey at the pleasure of the conductor aforementioned [. . .] **this narrative may embrace the opportunity of ascertaining the condition of Sir Mulberry Hawk**, and to what extent he had, by this time, recovered from the injuries consequent on being flung violently from his cabriolet, under the circumstances already detailed (Dickens, 1982: chapter 38)

> He stretched himself. He rose. He stood upright in complete nakedness before us, and while the trumpets pealed Truth! Truth! We have no choice left but confess – he was a woman.
> The sound of the trumpets died away and Orlando stood stark naked. No human being, since the world began, has ever looked more ravishing. [. . .] Orlando looked himself up and down in a long looking-glass, without showing signs of discomposure, and went, presumably, to his bath.
> **We may take advantage of this pause in the narrative to make certain statements.** Orlando has become a woman – there is no denying it. (Woolf 1989: 137–8)

> Mrs. Tow-wouse [. . .] began to compose herself, and at length recovered the usual serenity of her temper, **in which we will leave her, to open the reader the steps which led to a catastrophe**, common enough [. . .] yet often fatal to the repose and well-being of families, and the subject of many tragedies, both in life and on stage [i.e. adultery]. (Fielding, *Joseph Andrews* I, xvii)

> As we have now brought Sophia into safe hands, **the reader will, I apprehend, be contented to deposit her awhile, and to look a little after other personages, and particularly poor Jones**, whom we have left long enough to do penance for his past offences, which, as is the nature of vice, brought sufficient punishment upon him themselves. (Fielding, *Tom Jones*, Book XI, ch. 10)[12]

Fiction writers have for a long time been including in their narrative an extra-fiction concerning the narration itself. Those fictions have become classic. This extra-fictional move on the side of fiction writers requires considering the narrative itself as an embedded fiction and the narration itself as an embedding fiction. The excerpts which have just been mentioned show that the narrator who belongs to the embedding fiction is sometimes said to enter – or, as in the last excerpt, to intervene – into the embedded fiction, the narrated world. What is remarkable is that these metaleptic passages in no way disrupt the fictional involvement of the reader. Once again they are considered as classic.

It is true that our story about Superman and Sarah represents the intrusion not of a narrator but of a character belonging to an embedding fiction into an embedded fiction. And this certainly makes a difference with the excerpts just mentioned. Still one may easily find a continuity between metaleptic fictions of this kind and fictions in which, as in the excerpts mentioned, the narratee is invited to make-believe that he can leave some personages and look at other personages. As soon as one admits that there is such a continuity, the objection concerning the unorthodox status of metaleptic fiction is weakened.

8.2   Metarepresentation and transparency[13]

8.2.1   Recanati's 'transparency thesis'

According to Recanati, when a speaker characterizes how the world is according to somebody's beliefs, he does not characterize the actual world but, through mental simulation, someone else's belief world. In saying 'John believes that Morocco is a Republic', the speaker characterizes John by describing the world as it is according to him and the function of the prefix 'John believes that . . . ' is to shift the world with respect to which the fact represented at the primary level 'Morocco is a Republic' is evaluated.[14] On that basis, Recanati claims that what I call 'ascribed situations' are imaginary situations in the following sense:

> In metarepresentations, the fact represented at the primary level is located in the *imaginary* realm rather than in the actual world. (Recanati 2000: xiv)

According to Recanati, metarepresentations are intrinsically simulative. The simulative essence of metarepresentations follows from the intuitive observation that in order to metarepresent, to have a second-level belief about a first-level belief, one needs to display the content believed – the 'ascribed situation' – at the first level. This is what Recanati calls the 'iconic' dimension of metapresentations. Metarepresentations are 'iconic' in so far as they resemble or replicate the beliefs they are about.[15] The linguistic format of our belief reports, the way belief reports are displayed, is then, for Recanati, more evidence in favour of the simulation theory of metarepresentations.

The 'iconic' dimension of metarepresentations in turn explains why the ascriber needs first to entertain the content of the first-level representation he or she attributes to the ascribee. This last move leads Recanati to claim that metarepresentations are 'transparent' representations. Metarepresentations do not constitute an opaque interface between the ascriber and the ascribee's thoughts since the ascriber needs to entertain the semantic content of the representation he attributes – the 'ascribed situation' – to the other person. In my terminology, 'ascribed situations' are, for Recanati, transparently represented.

In all these moves, Recanati relies on the syntactic format of indirect discourse to deduce some of its semantic properties: the iconic presence in the metarepresentation at the syntactical level of the object representation or 'ascribed situation' entails, for Recanati, that in order to attribute a belief one needs first to entertain the semantic content of the ascribee's belief. This is the 'transparency thesis', the fact that whichever state of affairs the object representation represents, the metarepresentation also represents: whenever a metarepresentation displays the content x of an object-representation, then the metarepresentation is bound to be about x. According to Recanati, a genuine metarepresentation dS (where d is the tag and S the radical) satisfies the following schema:

Schema (I):
One cannot entertain the proposition that dS without entertaining the proposition that S.

For example:

One cannot entertain the proposition that John believes that grass is green without entertaining the proposition that grass is green. (Recanati 2000: 10)

8.2.2   An empathetic conception of simulation?

Recanati's proposal has for it a pre-philosophical intuition about the truth of our belief reports. According to that intuition, a true belief report contains a that-clause whose terms have the same *references* as the ones used by the subject of the report. As is well-known, this pre-philosophical intuition goes against what has now become the standard Fregean philosophical intuition according to which the that-clause of a belief report has to express some sort of conceptual content that the subject of the report believes in order for the report to be true. To use Davidson's phrase, Recanati tries to recover this 'pre-Fregean semantic innocence'.[16]

Recanati's proposal has also for it a long philosophical tradition when he stresses the vital role of simulation in belief reports and metarepresentations. In the now classic debate in the philosophy of mind about the cognitive mechanisms involved in 'mindreading',[17] the 'theory theorists' claim that the ability to think about other's mental states can be explained by our (maybe tacit) possession of a theory of the structure and functioning of the mind while the 'simulation-theorists' maintain that the ability to understand the mind of others is grounded in our ability to engage in mental simulation. Recanati is a friend of simulation theory. As other simulationists, Recanati has behind him a long philosophical history going back as far as Vico, Dilthey and Weber, an history which has recently enjoyed a resurgence in Quine (1960), Goldman (1989) and, most notably, in Gordon (1986).[18]

What is mental simulation? It is an exercise of the imagination commonly described as putting oneself or imagining being 'in someone else's shoes'. At least, two steps are involved in a simulation:

1. In this imaginary move, the simulator finds himself having certain feelings, certain beliefs and desires, he finds himself choosing a certain course of action . . .
2. The simulator is then in a position to judge that the simulatee is *actually* having such and such states, *similar* or at least *analogous* to the simulator's own imaginary states.

Is there in this very general description of an exercise of mental simulation some grounds in favour of Recanati's 'transparency thesis'? It is said in this general description that the process occurring in the simulator *models* the process occurring in the simulatee, or that the simulator uses his own mental states *to represent* another's mental states. But, contrary to Recanati's claim, nowhere is it said, that the simulator literally thinks what the simulatee thinks. Generally, it is said that when we engage in mental simulation, we attribute psychological states to others on the basis of our experience of the same psychological states, or at least *similar* or *corresponding* or *analogous* ones. All these phrases point towards the presence of a non-transparent or opaque ingredient in simulation. Simulation theory, as it is traditionally conceived, is non-transparent. Let's quote Goldman:

> Let us . . . describe the simulation heuristic . . . The initial step is . . . to imagine being 'in the shoes' of the agent . . . This means pretending to have the same initial desires, beliefs, or other mental states that the attributor's background information suggests the agent has. The next step is to feed these pretend states into some inferential mechanism, or other cognitive mechanism, and allow that mechanism to generate further mental states as outputs by its normal operating procedure. For example, the initial states might be fed into the practical reasoning mechanism which generates as output a choice or decision . . . More precisely, the output state should be viewed as a pretend or surrogate state, since presumably a simulator doesn't feel the *very same* affect or emotion as a real agent would. Finally, upon noting this output, one ascribes to the agent an occurrence of the output state. (Goldman 1995: 189)

Goldman rightly stresses that presumably a simulator doesn't feel the *very same* affect or emotion as a real agent would. One should add, following Goldman, that presumably a simulator doesn't think the *very same* thought as the simulatee. On that basis, one may doubt that simulation is as transparent and innocent as Recanati apparently believes it is. Actually, the very opposite may be true. Of course, it may happen that the shoes that the simulator occupy are enough like those of the simulatee.

In these circumstances, as Recanati suggests, the simulator can metarepresent in a transparent and innocent way. But one may wonder whether, in these particular circumstances, the simulation of the ascriber involves an imaginative experiment since, in these circumstances, imagining may not be necessary to think what the other thinks. Following simulationists like Goldman, Recanati claims that one needs to put oneself into someone else's shoes in order to entertain a genuine metarepresentation. But, unless one follows radical simulationists like Gordon and adopts *contra* Goldman what may be called an empathetic conception of simulation, the former claim does not by itself entail Recanati's 'transparency thesis', that is the thesis that the ascriber needs to think what the ascribee thinks.

There is here a risk of confusion between two different imaginative projects that may be involved in an exercise of simulation. To put oneself into someone else's shoes in the manner of Goldman is a very different imaginative project from the project of thinking what someone else thinks in the manner of Recanati. The main difference between the two imaginative projects is, according to Wollheim (1984: 76), that while the former leaves it open to the simulator at any moment to imagine himself being face to face with the simulatee, the latter rules out such possibility.[19] The distinction between these two projects is present in the phrase 'Imagining being X' which, at the conceptual level, is an ambiguous phrase. Its sense can vary between two extremes, from 'imagining *oneself* in X's place' to 'imagining that one is X *rather than oneself*'.[20] Only the latter project rules out for the imaginer to imagine being brought face to face with X. Following Mackie (1977), Goldie (1999) notes that what is characteristic of the modest 'imagining being X' in the sense of 'imagining *oneself* in X's place' is that, contrary to what is required by empathy, it involves a mixture of the imaginer's properties and of the X's properties.[21] And I believe an exercise of simulation – as it is traditionally conceived in simulation theory – shares many more characteristics with the modest imaginative project rather than with the other.

As a conclusion, I suggest that Recanati's conception of simulation is an empathetic conception. Only such a conception can motivate Recanati's 'transparency thesis' for it is only through a process like empathy that the ascriber can lose sight that he or she has a different point of view than the ascribee. For Recanati, empathy is a process by which a person imagines, not only the emotions and affects of another person, but also the thoughts of another person. But whereas there is no doubt that some degree of empathy is needed to detect someone else's affects and emotions, one may wonder whether the same mechanism is at work to ascribe beliefs.

Notes

1. Cf. Recanati (2000: 50).
2. See also Recanati (1996: § 6)
3. Cf. Lewis (1986: 69–81).
4. A non-philosopher would certainly claim that the Superman of (s_3) and the Superman of (s_1) do actually bear the same name. Moreover the non-philosopher would claim that both Supermen are the same individual and that, after all, the Superman of (s_3) exists.
5. The homonyms mentioned here are different from the ones Kripke has in mind when he allows that a name of a fictional object like 'Superman' is ambiguous between two uses, one of which is parasitic on the other. According to Kripke, as the name 'Superman' was originally introduced, it has no referent whatsoever and it is used all the way in pretense as a name for a person. At a later stage, this use in pretense ends up creating a fictional character which Kripke conceives as an abstract and existing artifact. In the end, this metaphysical move gives rise to a nonpretend use of another name 'Superman' to refer to that existing artifactual entity. In effect, there are for Kripke two different names 'Superman': one for a person which does not exist, one for an existing abstract entity. By contrast, the two names which are considered here as homonyms are two names for two different concrete individuals who bear different names with the same spelling.
6. Cf. Kripke (1972/1980: 157–8).
7. Recanati explains what he means by 'to support' in this context in the following way: 'Whenever a fact σ holds in a situation s, or equivalently, whenever a proposition is true at s, we say that the situation in question *supports* the fact or proposition. In symbols: $[s] \lfloor \sigma'$ (Recanati, 64).
8. Le Poidevin (1995) gives many illuminating instances of fictions of this kind.
9. In *At Swim-Two-Birds*, Flann O'Brien writes a story of this kind in which a fictional author, Dermot Trellis, creates the beautiful Sheila Lamont. Sheila Lamont is so beautiful that Trellis is said in the fiction to ravish her and to make her pregnant. On this example, see Le Poidevin (1995: 230–1).
10. Cf. Lewis (1986: 210–48).
11. Doug McLellan suggests that a defender of Lewis may claim that Superman and Sarah's meeting is proof that they must have been in the same world all along. It only seemed that they inhabit different worlds and meet later on, but the truth is that they must have been in the same world all along. To this reply, one may object that a fiction may be considered as metaleptic only if it satisfies the following two conditions: first, there exist two distinct possible worlds in which either the embedding fiction or the embedded fiction is truthfully told and, second, at one point the borders between these different possible worlds is said to dissolve. If one were to follow Lewis's defence presented by McLellan, I believe that one would be led to admit that the possible worlds in which the embedding and the embedded fiction are truthfully told are *not* different possible worlds, and as a consequence, that the fiction in which Superman and Sarah from the start belonged to the same world, is *not* metaleptic.
12. These literary excepts are quoted and discussed in Fludernik (2003). One may also find some comments on these literary excerpts in Pelletier (2003).
13. This part of the chapter is a sequel of Pelletier (2002).
14. Cf. Recanati (2000: 168).
15. On the iconicity of metarepresentations, cf. Recanati (2000: 9–12).
16. Cf. Davidson (1968: 108).

17. See Davies and Stone (1995a, 1995b), Carruthers and Smith (1996) and Dokic and Proust (2002).
18. On the philosophical antecedents of simulation theory, see Goldman (1995: 188–9).
19. '[I]magining myself in the Sultan's shoes (. . .) leaves it open to me at any moment to imagine myself brought face to face with the Sultan. And that is something that the imaginative project I have in mind [empathizing with the Sultan.] clearly rules out' (Wollheim 1984: 76).
20. Cf. Goldie (1999: 397).
21. To adapt Goldie's excellent example to our times, the question: 'What would I do if I were in G.W. Bush's shoes?' does not motivate an answer like 'Obviously, just as G.W. Bush would' nor an answer which supposes that I, with all my characteristics, am strangely catapulted into Bush's chair in the Oval Office. Cf. Goldie (1999: 412) and Pelletier (2004).

References

Carruthers, P. and Smith, P. (eds) (1996) *Theories of Theories of Mind*. Cambridge: Cambridge University Press.

Davidson, D. (1968) 'On Saying That' reprinted in his *Inquiries into Truth and Interpretation*. Oxford: Clarendon Press (1984), pp. 93–108.

Davies, M. and Stone, T (eds) (1995a) *Folk Psychology: The Theory of Mind Debate*. Oxford: Blackwell.

Davies, M. and Stone, T (eds) (1995b) *Mental Simulation: Evaluations and Applications*. Oxford: Blackwell.

Dickens, C. (1982) *Nicholas Nickleby*. Oxford: Oxford University Press

Dokic, J and Proust, J (eds) (2002) *Simulation and Knowledge of Action*, Advances in Consciousness Research series. Amsterdam/Philadelphia: John Benjamins.

Fludernik, M. (2003) 'The Diachronization of Narratology'. *Narrative*, 11(3): 331–48.

Genette, G. (1980) *Narrative Discourse: An Essay in Method*. Ithaca, NY: Cornell University Press.

Goldie, P. (1999) 'How We Think of Other's Emotions'. *Mind and Language* 14: 394–423.

Goldman, A.I. (1989) 'Interpretation Psychologized'. *Mind and Language* 4: 161–85.

Goldman, A.I. (1995) 'Empathy, Mind and Morals'. In M. Davies and T. Stone (eds) (1995b), *Mental Simulation: Evaluations and Applications*. Oxford: Blackwell, pp. 185–208.

Gordon, R. (1986) 'Folk Psychology as Simulation'. *Mind and Language* 1: 158–71.

Le Poidevin, R. (1995) 'Worlds within Worlds? The Paradoxes of Embedded Fiction'. *British Journal of Aesthetics*, 35(3): 227–38.

Kripke, S. (1972/1980) 'Naming and Necessity'. In D. Davidson and G. Harman (eds), *Semantics of Natural Language*. Dordrecht: Reidel (1972); republished in S. Kripke (1980) *Naming and Necessity*. Oxford: Basil Blackwell.

Lewis, D. (1978/1983) 'Truth in Fiction'. *American Philosophical Quarterly*, vol. XV, pp. 37–46. Reprinted in David Lewis (1983), *Philosophical Papers*, vol. 1. New York: Oxford University Press, pp. 261–80.

Lewis, D. (1986) *On the Plurality of Worlds*. Oxford: Basil Blackwell.

Mackie, J. (1977) *Ethics: Inventing Right and Wrong*. London: Penguin.

Pelletier, J. (2002) 'Reply to François Recanati'. In J. Dokic and J. Proust (eds), *Simulation and Knowledge of Action*. Amsterdam and Philadelphia: John Benjamins Publishing Company, Advances in Consciousness Research series, pp. 173–84.

Pelletier, J. (2003) 'Vergil and Dido'. *Dialectica.* 57(2): 191–203.

Pelletier, J. (2004) 'Analogical Uses of the First Person Pronoun: A Difficulty in Philosophical Semantics'. *Journal of Cognitive Science* 5: 139–55.

Recanati, F. (1996) 'Domains of Discourse'. *Linguistics and Philosophy* 19: 445–75.

Quine, W.V. (1960) *Word and Object.* Cambridge, MA: MIT Press.

Recanati, F. (2000) *Oratio Obliqua, Oratio Recta: An Essay on Metarepresentation.* Cambridge, MA: The MIT Press.

Walton, K. (1990) *Mimesis as Make-Believe: On the Foundations of the Representational Arts.* Cambridge, MA: Harvard University Press.

Wollheim, R. (1984) *The Thread of Life.* Cambridge, MA: Harvard University Press.

Woolf, V. (1989) *Orlando: A Biography.* San Diego: Harcourt, Brace, Jovanovich.

Recanati's Reply to Pelletier

I

According to Jérôme Pelletier, the property I appeal to in order to distinguish imaginary from real situations, viz. hyperinsulation, is nothing but (or follows from) the property of *spatiotemporal or causal disconnection*. Real situations are spatiotemporally or causally connected; but imaginary situations are not spatiotemporally or causally connected to real situations. It follows that what happens in the imaginary situation described by a certain book has no consequence on what happens in the real situation in which the book itself is written or read, and conversely. In particular, if there is a man who can fly in the imaginary situation, it does not follow that there is such a man in the real situation in which the imaginary situation is described. Now this is an example of what I call hyperinsulation: even facts that are 'persistent' in the logical sense (such as the fact that there is a man who can fly) do not necessarily persist when we move upward from imaginary situations to the real situations comprising them.

But the notion of causal disconnection is not itself crystal-clear. What happens to the author of the story in the actual world may have an impact upon what he writes and therefore upon what happens in the imaginary situations he describes; and what happens in the imaginary situation the author describes may have consequences for the real situation in which he writes. If Superman starts abusing children in the imaginary situation, anti-paedophile associations will boycott the Superman stories in the actual world. Is there, or is there not, a causal relation between the two facts? One might argue that what causes the boycott of the Superman stories is a real fact: the fact that they feature Superman as a paedophile. But this real fact is a fact about an imaginary situation: it is the fact that, in the imaginary situation described by the stories in question, Superman behaves as a paedophile. The idea that imaginary situations are causally disconnected from the actual world is not crystal-clear because certain real situations (e.g. books and other fictions) 'comprise' imaginary situations. When the causal consequences of a real situation (say, the publication of the new

179

Superman stories) are essentially tied to the properties that situation has in virtue of comprising an imaginary situation (say, a situation in which Superman behaves badly), there is a sense in which the imaginary situation itself has those consequences and causally affects the actual world, via the path that does exist between the real situation and the imaginary situation. That path is the comprise relation, which here takes the form of one situation containing a description of the other. To be sure, the path in question is not a spatiotemporal or causal path internal to the actual world, but an 'intentional' path which essentially involves a shift from the actual world to some other possible world. But this intuitive distinction is precisely what we are trying to make sense of: we are trying to make sense of the idea that some situations – those to which we have access through books and other representations – are merely 'imaginary'. My suggestion is that hyper-insulation is criterial: whenever the comprise relation between two situations s_1 and s_2 involves a world-shift, in such a way that s_2 is 'imaginary' with respect to the parent situation s_1, then even if a fact σ belongs to the persistent variety, its being a fact in s_2 does not entail that it is a fact also in s_1 (contrary to what happens when s_1 and s_2 belong to the same world).

II

Pelletier wonders whether the fact that imaginary worlds are insulated from the actual world and from each other prevents them from containing the same individuals. As is well-known, Kripke accepts trans-world individuals, while Lewis takes individuals to be 'world-bound'. For Kripke, however, only actual individuals can be stipulated to exist in other possible worlds, because nonactual individuals (e.g. fictional individuals) lack clear conditions of individuation:

> Granted that there is no Sherlock Holmes, one cannot say of any possible person that he *would have been* Sherlock Holmes, had he existed. Several distinct possible people, and even actual ones such as Darwin or Jack the Ripper, might have performed the exploits of Holmes, but there is none of whom we can say that he would have *been* Holmes had he performed these exploits. For if so, which one? (Kripke 1980: 158)

In Lewis' system, identity across possible worlds is ruled out on principle. No individual, whether actual or fictional, can exist in more than one possible world. But the inhabitants of one possible world may have 'counterparts' in other possible worlds. Fictional individuals are just like other individuals, in this respect. If an actual individual is found who is called 'Sherlock Holmes', performs the exploits of Holmes, has a friend named 'Watson' with such and such characteristics, etc., in the actual world, there will be no doubt that that person is a 'counterpart' of Sherlock Holmes in the actual world.

Pelletier takes both Kripke and Lewis to be insulationists who reject the possibility for fictional individuals to show up in the actual world ; and he thinks metaleptic narratives in which the author of a fiction meets one of his or her fictional characters cannot be handled consistently within Lewis's theory of fictional truth if one accepts insulationism. For Lewis, a sentence 'In fiction f, φ' is true iff φ is true at every possible world where f is told as known fact rather than fiction (Lewis 1983: 268). Pelletier objects that if one is an insulationist (as he takes Lewis to be), then there is no possible world in which a metaleptic narrative is told as known fact. I think that objection fails because Lewis is not really an insulationist: he can accept the possibility for the (actual or fictional) author of a fiction to meet a counterpart, in his world, of the fictional character he has created. The only argument for considering Lewis an insulationist is his wholesale rejection of trans-world identity in favour of a less demanding counterpart relation, but this is irrelevant to the issue about metalepsis.

Be that as it may, I need not take a stand on those issues because, contrary to what Pelletier suggests, my claim that imaginary situations are 'hyperinsulated' from the real situations containing them entails nothing regarding insulationism, as described by Pelletier. Hyperinsulation means that if Superman kisses Lois Lane in the imaginary situation, it does not follow that he kisses her in the actual situation in which the imaginary situation is described. This entails nothing regarding the possibility or impossibility for Superman and Lois Lane or for their counterparts to exist in the actual situation in question.

III

The last issue Pelletier raises regards simulation. I hold that metarepresentations are essentially simulative, for they contain the representation they are about as a proper part; hence one cannot, for example, entertain the thought that my cousin believes that Paris is a large city without *eo ipso* entertaining the thought that Paris is a large city. This implies that we cannot metarepresent the thoughts of creatures whose concepts we do not possess. Pelletier objects that when we metarepresent, the thought expressed by the embedded portion is not necessarily identical to the thought actually entertained by the ascribee. Perhaps my cousin does not literally entertain the thought 'Paris is a large city', but has a similar thought, which I report by saying (or thinking) that he believes Paris to be a large city. This is true, but so what? The metarepresenter cannot but entertain *the thought that he is ascribing*; whether this thought exactly or approximately corresponds to the ascribee's actual thought is another matter. Goldman writes that 'the output state [of the simulation procedure used in predicting an agent's emotion or affect in a given circumstance] should be viewed as pretend or surrogate state, since presumably a simulator doesn't feel the very same affect or emotion as a real agent would' (Goldman 1995: 189). In the same way, the thought which the metarepresenter ascribes and which (I claim) he is bound to entertain should perhaps be viewed as a pretend or surrogate thought, since it need not correspond exactly to the ascribee's thought. This is not a problem for me, and there is no reason to assume that my brand of simulationism is closer to Gordon's radical simulationism than it is to Goldman's, or that it corresponds to the imaginative project which Wollheim calls 'empathizing'.

References

Goldman, A. (1995) 'Empathy, Mind, and Morals'. In M. Davies and T. Stone (eds), *Mental Simulation*. Oxford: Blackwell, pp. 185–208.
Kripke, S. (1980) *Naming and Necessity*. Oxford: Blackwell.
Lewis, D. (1983) *Philosophical Papers*, vol. 1. New York: Oxford University Press.

9

Names for *Ficta*, for *Intentionalia*, and for Nothing

Alberto Voltolini

In his *Oratio Obliqua, Oratio Recta*, Recanati maintains two main theses regarding metarepresentational sentences embedding allegedly empty proper names. The first thesis concerns both belief sentences embedding allegedly empty names and (internal) metafictional sentences (i.e., sentences of the form 'in the story S, p')[1] embedding fictional, hence again allegedly empty, names.[2] It says that such sentences primarily have *fictive* truth-conditions: that is, conditions for their *fictional* truth. The second thesis is that a fictive ascription of a singular belief, assigning to a certain meta-representational sentence fictive truth-conditions, amounts to the factive ascription of a pseudo-singular belief, assigning to that very sentence factual truth-conditions as well. In what follows, I will first try to show that the first thesis is definitely correct only for a rather limited range of cases, i.e., cases of metarepresentational sentences embedding *absolutely* empty proper names. Second, I will claim not only that the notion of a pseudo-singular belief is not so clear as it may seem, but also that, for those cases for which the first thesis is correct, we do not really need the sentences involved to also have factive truth-conditions.

9.1 Fictive truth-conditions

According to Recanati, belief sentences embedding allegedly empty names – like 'Jean believes that Marcel is sleeping', reporting Jean's hallucination of an individual with that name as sleeping in front of her – as well as internal metafictional sentences embedding fictional, hence again allegedly empty, names – like 'In the story, Santa Claus lives in the sky', where Santa Claus is the character the well-known myth so names – primarily have *fictive* truth-conditions; that is, conditions for their *fictional* truth (cf. Recanati 2000: 215–20). This is to say that both sentences are fictionally true, that is, are true in a pretense, respectively iff, in a given pretense, there is an individual, whose name is 'Marcel', such that Jean believes that such an individual is sleeping and, in an(other) pretense of the same general kind, there is an individual, named 'Santa Claus', who the myth says lives in the sky. In actual fact, according to Recanati the utterers of the above sentences exploit what he calls a Meinongian pretense. In this general kind of pretense, such utterers respectively make believe that there are individuals like Marcel and Santa Claus who, unlike ordinary existents, have the property of being illusory or anyway fictional objects. So, in uttering the above sentences they respectively pretend that Jean has a belief about such a hallucinatory individual that it is sleeping and that the myth says of that fictional individual that it lives in the sky (cf. Recanati 2000: 220). Since both things are make-believedly the case, those sentences effectively are fictionally true.

For Recanati, this thesis on the fictive truth-conditions of the above sentences goes hand in hand with the idea that, when used in the above sentences, proper names like 'Marcel' and 'Santa Claus' undergo an *overall* contextual shift. First, these names must be taken to be uttered in a shifted context, the context of the Meinongian pretense in question. Moreover, this context is such that both the belief and the fictional operator respectively occurring in those sentences are also to be taken as uttered within such a context, so that their semantical contribution is given within that context as well (cf. Recanati 2000: 214–15). As a result, in the above sentences those names *really* refer to *nothing*, they refer *only fictionally*. Moreover, they so refer within the general Meinongian pretense, whose scope is wider than that of the relevant belief or of the narrower pretense constituted by the myth-telling.

Let me now call *absolutely* empty names those morphosyntactically simple singular terms that actually refer to nothing *at all* (i.e., in no context) – at most, they are merely misbelieved to have a referent. A prototypical example of a name of this kind may be the following.[3] Suppose I mishear a sentence saying that war is terrible, by taking 'war' as a proper name of someone. Asked to write what I heard, I scribble: 'War is terrible' (note the majuscule), using 'War' as a proper name and misconceiving it as referring to someone I do not know.

Now, I agree with Recanati that, as far as *these* names are concerned, *no* sentence containing them has real truth-conditions. As a result, a belief sentence containing one such name can merely have fictive truth-conditions. For in a situation like the one above, scribbling something on the ascribee's part would definitely not be enough in order for her to have a belief about something. Rather, it would count only *as if* she had such a belief. So, if someone said of me: 'A.V. believes that War is terrible' this sentence would not have real truth-conditions, hence a real truth-value, but merely fictive truth-conditions, hence a fictive truth-value.

We have now to see whether in the other cases of allegedly empty proper names we are in the same situation as the above one, as Recanati maintains.

Let me start from fictional names, i.e., names used primarily in *fictional* sentences ('Hamlet is a prince') as well as in *metafictional* sentences, both *internal* ('In *Hamlet*, Hamlet is a prince') and *external* ('Hamlet is a fictional character').[4] As some have remarked,[5] it is incorrect to assimilate fictional names to absolutely empty names. Indeed, they (allegedly) are at most *relatively* empty names: although *in reality* they do not refer at all, *in the context of the fiction* where they are primarily taken as uttered they do refer to something, namely to the individuals bearing those names in such a fiction.

Here Recanati would probably rejoinder that the fact that fictional names are relatively empty names does not make them really refer in internal metafictional sentences. For, as I have just said, *outside fiction* these names do not refer at all. As a result, for him such sentences fail to have *real* truth-conditions insofar as the fictional names in it do not yield any *real* truth-conditional contribution. This holds true of those terms in those sentences precisely once one maintains that, although those names refer *in the scope* of the general Meinongian pretense which those fictive truth-conditions mobilize, they *really* refer to *nothing*. So, Recanati accommodates their being relatively empty names by providing internal metafictional sentences embedding them primarily with fictive truth-conditions.

Yet there is a problem with assigning internal metafictional sentences primarily fictive truth-conditions. To be sure, a sentence of the form 'in the story S, p' may well have fictive truth-conditions. Definitely, moreover, this happens when it is uttered within the context of a pretense. Yet this occurs when, within a game of make-believe, one makes believe that there is another, typically narrower, game of make-believe in which something is pretended to be the case. Typically, these are cases of a play-within-a-play: within a certain piece of fiction, it is make-believedly the case that there is a(nother) fiction where something make-believedly happens. Now, suppose that a sentence such as the above, uttered in the broader game of make-believe, embeds a proper name. In so uttering that sentence, its utterer precisely pretends, *in the play*, that there is an individual designated by that name who is a fictional individual, and that such an individual is further pretended, *in the play-within-a-play*, to be a real individual doing certain things. For instance, suppose that in playing *Hamlet* it is uttered: 'In *The Murder of Gonzago*, Gonzago dies' (because, say, the utterer in the play wants to summarize the content of the play within it). In the play (*Hamlet*), the utterer pretends that there is an individual named 'Gonzago' who is a fictional individual, and that such an individual is further pretended, in the play-within-a-play (*The Murder of Gonzago*), to be a real individual who dies – as unfortunately happens to real things. So, in these cases a Meinongian pretense, in Recanati's sense, is exploited, so that the internal metafictional sentence has fictive truth-conditions. Yet definitely in a vast majority of cases, we do not use internal metafictional sentences in such a way. In all such cases, we feel that such sentences are really true, not fictionally true, hence that they have real, not fictive, truth-conditions. Indeed in all such cases, those sentence are not uttered in a play nesting another play, but uttered outside *any play whatsoever*.

Let me restate this point in a different and more general form. As it can be said by extending to sentences what Evans says about fictional names, fictional sentences can be used not only connivingly, i.e., as uttered within the pretense, but also *non*-connivingly, i.e., as uttered outside pretense.[6] Now, many maintain that in this latter use, a fictional sentence 'p' may well be taken as equivalent to the corresponding internal metafictional sentence of *degree 1* 'in the story S, p'.[7] Yet in order for such an equivalence to hold, this internal metafictional sentence must in its turn be used non-connivingly not only with respect to the story of degree 1 it refers to, but also *absolutely*, i.e., with respect to *any story whatsoever*. For it may turn out that such a sentence is used connivingly with respect to *another* story of degree 2, as in the 'play-within-a-play'-case. If this is the case, then we must again draw a distinction between the non-conniving use of the internal metafictional sentence merely with respect to the play of degree 1 and its absolute non-conniving use. In this latter use, the internal metafictional sentence of degree 1 will be equivalent to another internal metafictional sentence of *degree 2* 'in the story S', (it is the case that) in the story S, p'. As a consequence, the non-conniving use of the original fictional sentence will be equivalent to this latter internal metafictional sentence. Provided, of course, this sentence is in its turn used absolutely non-connivingly, i.e., non-connivingly with respect to any story whatsoever, and so on. Take 'Gonzago dies'. In its non-conniving use, this fictional sentence says the same as the internal metafictional sentence of degree 1 'In *The Murder of Gonzago*, Gonzago dies', provided this latter sentence is used *absolutely* non-connivingly. If this is *not* the case, that is, if this latter sentence is used connivingly with respect to a play of higher degree (as it may turn out if this sentence is uttered in *Hamlet*), then both the fictional sentence (in its non-conniving use) and the above internal metafictional sentence of degree 1 (in its absolute non-conniving use) are equivalent to the further internal metafictional sentence of degree 2 'In *Hamlet*, (it is the case that) in *The Murder of Gonzago*, Gonzago dies', in its absolute non-conniving use.

We can thus say that fictional sentences have both fictive and real truth-conditions, depending on whether they are used connivingly or non-connivingly. Yet the same holds also of internal metafictional sentences, depending on whether they are used either non-connivingly only with respect to the play of degree 1 the fictional sentences characterize or absolutely. In actual fact, fictional sentences non-connivingly used have the same real truth-conditions as the corresponding internal metafictional sentences of degree 1 absolutely non-connivingly used. As a result, it is true that internal metafictional sentences of degree 1 – sentences of the form 'in the story, p' where 'p' is a sentence not containing any further 'in the story'-prefix – have fictive truth-conditions. Yet this holds only when they are non-connivingly used merely with respect to a story of degree 1. As regards however the majority of their uses, namely when they are absolutely non-connivingly used, this is not the case; they then have real truth-conditions.

To be sure, the idea that fictional sentences as well as internal metafictional sentences have both fictional and real truth-conditions is well accepted in the context of an overall pretense-theoretic approach to fiction. Both Evans and Walton have indeed defended it.[8] In point of fact, Evans and Walton hold this truth-conditional thesis while sharing with Recanati the thesis that in the above sentences fictional names really refer to nothing. Yet Recanati gives up this theoretical possibility. Let us see why.

Leaving details aside, Evans-Walton truth-conditional account of fictional sentences (as I would add, in their non-conniving use) and metafictional sentences (in their absolutely non-conniving use) is simple. According to them, a fictional sentence is really true iff it is fictionally true, that is, iff it is true in the pretense.[9] If one likes, the fictional truth of the fictional sentence can be vividly described as the fact that such a sentence is true in the imaginary world postulated by the tale to which that sentence belongs, the world of the fictional story. Now, when this sentence contains a fictional name, this means that the referent that name has in such a world possesses in that world the property designated there by the predicate completing the sentence. Correspondingly, the metafictional sentence made of that fictional sentence and of a certain prefix of the form 'in the story S' is really true iff that fictional sentence is really true, that is, iff that sentence is fictionally true.[10] As a result, the fictional sentence in question, as well as its equivalent metafictional sentence, can be really true even if its fictional name really refers to nothing. For that real truth, it suffices that such a name fictionally refers to something, i.e., refers to something in the world of the fictional story.

Yet Recanati finds this proposal unsatisfying. First of all, he notes that this account of the real truth-conditions of fictional sentences, hence of the equivalent internal metafictional sentences, is very far from what these sentences, especially the second ones, literally seem to express.[11] Yet I suspect that there is for him a deeper drawback in such a proposal. To accept that internal metafictional sentences in particular have such real truth-conditions entails accepting that the prefixes of the form 'in the story S' they contain may not only be *circumstance-*, but also *context-shifting* operators. This may be shown to be independently problematic. Let me see this point in detail.

There is no trouble, says Recanati, in accepting that operators of the above form, as well as intensional operators in general (supposing for argument's sake that a prefix like the above is one such operator), are *circumstance-shifting*. Indeed, the typical way of accounting for the truth-conditions of a sentence of the kind 'IOp', where 'IO' expresses an intensional operator, is that such a sentence is true iff its embedded sentence 'p' is true in certain *non-actual* circumstances, hence in circumstances which are different from those in which the sentence characterized by that operator is true, namely *actual* circumstances (cf. Recanati 2000: 47–8). In the case of internal metafictional sentences, one might say with Recanati that this precisely obtains when the singular term occurring in the embedded sentence is a definite description. For then the whole sentence is true in the actual circumstances iff the denotation which that description has in the relevant non-actual circumstances, i.e., the world of the fictional story, also possesses in those circumstances the property designated there by the embedded predicate.

Yet theoretically speaking an operator may be not only a circumstance, but also a context-, shifting operator. This occurs insofar as an operator fixes the context with respect to which the semantic interpretation of the sentence it embeds is determined. In such a case, the truth-conditions of the sentence containing that operator again mobilize a shifted circumstance of evaluation of the sentence nested in such a sentence. Yet that operator triggers that very circumstance as a context relevant also to determine the content that sentence has in order to be so evaluated.

Now, if the singular term embedded in the metafictional sentence is a proper name, then the Evans-Walton truth-conditional account precisely makes it the case that the 'in the story'-operator is not only a circumstance-, but also a context-shifting operator. For then the whole sentence is true iff the referent which that name, *once it is taken to be uttered in the relevant non-actual circumstances* (i.e., the world of the fictional story), has in such circumstances, also possesses in those circumstances the property designated there by the embedded predicate.[12]

In point of fact, accounting for 'in the story'-prefixes as context-shifting operators is unavoidable once one both (i) endorses a direct-referential conception of proper names, (ii) takes fictional names as relatively empty names, and (iii) takes internal meta-fictional sentences as having real truth-conditions. For insofar as a fictional name really is an empty name and proper names are taken to be direct-referential expressions, then such a name should remain empty with respect to any alternative circumstance of evaluation of the sentences in which it figures. As Salmon maintains, an actually empty name is a rigid *non*-designator (cf. Salmon 1998: 287, 291–2). So, one can assign it a referent in an alternative circumstance, as 'referential relativists' like Evans and Walton do in order to assign real truth-conditions to an internal metafictional sentence embedding it, only by presupposing that such a name is taken to be uttered not from our perspective, the actual one, but precisely from the standpoint of that alternative.

Yet, comments Recanati, accepting that there are not only circumstance-, but also context-shifting operators, is rather problematic. For, as Kaplan has shown (cf. Kaplan 1989: 510), in the case of embedded indexicals no such shift is possible. If I say 'in *Remembrance of Time Past*, for a long time I used to go to bed early', there is no chance for that sentence to be true iff in the imaginary world postulated in Proust's *Recherche*, the imaginary narrator used to go to bed early for a long time. For this to be the case, the context of utterance of the embedded sentence 'for a long time I used to go to bed early' should be shifted in such a way that the content of such a sentence also shifted to a proposition such that 'I' referred to the imaginary narrator of the *Recherche* as the objectual component of such a proposition. Yet the 'in the story'- prefix does not manage to shift the reference of 'I' to that imaginary narrator, but is forced to have it refer to *me*, its actual utterer.

On behalf of the overall pretense-theoretic approach to fiction, one might think that this problem is circumscribed to indexicals. Yet, Recanati thinks, it is preferable to find a general truth-conditional account of internal metafictional sentences that refrains from taking 'in the story'-prefixes, hence intensional operators as a whole, as context-shifting operators. For this goes against a 'semantically innocent' approach to intensional contexts in general (cf. Recanati 2000: 250–1). As a result, his own truth-conditional account of internal metafictional sentences sticks to the theses (i)–(ii) above while rejecting thesis (iii): fictional names are direct-referential expressions that really refer to nothing insofar as also internal meta-fictional sentences primarily have fictive truth-conditions.[13]

I independently agree with Recanati that the Evans-Walton truth-conditional account of both fictional sentences (in their non-conniving use) and metafictional sentences fails to convince. To my mind, indeed, for a sentence possibly embedded in a certain internal metafictional sentence to be true in a fictional circumstance is just a necessary, but not a sufficient, condition for its truth in its non-conniving use, hence for the truth of that metafictional sentence (cf. Voltolini 2006).

So, I agree with Recanati that theses (i)–(iii) cannot be satisfactorily held together, as 'relativists' like Evans and Walton believe. Yet, since I think that Recanati's approach to internal metafictional sentences is also unsatisfying, I hold that another possibility of revising theses (i)–(iii) deserves scrutiny – namely to stick to theses (i) and (iii) while rejecting thesis (ii). That is, insofar as fictional names are direct-referential expressions that really refer to something, i.e., *fictional objects*, internal metafictional sentences may well have real truth-conditions that precisely involve such entities. These are the same truth-conditions that affect a fictional sentence in its non-conniving use. A fictional sentence containing a fictional name in its non-conniving use, as well as its equivalent internal metafictional sentence, is really true iff what that name really refers to, i.e., *a certain fictional object*, possesses the property designated by the predicate figuring in that sentence.[14]

Incidentally, I have formulated in the above way the truth-conditions of a fictional sentence containing a fictional name in its non-conniving use as well as of the corresponding metafictional sentence, for I believe that prefixes of the form 'in the story S' not only are no context-, but also they are no circumstance-shifting operator either; in a nutshell, they are no intensional operators.[15] Indeed, in the above truth-conditional account, there is no circumstance shift which is required to evaluate the (possibly) embedded fictional sentence.[16]

Up to now, we have found two paradigmatic situations of allegedly empty names: allegedly empty names which are thoroughly such, i.e., absolutely empty names, and allegedly empty names which were taken as such only relatively, i.e., fictional names, but that we may now legitimately describe as fully referential expressions. As far as the former expressions are concerned, Recanati's proposal seems to me correct: metarepresentational sentences embedding them have merely fictive truth-conditions. As far as the latter expressions are concerned, on the contrary, I disagree with Recanati. Like Evans-Walton, metarepresentational sentences embedding them have real truth-conditions. However, unlike Evans-Walton, such truth-conditions commit one to *ficta*.

Bearing this in mind, we are theoretically able to account for a third case of allegedly empty names, i.e., names purportingly designating intentional objects, as well as for metarepresentational sentences embedding them – typically, attitudinal sentences ('LochNessians fear that Nessie comes out of the lake'). For we can now say that only two options are available. Either we assimilate such names to the case of absolutely empty names. Then we will *eo ipso* deny that they refer to something in the metarepresentational sentences embedding them. As a result, we will be ready to accept Recanati's truth-conditional proposal as covering these metarepresentational sentences as well. In such a case, these sentences have merely fictive truth-conditions. Or we take these names as again being *merely* allegedly empty names, as fictional names have turned out to be. More specifically, we take these names as really referring to intentional objects when embedded. As a result, we will be ready to ascribe real truth-conditions to metarepresentational sentences embedding those names.

Here I want to remain neutral between the two options.[17] Let me note just two consequences of the committal alternative. First of all, in such a perspective one has to accept that the attitudinal prefixes occurring in the relevant metarepresentational sentences are intensional operators. For in this perspective, a sentence containing one such prefix is true iff what the embedded name really refers to, i.e., a certain intentional object, possesses *in the alternative circumstance* the property designated there by the embedded predicate. Moreover, in such a perspective attitudinal prefixes are not only circumstance-, but also risk to be context-, shifting operators. For when their embedded sentence is taken *per se* – e.g. 'Nessie comes out of the lake' – the name occurring in it has no referent, hence the sentence does not have a complete truth-conditional meaning. Yet when the sentence figures in its embedding metarepresentational sentence, the name has the same referent it has *qua* embedded in such a sentence, namely a certain intentional object. As a result, the sentence must be taken as uttered in a context that makes it have a complete truth-conditional meaning, the context determining a certain unactual circumstance as its alternative circumstance of evaluation.[18]

9.2 Factive truth-conditions

So, I partially accept Recanati's truth-conditional account of metarepresentational sentences embedding proper names that do not refer to actual concrete individuals in terms of fictive truth-conditions; namely, only when these sentences contain in their subordinate clauses *absolutely* empty names.

Yet Recanati is discontent with an obvious consequence of his approach to metarepresentational sentences, namely that, insofar as they have fictive, but not real, truth-conditions, such sentences do not have a real truth-value. This leads him to defend a further idea, namely that, whenever a metarepresentational sentence embeds allegedly empty proper names, the *fictive* ascription via that sentence of a singular belief amounts to the *factive* ascription, again via that very sentence, of a pseudo-singular belief (Cf. Recanati 2000: 226). This means that for him, over and above their primarily having fictive truth-conditions, metarepresentational sentences may also be seen as having factive truth-conditions, different from the fictive ones. This allows such sentences to also have a real truth-value. Moreover, it suggests that for him, those sentences are provided factive truth-conditions via their already having fictive truth-conditions. Indeed, he says that the factive ascription 'is not directly expressible save by appealing to the pretense' (2000: 226).

In this respect, metarepresentational sentences behave for him like metaphorical utterances. For in the case of a metaphorical utterance of a certain sentence, he says, we may precisely ascribe it factive over and above fictive truth-conditions. Moreover, it is clear that the fictive truth-conditions prompt the different factive ones. In his own example, 'That mountain range goes from Canada to Mexico' is fictionally true iff in the pretense, that mountain range moves from Canada to Mexico, yet it is factively true iff that mountain range *lies between* Canada and Mexico; and the former prompts the latter (cf. Recanati 2000: 222–4).

To be sure, since for me internal metafictional sentences (in their absolutely non-conniving use) have real truth-conditions from the very beginning, with respect to them this distinction between primary fictive and secondary factive truth-conditions does not apply. Yet we may well expect that things go this way as far as attitudinal sentences embedding absolutely empty proper names are concerned. In point of fact, in saying that over fictive truth-conditions, metarepresentational sentences also have distinct factive truth-conditions (as prompted by the former ones), Recanati precisely focuses on such attitudinal sentences. As I said above, for him the fictive ascription of a singular belief, that lets a certain attitudinal sentence embedding an absolutely empty name have fictive truth-conditions, amounts to the factive ascription of a pseudo-singular belief, that lets that very sentence have factive truth-conditions.

In order to check whether as far as attitudinal sentences are concerned Recanati's further thesis is correct, we must first scrutinize what a factive ascription of a pseudo-singular belief is. We already know what is a fictive ascription of a singular belief. To fictively ascribe to someone a singular belief by means of that sentence is to make believe that the ascribee has a belief whose content involves an object. This lets the sentence have certain fictive truth-conditions. Correspondingly, a factive ascription of a pseudo-singular belief should be the real ascription to the ascribee of a genuine belief which however is make-believedly singular, i.e., whose content pretends to involve an object. As Recanati (2000: 225) himself says, the belief in question 'purports to be singular'. This should allow that sentence also to have factive truth-conditions. Yet if the content of the belief ascribed is just make-believedly, but not in reality, singular, what content effectively has such a belief, hence what belief is it really?

A natural way to intend the pseudo-singular belief would be to take it as a belief whose content actually is a general existential proposition; hence, to take that belief as a general belief (cf. McDowell 1998: 475–6, 482–3). However, Recanati explicitly rejects this possibility. So, what else it may be?

In point of fact, Recanati describes the ascribee of a pseudo-singular belief as taking herself to believe a singular proposition (cf. Recanati 2000: 226). Or, as he alternatively says, the ascribee takes herself to entertain a singular sentence as tokened in her belief box (*ibid.*). So, Recanati describes the subject of a pseudo-singular belief as a subject entertaining a second-order belief: a belief that subject has of believing a singular proposition. Is the pseudo-singular belief this second-order belief, as Recanati seems to suggest?

This is hardly the case. Note indeed that a subject entertains one such second-order belief also when she really has a singular belief. Simply, in this case the second-order belief is a correct belief, for the subject really believes a singular proposition. Whereas in the case in question, the second-order belief is a mis-belief, for the subject actually fails to believe a singular proposition. Now, when the subject really has a singular belief, it is obvious to take the second-order belief as another belief accompanying the first one. So, why things should be different in the case in which the subject does not have a singular belief, but has a pseudo-singular belief? That is, why her second-order belief should not accompany another belief of hers also in that case? Yet if this is the case, the second-order belief, the accompany*ing* belief, cannot be the pseudo-singular belief. For otherwise it should be identical with that belief also when it is correct, which is obviously impossible. For, if it is correct, then the subject really has a singular, not a pseudo-singular, belief. But then in that case the pseudo-singular belief is not the accompani*ed* belief either. For the only belief which in the case in question the second-order belief may accompany is a general existential belief (cf. McDowell 1998: 475–6, 482–3). Yet Recanati has already rejected that the pseudo-singular belief is a general existential belief. So, it finally seems that we have moved in a circle, without finding any plausible candidate for a pseudo-singular belief.

At this point, I think that Recanati's theoretical conceptual repertoire enables us to explore the following alternative suggestions. He might say that the factive ascription of a pseudo-singular belief is *no* ascription of a belief at all, but rather of something like a *quasi*-belief – as in the case of a deferential belief ascription like 'the teacher believes that Cicero's prose is full of "synecdoches"' (cf. Recanati 2000: 278). Or he might say that it is the ascription of a belief in which a *local* pretense occurs as affecting the embedded name – as in the case of 'James believes that "Quine" has not finished writing his paper' (cf. Recanati 2000: 238–9, 249–51).

However, neither option seems to me particularly appealing. For both in the case of a quasi-belief and in the case of a belief affected by local pretense, according to Recanati every element in the representation attributed to the ascribee as entertained by her contributes a content to such a representation. Yet it is hard to see which content could be contributed to the representation possibly entertained by the ascribee by the absolutely empty name embedded in the attitudinal sentence.[19] For insofar as it is absolutely empty, such a name utterly has no referent, hence no meaning at all.[20]

To be sure, this does not prevent other suggestions to the role of a pseudo-singular belief from being put forward.[21] Yet in the absence of such suggestions, the very notion of a pseudo-singular belief remains hardly scrutable.

This prompts me to formulate a more general question. In the cases of attitudinal sentences whose embedded name is empty, do we really need a factive over and above a fictive ascription? If the name in question is absolutely empty, it seems that we can rest content with the mere fictive ascription. Take the aforementioned example 'A.V. believes that War is terrible'. Why should my mishearing a noun as a name prompt us to think that, in uttering that attitudinal sentence, the reporter does more than fictively ascribe a singular belief? Rather, it is precisely because I am not meaning anything by uttering 'War is terrible', and am doubtful that I mean anything, that prompts reporters to do no more than pseudo-ascribe a singular belief to me. If we are not content with that, it is because we feel that the name is not empty after all, for we rather suspect that it refers to something like an intentional object. This is the case of e.g. 'LochNessians fear that Nessie comes out of the lake'. Yet, as we have seen at the end of the previous section, there is a more radical way to account for the idea that one such sentence has factive truth-conditions. That is, we can ground that referential feeling by refraining from assigning that sentence fictive truth-conditions and rather straightforwardly yielding it *committal* factive truth-conditions, involving precisely a full-fledged intentional object.[22]

Notes

1. I slightly modify Recanati's terminological distinction between *fictional* sentences, i.e., sentences occurring directly or indirectly in a story, and *metafictional*

sentences, i.e., sentences of the form 'in the story S, p'. For I prefer to let his distinction interact with Bonomi's parallel yet threefold distinction between *textual* (roughly, fictional), *paratextual* (roughly, to be paraphrased as metafictional), and *metatextual* sentences. The latter sentences are those apparently concerning a fictional individual yet mobilizing no story, either directly or indirectly; for instance, 'Hamlet is a fictional character'. cf. Bonomi (1999). As a result, we may speak of *fictional* (i.e., Bonomi's textual), *parafictional* (i.e., Bonomi's paratextual), *internal meta-fictional* (i.e., Recanati's metafictional) and *external metafictional* (i.e., Bonomi meta-textual) sentences.

2. For the scope of this chapter, I speak as if there were a distinction in the general category of proper names between full and empty names. Moreover, I will further divide the latter into absolutely non-referential and relatively non-referential names, where fictional names belong to this second group. In actual fact, however, I hold that in the general category of proper names there are no such subdistinctions. Proper names actually are a special kind of indexicals. Insofar as this is the case, one and the same proper name may have both referentially full and referentially empty occurrences. Cf. e.g. Voltolini (1995). Yet Recanati would more or less share this idea: cf. his (1993). Moreover, even under this proviso I speak of 'allegedly empty proper names' for to my mind many of those names actually are full ones: see below.

3. I reformulate a similar example given by Kripke (1973) with the term 'Moloch'. For other similar examples of – as he labels them – thoroughly non-referring names, cf. Salmon (1998: 305–6).

4. See note 1 above.

5. Cf. Almog (1991: 608n.13), Bach (1985/6: 366–7) and Parsons (1980: 113–14).

6. For Evans' distinction between a conniving and a non-conniving use of a proper name, cf. Evans (1982: 365–6). This distinction fits Currie's distinction between fictional and metafictional use of names, that Currie himself extends to sentences. Cf. Currie (1988, 1990).

7. At least from Lewis (1978) onwards.

8. To be sure, they do not seem to appeal to a distinction between conniving and non-conniving use of a fictional sentence. Yet they stick to the distinction between fictive and real truth-conditions of such a sentence. Indeed according to them, in uttering one such sentence, by fictionally saying that something is the case, one also really says that something (else) is the case. Cf. Evans (1982: 362–4), Walton (1990: 399–400).

9. For this simple reconstruction, cf. Crimmins (1998: 2–8). But see also the more complex formulations of Evans (1982: 362–4) and Walton (1990: 399–400).

10. According to Walton, the fictional sentence really says the same as the corresponding metafictional sentence, provided one remembers that the fictional sentence (in its non-conniving use, I would add) is 'primary' (1990: 402).

11. Cf. Recanati (2000: 218). The second explicit objection he raises there against the Evans-Walton account seems to me misguided. Recanati says that what makes an internal metafictional sentence fictionally true cannot be the same as what makes the embedded fictional sentence fictionally true. In this, I utterly agree with him. In point of fact, my account of the fictional truth of an internal metafictional sentence in its conniving use is precisely based upon this idea. Yet this cannot be an objection against Evans-Walton. For they want to give the *real*, not the *fictional*, truth-conditions of an internal metafictional sentence in terms of the fictional truth-conditions of the embedded fictional sentence.

12. Cf. Recanati (2000: 176). Recanati (2000: 206) seems to ascribe this position to Predelli (1997). Yet Predelli specifies that in such cases, context-shift does not affect the interpretation, but only the evaluation, of the shifted sentence (1997: 75). As Predelli moreover adds in (2002), both when evaluated with respect to an actual circumstance and when evaluated with respect to a fictional circumstance, a fictional sentence containing a fictional name has this name referring to the very same *fictional object*. Bonomi (1999) may instead be taken as a genuine sustainer of this position. For according to him the contextual shift in question also affects the very content of the shifted sentence. This sentence thereby passes from really being about nothing, hence from really having no truth-value, to be about a fictional object, hence to have a definite truth-value.

13. Recanati admits another possibility, which on the one hand gives an internal metafictional sentence real truth-conditions and on the other does not contravene Kaplan's thesis that there are no context-shifting operators. Yet such a possibility consists in endorsing a metalinguistic account of internal metafictional sentences, according to which the embedded material has to be taken as quoted material. Cf. Recanati (2000: 206).

14. To make this account credible, I follow some Neo-Meinongians in holding that the properties predicated of *ficta* in non-connivingly used fictional sentences are predicated of, hence possessed by, such entities in the *internal* mode of predication. On such a mode, cf. Castañeda (1989), Rapaport (1978), Zalta (1983). I cannot deal with this point here. See my Voltolini (1994, 2006).

15. Theoretically speaking, one may hold both that such prefixes are intensional operators and that fictional names really refer to fictional objects in internal metafictional sentences. If this were the case, one might give the truth-conditions of such sentences as follows: one such sentence is true iff *what the embedded name really refers to*, i.e., a certain fictional object, possesses *in the world of the story* the property designated there by the embedded predicate. The artifactualist approach to *ficta* goes along these lines: cf. Salmon (1998: 300–3), Thomasson (1999: 105–7). Yet in actual fact, I do not share this approach. For I do not believe that in the worlds of the fictions the properties in question are possessed by *fictional* objects; in such worlds, those properties are possessed by individuals concretely existing in them. Cf. Voltolini (2006).

16. In point of fact, when an internal metafictional sentence is used absolutely nonconnivingly, these prefixes work as specifying locatives. For they say precisely *where*, in the actual circumstances, the proposition explicitly expressed by the corresponding fictional sentence in its non-conniving use is located: namely, in a story taken as an abstract object, i.e., as a set of propositions. One may see the relation between a fictional sentence non-connivingly used and the corresponding internal metafictional sentence as roughly the same as the relation between an incomplete sentence uttered in a certain context whose location is a certain place (say, 'it rains' uttered in Paris) and the corresponding complete sentence where that place is explicitly referred to ('it rains *in Paris*'). That is, stories *qua* abstract objects are unarticulated constituents of the propositions thoroughly expressed by fictional sentences in their non-conniving use.

17. I have, however, defended the second one in Voltolini (2000, 2005).

18. To avoid this risk, one has again to appeal to an indexical conception of proper names (cf. note 2). For then one may say that a simple sentence containing a name like 'Nessie' has different occurrences respectively containing empty and full tokens of that name, the latter referring to a certain *intentionale*. In such a case, no contextual shift is required to assign the corresponding token of that sentence

when figuring as embedded in the attitudinal sentence's truth-conditions the very same referent.

19. To be sure, Recanati admits that there are what he calls 'Sperberian' cases of deferential beliefs in which the terms embedded in the corresponding belief ascription contribute no content at all to the embedded sentence, hence to the meta-representation as well, but at most a (deferential) character. Take for instance 'Lacanians believe that the unconscious is structured like a language' or 'my three-year-old son believes that I am a "philtosopher"'. Cf. Recanati (2000: 273–4). Perhaps this fits cases of attitudinal sentences like 'A.V. believes that War is terrible'. Yet attitudinal sentences like 'LochNessians believe that Nessie comes out of the lake' hardly are cases of this kind. For here the ascribee may be seen as referring to something by means of the embedded name, hence as contributing a content by means of it.

20. To be sure, one may find cases in which the ascribed belief precisely is a belief that merely pretends to have a singular content for its embedded name refers to nothing at all. For instance, ascribing to someone a belief that *it* rains is ascribing a belief that pretends to have a singular content in this sense. We may assimilate such cases to cases of local pretense. Such an ascription indeed counts as 'S believes that *it* rains', where the pronoun occurs as uttered in the scope of a *local* pretense, the pretense in which 'it' refers to something. This would be clearer if the ascription were nowadays made in Latin. One would then have to say 'S putat Jovem pluvere', where 'Jovem' refers to something only in the scope of a pretense. Yet in such cases, the real content of the ascribed belief is a possible impersonal event. Nothing similar may be imagined in cases of attitudinal sentences like 'A.V. believes that War is terrible' or 'LochNessians fear that Nessie comes out of the lake'.

21. A suggestion might be to equate a pseudo-singular belief with a gappy belief, i.e., a belief whose content is the incomplete content of an open sentence. On gappy beliefs, cf. Adams and Stecker (1994: 391).

22. I thank François Recanati for having clarified to me his point in discussion, as well as participants in the XIII Inter-University Workshop on Philosophy and Cognitive Science Granada (Spain), 25–7 February 2003, where I presented a preliminary version of this chapter, for their stimulating questions.

References

Adams, F. and R. Stecker (1994) 'Vacuous Singular Terms'. *Mind and Language* 9: 387–401.

Almog, J. (1991) 'The Subject-Predicate Class I'. *Noûs* 25: 591–619.

Bach, K. (1985/6) 'Failed Reference and Feigned Reference: Much Ado About Nothing'. *Grazer Philosophische Studien* 25(6): 359–74.

Bonomi, A. (1999) 'Fictional Contexts'. *Selected Papers from the Second International and Interdisciplinary Conference on Modeling and Using Context, held in Trento, Italy, 1999.* Stanford: CSLI Publications.

Castañeda, H.-N. (1989) 'Fiction and Reality: Ontological Questions about Literary Experience'. *Thinking, Language, and Experience.* Minneapolis: University of Minnesota Press, pp. 176–205.

Crimmins, M. (1998) 'Hesperus and Phosphorus: Sense, Pretense, and Reference'. *The Philosophical Review* 107: 1–47.

Currie, G. (1988) 'Fictional Names'. *Australasian Journal of Philosophy* 66: 471–88.

Currie, G. (1990) *The Nature of Fiction*. Cambridge: Cambridge University Press.

Evans, G. (1982) *The Varieties of Reference*. Oxford: Clarendon Press.

Kaplan, D. (1989) 'Demonstratives'. In J. Almog *et al.* (eds), *Themes from Kaplan*. Oxford: Oxford University Press, pp. 481–563.

Kripke, S. (1973) *The John Locke Lectures 1973*. Unpublished typescript.

Lewis, D. (1978) 'Truth in Fiction'. *American Philosophical Quarterly* 15: 37–46.

McDowell, J. (1998) 'Having the World in View: Sellars, Kant, and Intentionality'. *The Journal of Philosophy* 95: 431–91.

Parsons, T. (1980) *Nonexistent Objects*. New Haven and London: Yale University Press.

Predelli, S. (1997) 'Talk about Fiction'. *Erkenntnis* 46: 69–77.

Predelli, S. (2002) ' "Holmes" and Holmes. A Millian Analysis of Names from Fiction'. *Dialectica* 56: 261–79.

Rapaport, W.J. (1978) 'Meinongian Theories and a Russellian Paradox'. *Noûs* 12: 153–80.

Recanati, F. (1993) *Direct Reference*. Oxford: Blackwell.

Recanati, F. (2000) *Oratio Obliqua, Oratio Recta*. Cambridge, MA: The MIT Press.

Salmon, N. (1998) 'Nonexistence'. *Noûs* 32: 277–319.

Thomasson, A.L. (1999) *Fiction and Metaphysics*. Cambridge: Cambridge University Press.

Voltolini, A. (1994) 'Ficta versus Possibilia'. *Grazer Philosophische Studien* 48: 75–104.

Voltolini, A. (1995) 'Indexinames'. In J. Hill and P. Kot'àtko (eds), *Karlovy Vary Studies in Reference and Meaning*. Prague: Φιλοσοφια-Filosofia Publications, pp. 258–85.

Voltolini, A. (2000) 'Is It Merely Loose Talk? A Bizarre Solution to the Opacity Puzzle'. *Dialectica* 54: 51–72.

Voltolini, A. (2005) 'How to Get Intentionality from Language'. In G. Forrai and G. Kampis (eds), *Intentionality: Past and Future*. Amsterdam: Rodopi, pp. 127–41.

Voltolini, A. (2006) *How Ficta Follow Fiction: A Syncretistic Account of Fictional Entities*. Berlin: Springer.

Walton, K.L. (1990) *Mimesis as Make-Believe*. Cambridge, MA: Harvard University Press.

Zalta, E.N. (1983) *Abstract Objects*. Dordrecht: Reidel.

Recanati's Reply to Voltolini

When a storyteller tells a story he pretends to report facts (Lewis 1978). But those facts are not really facts; they are fiction. In particular, when the characters that are mentioned as part of the fiction do not really exist, the storyteller does not really refer to them – he merely pretends to do so.

Fictional names are empty names, because they 'refer' only fictively. It follows that the fictional sentences issued by the storyteller, insofar as they involve such names, do not really express singular propositions, but merely pretend to do so.

What about metafictional sentences, such as 'In *Les Misérables*, Jean Valjean worries about Cosette'? The names 'Jean Valjean' and 'Cosette' are both fictional names – they refer only fictively. Neither Jean Valjean nor Cosette exist. Does it not follow that the metafictional sentences themselves lack content and fail to express the singular propositions they pretend to express? I think that consequence follows, unless one accepts to drop at least one of the following principles:

- Names (including fictional names) are directly referential expressions.
- A sentence such as 'Jean Valjean worries about Cosette' (and each of its constituents) keeps the same meaning in all of its occurrences; in partic-ular, the sentence has the same meaning whether it occurs in isolation or as a constituent in a more complex sentence.
- There is no context-shifting operator in English.

The problem is that there is a strong intuitive difference between a fictional sentence as it occurs in, say, *Les Misérables* ('Jean Valjean worries about Cosette') and the corresponding metafictional sentence ('In *Les Misérables*, Jean Valjean worries about Cosette'). The former arguably lacks content and only pretends to express a singular proposition, hence it is not truth-evaluable; but the latter seems to say something true or false about the fiction. This suggests that there *is* something wrong with at least one of the three principles listed above.

The principles are not sacrosanct, but we may be reluctant to give up any of them. Assuming that is so, what can we do? In 'Talk about fiction' and *Oratio Obliqua, Oratio Recta*, I sketched a possible solution, which Alberto Voltolini criticizes. According to that solution, metafictional sentences also rest on pretense. They are not literally truth-evaluable. Like fictional sentences, they fail to express a definite content whenever the names they contain are empty. The intuitive difference with fictional sentences is due to the fact that, in the metafictional case, the pretense at stake is of the 'shallow' type (Crimmins 1998): it is unavailable to consciousness because it is built into our ordinary ways of speaking and thinking. This is similar to certains sorts of metaphor that are not perceptible because they permeate our ordinary talk. Thus we say that the mountain range 'goes from Mexico to Los Angeles', without even realizing that we use a motion verb to describe a static relation (Talmy 1996).

The pretense at work in metafictional sentences I call the Meinongian pretense. It consists in treating existence as a property which some things (the 'real' objects) have and others don't. We do as if there were two sorts of objects in the world: the real objects, which exist, and another sort of object – fictional objects, intentional objects, etc. – that are ghostlike in that they lack the property of real existence but have other properties nonetheless. Thus a fictional character such as Jean Valjean does not really exist, but that does not prevent us from referring and ascribing properties to him, as in metafictional talk. Were it not for the Meinongian pretense, we could not do that. Jean Valjean's nonexistence would block any reference to him.

By relying on the Meinongian pretense and saying something that is not literally truth-evaluable (because the names do not really refer), we manage to communicate something that *is* true or false. Thus by fictively referring to Jean Valjean and Cosette and saying that, in the story, the former worries about the latter, we ascribe to the story properties which it really has: the property of featuring two individuals x and y with a certain number of properties (including the property of being called respectively 'Jean Valjean' and 'Cosette'), such that x worries about y. Similarly, when I say that my four-year-old child believes that Santa Claus will come tonight, I rely on the Meinongian pretense to ascribe to a nonexistent individual (Santa Claus) the property that my child believes he will come tonight; and by thus fictively ascribing to my child a singular belief, I manage to convey something true about the state of mind he is in. As I put it in *Oratio Obliqua, Oratio Recta*, 'the fictive ascription of a singular belief . . . amounts to the factive ascription of a pseudo-singular belief' (Recanati 2000: 226). (The fictive/factive terminology, like the 'mountain range' example of fictive motion, comes from Talmy 1996.)

Voltolini thinks this account goes too far, or not far enough, depending upon the cases. In some cases, he argues, there is indeed pretense, but there is nothing more. He gives the following example:

Suppose I mishear a sentence saying that war is terrible, by taking 'war' as a proper name of someone. Asked to write what I heard, I scribble: 'War is terrible' (note the majuscule), using 'War' as proper name and misconceiving it as referring to someone I do not know... If someone said of me: 'A.V. believes that War is terrible' this sentence would not have real truth-conditions, hence a real truth-value, but merely fictive truth-conditions, hence a fictive truth-value.

Voltolini denies that, in such a case, the sentence 'A.V. believes that War is terrible' acquires factive truth-conditions on top of its fictive truth-conditions. In the described circumstances, the ascribee does not believe anything, Voltolini holds, even if he takes himself to believe something. The ascribee takes himself to believe a singular proposition involving the individual named 'War', but there is no such individual, hence there is no singular proposition either. It follows that no (first-level) belief can be seriously (i.e. nonfictively) ascribed to the subject in such circumstances.

I think this criticism misses its target. When I say that, in such circumstances, the fictive ascription of a singular belief amounts to the factive ascription of a pseudo-singular belief, I explicitly acknowledge the fact that no genuine singular belief can be ascribed to the subject. By 'pseudo-singular belief' I mean a state of mind that is precisely not a genuine belief, because it lacks a definite content. By overtly pretending that there is an individual, named 'War', of whom A.V. believes that he is terrible, the speaker manages to communicate that A.V. takes *war* as a proper name of someone and (spuriously) 'believes' of that person that 'he' is terrible. All this, which is true and could be spelt out in a more technical vocabulary (without scare quotes), is conveyed through the pretense. This is what I mean when I say that the fictive ascription of a singular belief amounts to the factive ascription of a pseudo-singular belief.

Voltolini grants that, in some cases, we definitely want to ascribe beliefs to the subject though the names at stake do not refer to flesh-and-blood individuals. Thus we really want to ascribe to my son a belief to the effect that Santa Claus will come tonight, even though Santa Claus does not exist. In such cases a 'factive' ascription is made, which can be evaluated as true or false. Whenever that is so, Voltolini points out, this shows that 'the name is not empty after all'. It does not refer to a flesh-and-blood individual, but it refers to something nonetheless: a fictional individual or 'character' in the Jean Valjean example, or an 'intentional object' in the Santa Claus example. No 'Meinongian pretense' needs to be appealed to to account for such cases: we do not have to 'pretend' that fictional and intentional objects are part of our ontology, because they *are* part of our ontology. That is Voltolini's line.

I confess that I have some sympathy for this view, at least if the 'ontology' we're talking about is the actual ontology that underlies our ordinary way of speaking and thinking. As Godehart Link wrote in a very influential paper, 'our guide in ontological matters has to be language itself' (Link 1998: 13). That is why Link decided to posit 'plural objects' in the ontology alongside ordinary objects. Thus the coins on this table are (formal semanticists tell us) an object distinct from the individual coins that are its parts even though they are 'materially' identical. If we are prepared to say that, we should also be prepared to say that Superman and Clark Kent are two distinct objects even though, in some sense, they are the same individual. According to Crimmins (1998), we 'do as if' Superman and Clark Kent were two distinct objects: a pretense is involved. But if the pretense is so 'shallow' and natural that we are not even conscious of it, why not simply decide to enrich the formal ontology with the relevant sort of objects? Why not accept guises and personalities and fictional objects alongside ordinary individuals?

In the case of fictional objects, we can't do without pretense, for fictional objects exist only through the pretense that is constitutive of storytelling. In storytelling, we pretend to be referring to flesh-and-blood individuals. Yet, it can be maintained, this very activity creates fictional characters to which we can factively refer. In this regard there is a useful convention: whenever a fictional character has come into existence through the fictive use of a name NN in storytelling, it is possible to use the same name NN factively to refer to that fictional character. Fictional names therefore turn out to have a dual use: in the pretense-internal use they fictively refer to flesh-and-blood individuals that do not really exist; but in the pretense-external use they factively refer to fictional individuals which do exist (as entities distinct from flesh-and-blood individuals). This means that we give up the second of the three principles mentioned above: the name 'Jean Valjean' does not behave in the same way in the fiction (where it is empty and only pretends to refer) and outside the fiction (where it is not empty, but refers to a character). This I take to be Voltolini's position, and, again, I have sympathy for it. After all, many words have distinct, though related, uses. For example, the word 'wish' has a psychological sense (meaning *desire*). That sense is at work in the optative use of the verb in sentences such as 'I wish that you will soon recover'. Now that optative use gave rise, through 'delocutive derivation', to a new sense for 'wish': the sense *express wishes*, as in 'He wished me good luck'.[1] Something similar to delocutive derivation may account for the transition from the fictive to the factive use of fictional names.

Between the two theories – the pretense-based theory, and the true Meinongian theory – the difference is not as big as one might have thought. I am not even sure that they are not notational variants, for two reasons. First, the fictional objects that the Meinongian posits as part of our ontology supervene upon our simulative practices targeted toward ordinary objects. This gives them a derived status that deprives them of first-class citizenship in our ontology. Second, even the pretense-based theory as stated in *Oratio Obliqua, Oratio Recta* acknowledges something like a dual use for fictional names; for the metafictional use of fictional names rests on a different sort of pretense (the Meinongian pretense) than that which underlies their fictional use.

Note

1. See my *Meaning and Force*, chapter 4, and the references therein.

References

Crimmins, M. (1998) 'Hesperus and Phosphorus: Sense, Pretense, and Reference'. *Philosophical Review* 107: 1–47.
Lewis, D. (1978) 'Truth in Fiction'. *American Philosophical Quarterly* 15: 37–46.
Link, G. (1998) *Algebraic Semantics in Language and Philosophy*. Stanford: CSLI Publications.
Recanati, F. (1987) *Meaning and Force*. Cambridge: Cambridge University Press.
Recanati, F. (1998) 'Talk about Fiction'. *Lingua e Stile* 33: 547–58.
Recanati, F. (2000) *Oratio Obliqua, Oratio Recta: An Essay on Metarepresentation*. Cambridge, MA: MIT Press/Bradford Books.
Talmy, L. (1996) 'Fictive Motion in Language and "Ception"'. In R. Bloom *et al.* (eds), *Language and Space*. Cambridge, MA: MIT Press, pp. 211–76.

10
Situated Representations and *Ad Hoc* Concepts[1]

Jérôme Dokic

Introduction

Situation theorists such as Jon Barwise, John Etchemendy, and (at one time) John Perry have advanced the hypothesis that linguistic and mental representations are 'situated' in the sense that they are true or false only relative to partial situations. François Recanati has done an important task in reviving and in many respects deepening situation theory. In this chapter, I would like to explore some aspects of Recanati's own account. I shall focus on situated mental representations, and stress the connection between them and *ad hoc* or temporary concepts. First, I introduce the notion of unarticulated constituent, due to John Perry. I suggest that the question of whether there really are such constituents should be divided into two issues, one concerning language and the other concerning thought (Section 10.1). Then I formulate a dilemma that any friend of cognitive unarticulated constituents must face: alleged unarticulated constituents seem to be either articulated or non-constituents after all (Section 10.2). The dilemma is strengthened by the fact that unarticulated constituents cannot be inferentially relevant (Section 10.3). In order to show, hopefully, that the dilemma can be avoided, I give two illustrations of what I take to be genuine unarticulated constituents. In the first, thoughts like *It's raining* and *It's over* are implicitly related to spatiotemporal situations via practical capacities for keeping track of particular places or times (Section 10.4). In the second, more tentative illustration, the relevant situations are not given, but stipulated, as with *In Constance, it's raining* (Section 10.5). In the last section, I argue that the notion of situation which emerges from the previous discussion is rather different from the one used by Recanati himself.

10.1 Unarticulated constituents: language and thought

Consider the following sentences (Perry 2001: 44):

    (1) It is raining
    (2) They are serving drinks at the local bar

Many utterances of (1) are true if and only if it is raining at a particular place, typically where the speaker is. Similarly, many utterances of (2) are true if and only if the people referred to by 'they' are serving drinks at a particular bar, typically located in the speaker's neighbourhood. Nevertheless, there is no item in the sentence (1) that designates the place where it is raining, just as there is no item in (2) that designates the location relative to which the bar is described as local.

In Perry's terminology, the relevant places are *unarticulated constituents* of the propositions expressed by utterances of (1) and (2). For instance, the place where it is raining 'is a constituent, because, since rain occurs at a time in a place, there is no truth-evaluable proposition unless a place is supplied. It is unarticulated, because there is no morpheme that designates the place' (2001: 45). The idea is that the interpreter has to look to the context *after* she has identified all the words and their meanings in the sentence; the context is used in a 'content-supplemental' way. In this respect, (1) and (2) differ from the explicitly indexical sentences 'It is raining here' and 'They are serving drinks at the bar in this neighbourhood', which articulate the relevant places.

It is worth distinguishing here two issues that are *prima facie* independent, although Perry himself often has both in mind. The first issue is about language, whereas the second is about thought.[2] At the level of language, the relevant question is whether what is literally said by an utterance of 'It's raining' (the 'official' proposition expressed by the sentence in context) can involve an implicit reference to a particular place even though there is no item, context-sensitive or not, corresponding to it in the syntactic or sub-syntactic structure of the sentence uttered. In other words, can one literally say that it is raining at a particular place by using only a one-place predicate 'rain' true of times? If the answer is 'yes', the place is a *semantic* unarticulated constituent of the linguistic representation 'It is raining'. Some authors, like Stanley (2000, 2002), doubt that there are unarticulated constituents in this sense, and defend the view that all alleged unarticulated constituents turn out to be articulated at a deeper level of syntactic structure or logical form.

The issue at the level of thought, as I see it, is whether what is *thought* in an utterance of 'It is raining' can involve an implicit reference to a particular place even though no constituent of the thought designates it. Let us say that the constituents of thoughts are *concepts* or *modes of presentation* of various objects and properties.[3] When a subject thinks *It's raining*,[4] can her thought in some sense concern a particular place while she does not grasp any mode of presentation of that place? Can she just deploy in thought the one-place concept *rain*, saturated by a mode of presentation of the present time?[5] If the answer to these questions is 'yes', the place is a *cognitive* unarticulated constituent of the thought *It's raining*.

Interestingly, the two issues might be independent. Even if Stanley is right and there is no English predicate 'rain' true of times only, *some* thoughts naturally expressed by 'It's raining' might involve the one-place concept *rain*. Conversely, if Stanley is wrong, as Recanati has recently argued (2002a), and the sentence 'It's raining' can involve a one-place predicate true of times, it is still possible that the thought naturally expressed by this sentence involves a mode of presentation of a particular place.

Consider Stanley's main argument to the effect that all constituents are articulated in some sense. This is the *Argument from Binding*. Stanley claims that if there are unarticulated constituents, they cannot vary with the values introduced by operators in the sentence uttered. Now, it is possible to prefix 'It's raining' with a spatial operator, like in 'Everywhere I go, it's raining'. In the last sentence, 'rain' is supposedly a two-place predicate, for the operator must bind a variable for a place. However (the argument goes on), in the original sentence as well, 'rain' is a two-place predicate, for there seems to be only one predicate 'rain' in English. Thus, an utterance of 'It's raining' does not introduce any unarticulated spatial constituent; the place *is* articulated, at least in the form of a variable.[6]

I think that Stanley's argument is best viewed against the background assumption that language is *modular*, at least to some extent. The modularity of language implies that predicates are lexically given independently of the cognitive context. Now I want to contrast linguistic modularity with cognitive flexibility. One of the most interesting claims of recent cognitive science is that concepts are very often constructed 'on the fly', depending on the current cognitive task. In addition to the 'stable' concepts that can be encoded by words, there are *ad hoc* or *occasional concepts*, namely temporary constructions in working memory. These cognitive constructions have been postulated in many areas of cognition (Sperber and Wilson 1998; Barsalou 1999; Carston 2002; Prinz 2002). Here is a recent statement of the context-sensitivity of concepts:

> [W]e all have countless DOG concepts... The way one represents a dog depends on whether one is thinking about the artic tundra or Central Park. The way one represents an elephant depends on whether one is at a circus, in a zoo, or on a safari. (Prinz 2002: 152–3)

If we take the idea of *ad hoc* concepts seriously (as I think we should), there are many concepts of rain varying with the cognitive context. Thus, even if the thought *Everywhere I go, it's raining* involves a concept of rain which demands a spatial mode of presentation, the simpler thought *It's raining* might well involve, in some contexts, a spatially neutral conception of rain.

Without exaggerating the gap between language and thought, we should be open to the possibility that a truth-conditionally relevant parameter is unarticulated at the semantic level while being articulated at the cognitive level, and vice versa. Table 10.1 summarizes the four possible cases.

In case (a), the relevant constituent is articulated both at the level of the sentence and at the level of thought. This case covers utterances of 'It

Table 10.1   The four possible cases of a truth-conditionally relevant parameter

	(a)	(b)	(c)	(d)
Level of the sentence (linguistic meaning)	+	−	+	−
Level of thought (conceptual content)	+	+	−	−

is raining here' and 'It is raining in Paris' when the place which is explicitly referred to is also singled out in thought. The existence of case (b) is more controversial. If we accept Recanati (2002)'s analysis of 'It's raining', according to which it need not introduce anything more sophisticated than a one-place predicate 'rain', we can imagine a scenario in which the subject uses this sentence but articulates the place in her thought. This may happen if the place has been explicitly introduced earlier in the conversation, so that it is now obvious to the speaker and the hearer which place is in question. As an example of case (c), take a subject who uses a two-place predicate 'rain' true of times and places, but does not bother articulating the place in thought, perhaps because the current cognitive task does not require it. Finally, in case (d), a truth-conditionally relevant constituent is unarticulated both at the level of sentence and at the level of thought.

10.2   A dilemma

Still, the claim that there are cognitive unarticulated constituents is controversial. There is a fundamental dilemma that any friend of such constituents has to face. Either the alleged unarticulated constituent is *cognitively relevant*, or it is not. In the former case, it can be a constituent of what is represented, but it seems to be *articulated* in the subject's cognitive life after all. So it looks as if the alleged unarticulated parameter must be cognitively irrelevant. However, in this case, it can no longer be considered a *constituent* of what is represented, for there is in principle a more accurate interpretation available.

Perry (2001: 46–7) draws a distinction among cases where he says there is an unarticulated constituent, between those where 'there is nothing insightful or innovative about articulating it', and those where a conceptual innovation is called for. The former cases include 'It is raining' and 'They are serving drinks at the local bar', which can easily be transformed into, say, 'It is raining in Paris' and 'They are serving drinks at the bar in this neighbourhood'. The first horn of the dilemma is doing its work here: since we all know that rain is a spatially located phenomenon and that something counts as local only relative to some reference location, the sense in which the thoughts expressed by these utterances are not fully articulated is at best unexplained.

In the other cases, the relevant constituent cannot easily be articulated save by using some general purpose phrase like 'relative to' or 'according to'. However (and this is the second horn of the dilemma), I would say that at least some of these cases really do not involve unarticulated *constituents*. Consider the following examples, all discussed by Perry:

(1) *These two flashes of light were simultaneous*, as thought by someone who has no idea of the theory of relativity.
(2) *It's two o'clock*, as thought by a young child who does not yet have the concept of a time-zone.
(3) *It's raining*, as thought by a Z-lander. (Perry 1993)

According to the theory of relativity, simultaneity has three argument roles: two events are simultaneous relative to an inertial frame. However, the folk notion of simultaneity does not involve any concept or mode of presentation of a frame. Does it follow that the frame is a cognitive unarticulated constituent? The answer depends on whether it is plausible to say that what is thought is made true, when it is true, by facts involving the triadic relation of simultaneity which the theory of relativity talks about. This is not very plausible for ordinary thinkers who have never heard of this theory. From the perspective of the theory of relativity, these thinkers have a naïve and confused view of physical reality. So, strictly speaking, a thought like (1) does not record an instance of physical simultaneity, but (perhaps) an experienced temporal coincidence. Of course, an educated semanticist can give (1) truth-conditions that are *relative* to an inertial frame. This interpretation is literally incorrect, but harmless if the validity of the thinkers' inferences and the success of their actions do not hinge on the identity of the underlying frame. In fact, they do not move, either in reality or in imagination, between frames.

Similarly, what is thought by the child does not have a particular time-zone as a cognitive *constituent*. When she eventually masters the concept of a time-zone, she can then *reinterpret* her earlier thoughts about the time as being true or false relative to a particular time-zone. Still, her temporal thinking before the conceptual change showed no sensitivity to time-zones, and belonged to a more primitive way of responding to the world.

Consider finally the third case. Perry (1993) imagines a community of primitive thinkers, called 'Z-landers', who do not travel and do not have the conception of a particular region as opposed to another. In particular, they always conceive of rain as a monadic property of times. For them, it just rains or not (at a given time). Z-landers' judgements about meteorological phenomena have a kind of primitiveness analogous to that of our ordinary judgements about simultaneity. We just don't have the same official ontology of rain. Their concept *rain* is not a concept *of* particular spatial regions.

So their thoughts *It's raining* do not embody a conception of objective, re-identifiable places at all, but belong to a feature-placing mode of thinking in Strawson's (1959) sense.

Thus, *pace* Perry and Recanati, the examples (1)–(3) do not introduce unarticulated constituents because in each case there is a better interpretation which makes the relevant utterances and thoughts completely articulated after all, although[8] expressive of a more primitive ontology.

10.3   Inferential roles

The dilemma just presented can be strengthened by considering the connection between thought and inference. A thought explicitly represents something if and only if it contains a concept or mode of presentation of that thing. A thought is composed of as many concepts as it has *inferentially relevant aspects* (Crane 1992). When something is explicitly represented, there will be inferences hinging on the identity of what is represented. For instance, the thought *Claire is upset* has at least two constituents (*Claire* and *is upset*) because it can participate in formal inferences such as the following, where these constituents figure separately in other thoughts:[7]

(1) *Claire is upset. Claire is my sister. So my sister is upset.*

One can accept that there is an internal relation between thought and inference even if one does not believe that inferential role can be characterized independently of conceptual content. Perhaps inferential role flows from a more basic account of conceptual content. The point is rather that whatever notion is fundamental (perhaps both are), a thought is individuated by its role in inferences hinging on its conceptual constituents.

Conversely, if there are unarticulated constituents, they cannot be inferentially relevant. For instance, if the thought *It's raining* is only implicitly related to a particular place, it cannot participate in inferences hinging on the identity of that place. This may cast doubt on the existence of unarticulated constituents. How can there be room for a thought to have constituents which cannot play any role as middle terms in inferences?

One can specify in advance the general form that a convincing answer to this question should have. The propositional content of a particular mental representation is determined, at least partly, by the way it is used or 'consumed' by the cognitive system (Millikan 1993). One way of using the representation is in inferences. One can infer the representation from other representations, and one can infer other representations from it. However, the representation's inferential role, which determines the inferences in which it *can* participate, does not exhaust the absolute proposition expressed (its 'official' content) if there are other ways of using it that are semantically relevant too.[8] In what follows, I shall give two illustrations of how this can arise. In the first illustration, representations are anchored to situations via practical capacities for keeping track of times and places. In the second illustration, the situation is explicitly represented, but situated representations are still used in chains of thoughts. In both cases, some aspects of the representations' inferential roles are silenced, generating *ad hoc* concepts.

10.4   Placing features

Perry insightfully points out that 'there is a little of the Z-lander in the most well-travelled of us' (1993: 216). In other words, there are circumstances in which I think and act *as if* I were a Z-lander: I look out the window, judge *It's raining*, want to stay dry, believe that if I deploy my umbrella over my head, I will stay dry, and eventually deploy my umbrella. In this mode of practical reasoning, the question of which particular place is in question is *never* raised. The inferences involving the thought *It's raining* do not hinge on the identity of a particular place. This kind of cognitive task does not involve anything more sophisticated than a one-place concept of rain, true of times.

Similar considerations apply to the temporal counterparts of thoughts like *It's raining*. As Prior (1976) emphasized, there are contexts in which the thought *It's over*, formed in referring to some painful event I have just gone through, immediately modifies my action tendencies and makes me feel relief. In these contexts, *It's over* is a temporary construction which does not involve a temporal mode of presentation.

Thoughts like *It's raining* and *It's over* belong to a mode of perceiving, thinking and acting on the world which is relatively *neutral* from a spatiotemporal point of view. In that mode, I can acquire information that some property is instantiated, but I cannot acquire the information that it is instantiated in my perceptual field *considered as a particular place among others*. In order to make sense of the latter information, I have to impose on my perception a cognitive map that contrasts the local place with other places, not currently perceived. Similarly, I can acquire perceptual information that some event is completed, but I cannot acquire the information that it happened *at a particular time*. In order to make sense of the latter information, I normally invoke a linear conception of time that contrasts the present time with other times. The uses of a cognitive map and a linear conception of time involve more sophisticated thoughts like *It's raining here* and *It's over now*, which are explicitly about particular places or times.[9]

The fact that I use representations such as *It's raining* and *It's over* does not mean that I adhere to Z-landers' ontology of rain, or that I indulge in a doubtful temporal ontology in which being over is an absolute property of events. My use of such representations is restricted to particular situations, in which the source of perception is roughly the same as the target of action. For instance, I would not go into the described inferential transitions if

I believed that the place of perception has become significantly different from the place of action. In contrast, Z-landers would make the same judgements if they were nomads, unknowingly changing places. Similarly, even though my thought *It's over* is not explicitly about the present time, the fact is that I use it only for an instant. In particular, it is never stored in that form in long-term memory for later use.

In other words, two dimensions can be distinguished in our use of the relevant representations. On the one hand, they have inferential roles characteristic of a feature-placing (spatial or temporal) mode of thinking. On the other hand, these roles are constrained by the subject to apply in specific spatiotemporal contexts. My suggestion is that the thoughts' 'official' contents are jointly determined by both dimensions, so that *It's raining* is true if and only if it is raining at a particular place, and *It's over* is true if and only if it is over at a particular time.

It is plausible that these representations are derived from more stable ones by cancelling some cognitive features of the latter. For instance, the concept $RAIN_1$, true of times only, might be derived from the stable concept $RAIN_2$, true of times and places, by silencing our ability to distinguish one rain event from another (at a given time), leaving only our ability to distinguish rain from non-rain. What makes the relevant representations *ad hoc*, though, is that they are *temporary* constructions, opportunistically used only as long as a particular cognitive task is carried out.

10.5   Situating inferences

On the foregoing account of Perry-like scenarios, the relevant thoughts are anchored to spatio-temporal situations via practical capacities for keeping track of the subject's own movements in space or the passage of time. However, there are more sophisticated cases in which the situation is not given but *stipulated*. Consider the complex thought *At Lake Constance, it's raining*. On the traditional analysis, the concept *rain* calls for a spatial mode of presentation, which here determines Lake Constance. Following Karl Bühler, Recanati argues on the contrary that when one entertains a representation like 'At Lake Constance, it's raining', 'one simulatively entertains a representation decoupled from the egocentric situation' (2002b: 162) in such a way that Lake Constance is *'presentified* through an act of the imagination' (2000: §6.5). So *within the context of simulation*, only a spatially neutral concept of rain is involved – the same as in the self-standing thought *It's raining*.

The difference between the two analyses is not obvious when a single representation is concerned. However, the merit of the second analysis emerges when we turn to more complex cases. Consider the following chain of thoughts:[10]

> (1) *I've just had news from my friend in Constance. It's raining heavily, so the streets are slippery. Everybody has to drive very carefully.*

The first thought in the chain explicitly introduces the anchor to which the rest of the reasoning is attached. The thoughts *It's raining heavily, The streets are slippery* and *Everybody has to drive very carefully* are then all true relative to Constance. Intuitively, it would be redundant, from a cognitive point of view, to articulate the reference to Constance at each step of the inference process, as in (2):

(2) *It's raining heavily in Constance, so the streets of Constance are slippery. Everybody in Constance has to drive very carefully.*

The question is how to spell out this intuitive argument in favour of the existence of situated reasoning such as (1).

Consider first the thought *It's raining heavily* as it occurs in (1). Just as in the simpler Perry-like scenarios, two cognitive dimensions can be distinguished in its grasping. First, it has the inferential role of a feature-placing thought. Second, I am nevertheless not ready to draw all the inferences that would be licensed by a genuine feature-placing thought. I restrict my reasoning to selected ways of establishing the thought, and ways of drawing consequences from it. For instance, as my simulation of Constance is decoupled from actual perception and action, my current experience of rain, say in Paris, does not establish the truth of *It's raining*, just as the latter does not lead to my opening an umbrella where I am. In fact, since the situation is stipulated to be Constance, my reasoning does not have to be sensitive to actual changes in my spatial relation to Constance, whatever it is.

Within the context of my simulation of Constance, the move from *It's raining heavily* to *The streets are slippery* makes perfectly good sense given the inferential role of the premise. As contrasts between Constance and other cities cannot be drawn within such a simulation, there is no question as to whether the place where it is raining is the same as the place where the relevant streets are. In general, it may be cognitively more manageable to cope with a partial situation rather than with the whole world when the difference between them is irrelevant to the success of one's theoretical and practical projects. For instance, in a Perry-like scenario, the thought *It's raining* can be directly geared to local rain-protecting action because the success of the latter does not depend on the weather elsewhere in the world.

There is some analogy to be made here with logical reasoning with arbitrary objects (cf. Fine 1985). When I reason with an arbitrary object, I have to make sure that the latter is representative of the domain of quantification. In other words, I have to control my reasoning so that it does not trade on special assumptions about the object. I can introduce the universal quantifier only if the difference between the arbitrary object and the other objects in the domain is irrelevant to the validity of my argument.

Of course, in the absence of a substantial theory of cognitive effort, the foregoing remarks remain speculative. There is an *a priori* requirement on the possibility of situated reasoning such as (1), which is that the cognitive *cost* of monitoring the inferences in (1) should be *below* that of the corresponding detached reasoning in (2), which articulates the reference to Constance at each step of the inferential process. Indeed, if each step of the inferential process in (1) were directly monitored by a full representation of the relevant situation, namely Constance, the difference between (1) and (2) would collapse. The fact that this requirement is met may be difficult to establish in particular cases, for unlike logical reasoning with arbitrary objects, there are often no strict rules saying which inferences may be drawn and which should be inhibited.

In the case of (1), the move from *It's raining heavily* to *The streets are slippery*, as well as the move from the latter to *Everybody has to drive very carefully*, are licensed only if the following dispositional condition is met: if I were to produce the detached versions of these thoughts, they would be organised as a piece of reasoning about Constance, as in (2). In other words, one can make such moves because one is disposed to detach the thoughts in the same way, i.e., to consider them as being implicitly related to the *same* constituent. Perhaps setting up such a dispositional connection requires less cognitive effort than explicity articulating Constance at each step in the chain of thoughts.

As a different illustration, consider the last thought in (1), *Everybody has to drive very carefully*. Arguably, two dimensions can be distinguished in the grasping of the quantified concept *everybody*. On the one hand, this concept is associated with the usual introduction and elimination rules. It has the inferential role of an absolute (unrestricted) universal quantifier. On the other hand, the application of these rules is opportunistically monitored, which makes *everybody* an *ad hoc* concept. The move from *Everybody is F* to *a is F* is made only if *a* belongs to the paradigm defining the situation, namely the set of objects that can be identified within it, and the move from *a is F* to *Everybody is F* is made only if *a* is representative of the objects in this paradigm. However, it is not clear that such inferential monitoring is more economical, from a cognitive point of view, than reasoning with a detached version of the thought, such as the last thought in (2), in which the domain of quantification is explicitly restricted.

Perhaps there is another way of looking at things. Here is a tentative suggestion. Suppose that *b* refers to somebody I take to be outside Constance at the relevant time. Then the inference from *Everybody is F* to *b is F* cannot be drawn within my simulation of Constance. However, the reason why it cannot be drawn is not that I have explicitly excluded *b* from the paradigm defining the situation. Rather, the inference cannot be drawn because the thought *b is F* cannot even be *grasped within the simulation*. The cognitive resources deployed within the simulation can at best identify a person *as opposed to others in the paradigmatic set*. In other words, modes of presentation of relevant individuals in the simulation are *ad hoc*. If one adds to the simulation the concept of a new person, additional cognitive resources are necessary because new contrasts become possible. This might be why it can be more economical to fix a situation once for a whole simulation project rather than making it explicit at each step of the inference process.

10.6 Austinian semantics and non-persistent facts

In Recanati's picture, the claim that there are unarticulated constituents has a place in a more general framework, inspired by situation semantics, more precisely the version of situation theory called 'Austinian semantics'.[11] In this framework, any representation concerns, without explicitly representing, a partial situation. Whenever there is a representation, two semantic dimensions should be distinguished:

(1) $< s, \sigma >$

In (1), σ is a (linguistic or mental) representation, and s is the situation relative to which σ is presented as true or false. Just as *It's raining*, in a context in which it is true or false relative to Paris, does not represent Paris (at least explicitly), σ does not represent the situation s it concerns.

In Austinian semantics, a situation is or generates a set of facts, including the fact stated by σ when it is true. A true representation σ is said to be 'supported' by the situation it concerns. The support relation, between a situation and the corresponding representation, is symbolised by the semantic turnstile:

(2) $s \models \sigma$

Recanati himself gives a more precise, set-theoretic characterization of the support relation (2000: 69):

Support relation
A situation s supports an atomic fact σ with respect to a world w if and only σ belongs to $W(s)$.[12]

One worry with this characterization is that it seems to carry a commitment to perspectival or non-persistent facts. Consider again the mental representation *It's raining*. It concerns a partial situation which includes facts about Paris, something that we can represent as follows:

(3) $s \geq W(\text{Paris}) \models \textit{It's raining}$

In (3), W is a function that takes as input an object and gives as output a set of facts about that object. Thus, W(Paris) refers to a set of facts about Paris, which is included in, or is identical with, the set of facts constituting s. Now, suppose the representation is true: it is actually raining in Paris. What is, then, the fact stated by *It's raining*? On Recanati's characterization, it appears to be *the fact that it is raining*. This is a perspectival fact, in the sense that it holds only within the partial, Parisian situation. This can give rise to non-persistence phenomena. For instance, that it is raining is a fact in the Parisian situation, but it may not be a fact in a larger situation, such as France. The fact that it is raining in Paris is compatible with the fact that it is *not* raining in France in general. (I assume that it is raining in a given situation s only if there is a fair distribution of rain within s.)

Much of what I have said in this chapter seems to me to be independent of the existence of non-persistent facts. Thus, either there is an alternative characterization of the support relation which does not carry a commitment to such facts, or the relation between a situation and its representation is not one of truth-making. If one follows the first option, one can still give a set-theoretical characterization of the support relation. Roughly, a situation s supports σ if and only if the fact stated by σ (in the relevant context) is included in s. However, the latter fact is persistent; it is the fact that in s, σ. For instance, the fact stated by *It's raining*, in the relevant context, is the persistent fact that it is raining in Paris.

However, the second option seems to me to be preferable, which makes my notion of situation different from Recanati's. On my definition, a situation includes all the facts that are responsible for the representation's expressing an absolute proposition. For instance, the situation of the representation *It's raining*, as used in a particular context to express the proposition that it is raining in Paris, includes various facts about the relation between the representation and Paris. What I have suggested in this chapter is that the facts that make the representation *concern* Paris are not the same as the facts which make the representation explicitly *about* rain. The latter have to do with inferential role, whereas the former concern the subject's restricted use of the representation. The situation includes both kinds of facts. The claim that it contains in addition the fact that it is raining in Paris if the representation is true does not seem to have much explanatory value.

10.7   Conclusion

In this chapter, I have followed Recanati's lead in arguing for the relevance of the notion of a situated representation. Two points have been particularly stressed. First, the notion of situated representation is intimately linked with that of *ad hoc* or temporary concepts. We have the ability to silence some aspects of the inferential roles of our representations and make explicit only what is in fact needed in a particular context. We thus create *ad hoc* concepts, which we use in representation only with respect to partial situations. Second, the notion of situation can be dissociated from the conception of perspectival or non-persistent facts, which Recanati seems to follow Barwise in endorsing. On the present account, a situation comprises complex relational facts between a representation and its propositional constituents, articulated and unarticulated, but need not in general include the fact stated by the representation when it is true.

Notes

1. Versions of this chapter were presented at the Summer School of Analytic Philosophy organized by Pascal Engel in July 2002, in Oslo in November 2002, and in Granada in March 2003. I thank the audiences there, as well as Eros Corazza, Dick Carter, Steven Davis, Pascal Engel, Elisabeth Pacherie, Stefano Predelli, Joëlle Proust and François Recanati for helpful comments and discussion.
2. On the difference between unarticulated constituents at the level of language and unarticulated constituents at the level of thought, see also Corazza (2002), to which I am indebted in what follows.
3. The notion of concept used here is non-Fregean; it concerns the level of sense, not the level of reference. 'Concept' and 'mode of presentation' are used as synonyms.
4. I shall adopt the convention of using italics for descriptions of mental representations.
5. I shall pretend, for simplicity's sake, that the temporal parameter is genuinely articulated in the thought *It's raining*, but in fact it need not be. As Kaplan (1989: 504), puts it, ' "It's raining" seems to be locationally as well as temporally and modally neutral'. The same is true of the mental representation *It's raining*.
6. In Recanati's (2002a) terminology, the place is 'weakly' articulated.
7. This is related to Evans's (1982) Generality Constraint.
8. By 'absolute proposition', I mean a proposition whose truth-value is not relative to anything but a possible world.
9. Cf. Recanati (1997: 54–5) for the connection between explicit representation and the possibility of contrasting the referent with others in the relevant paradigmatic set.
10. This is a variation on Recanati's example 'Berkeley is a nice place. There are bookstores and coffee shops everywhere' (2000: 67).
11. The original inspiration is John L. Austin's essay 'Truth', reprinted in Austin (1971). See Barwise and Etchemendy (1987), and Recanati (1997, 2000).
12. $W(s)$ is the set of facts associated with s. In what follows, I ignore the relativization of the support relation to a world.

References

Austin, J.L. (1971) 'Truth'. In *Philosophical Papers*, 2nd edn. Oxford: Oxford University Press.

Barsalou, L. (1999) 'Perceptual Symbol Systems'. *Behavioral & Brain Sciences* 22: 577–660.

Barwise, J. (1989) *The Situation in Logic*. Stanford: CSLI.

Barwise, J. and Etchemendy, J. (1987) *The Liar: An Essay on Truth and Circularity*. Oxford: Oxford University Press.

Barwise, J. and Perry, J. (1983) *Situation and Attitudes*. Cambridge, MA: MIT Press.

Carston, R. (2002) *Thoughts and Utterances: The Pragmatics of Explicit Communication*. Oxford: Blackwell.

Corazza, E. (2002) 'Thinking the Unthinkable: An Excursion into Z-land'. In M. O'Rourke and C. Washington (eds), *Situating Semantics: Essays on the Philosophy of John Perry*. Cambridge, MA: MIT Press.

Crane, T. (1992) 'The Non-conceptual Content of Experience'. In T. Crane (ed.), *The Contents of Experience*. Cambridge: Cambridge University Press.

Evans, G. (1982) *The Varieties of Reference*. Oxford: Clarendon Press.

Fine, K. (1985) *Reasoning With Arbitrary Objects*. Oxford: Blackwell.

Kaplan, D. (1989) 'Demonstratives'. In J. Almog, J. Perry and H. Wettstein (eds), *Themes from Kaplan*. Oxford: Oxford University Press.

Millikan, R.G. (1993) *White Queen Psychology and Other Essays*. Cambridge, MA: MIT Press.

Perry, J. (1993) 'Thought Without Representation'. In *The Problem of the Essential Indexical and Other Essays*. Oxford: Oxford University Press.

Perry, J. (2001) *Reference and Reflexivity*. Stanford: CSLI Publications.

Prinz, J.J. (2002) *Furnishing the Mind: Concepts and their Perceptual Basis*. Cambridge, MA: MIT Press.

Prior, A.N. (1976) 'Thank Goodness That's Over'. In P.T. Geach and A. Kenny (eds), *Papers on Logic and Ethics*. London: Duckworth, pp. 78–84.

Recanati, F. (1997) 'The Dynamics of Situations'. *European Review of Philosophy* 2: 41–75.

Recanati, F. (2000) *Oratio Obliqua, Oratio Recta: An Essay on Metarepresentation*. Cambridge, MA: MIT Press.

Recanati, F. (2002a) 'Unarticulated Constituents'. *Linguistics and Philosophy* 25: 299–345.

Recanati, F. (2002b) 'Varieties of Simulation'. In Dokic and Proust (eds), *Simulation and Knowledge of Action*. Amsterdam: John Benjamins.

Sperber, D. and Wilson, D. (1998) 'The Mapping Between the Mental and the Public Lexicon'. In P. Carruthers and J. Boucher (eds), *Language and Thought*. Cambridge: Cambridge University Press.

Stanley, J. (2000) 'Context and Logical Form'. *Linguistics and Philosophy* 23: 391–434.

Stanley, J. (2002) 'Making it Articulated'. *Mind and Language*, 17(1/2): 149–68.

Strawson, P.F. (1959) *Individuals*. London: Methuen.

Recanati's Reply to Dokic

I

Do thoughts involve unarticulated constituents? Dokic attempts to weaken the case for unarticulated constituency in thought, by arguing that the proto-typical examples invoked by Perry should be reinterpreted. Those examples 'do not introduce unarticulated constituents because in each case there is a better interpretation which makes the relevant utterances and thoughts completely articulated after all, although expressive of a more primitive ontology'.

Dokic discusses three examples: simultaneity, time-zones, and Z-land. He points out an alleged difficulty for Perry's position or mine. Ordinary subjects do not have inertial frames in their ontology, five-year-olds do not have time-zones in their ontology, and Z-landers do not have places in their ontology. According to Dokic, we should straightforwardly acknowledge the fact that the subject's ontology is more primitive than ours, instead of claiming that the subject's thought involves 'unarticulated constituents' which he or she is not even able to articulate. By positing unarticulated constituents in the subject's thoughts we – the theorists – unduly force our own ontology upon them.

Let me mention a fourth example that corresponds to the sort of case Dokic has in mind. Let us assume a primitive organism that lives in the present, constantly reacting to what is currently taking place, without ever thinking about the past or the future. Let the organism think 'it's cold' at time t_1, and 'it's hot' (or 'it's not cold') at time t_2. Dokic would say, correctly I believe, that the organism's ontology contains only objects and properties, and possibly places, but not times. This is the exact temporal analogue of the Z-land case. In the light of this example, however, Dokic's argument that the subject's thought in such situations does not involve unarticulated constituents turns out to be untenable. For we must account for the organism's rationality. If we don't relativize the organism's thoughts to times, by construing them as 'concerning' particular instants, we cannot capture the fact that the organism does not contradict himself even though he thinks 'it's cold' and 'it's not cold'. He does not contradict himself because his thought that it is cold is true iff it is cold at time t_1 (when the thought is tokened), while the thought that it's not cold is true iff it's not cold at t_2.

The notion of an unarticulated constituent enables us to capture the truth-conditions of the organism's thoughts by bringing environmental facts into play, without imputing to the organism the ability to conceptualise or mentally articulate those facts. It follows that the primitiveness of one's ontology has no bearing on the issue, whether or not one's thought involves unarticulated constituents (thus understood). Of course the organism's ontology does not encompass times; but this does not show that his thoughts do not *concern* times.

II

Dokic thinks one should accept unarticulated constituents only when they make a cognitive difference to the subject. This he calls the 'Anchoring Constraint':

> *Anchoring Constraint:*
> A mental representation is not related to the situation it concerns in a purely external manner but by way of cognitive facts about the subject.[1]

In the Z-land case Dokic denies that the place is an unarticulated constituent of the thought because the subject's relation to the place of thinking is 'purely external': the place has no cognitive reality for the subject. The situation is different for us, since we have a sophisticated ontology and can think about places. Still, we often do not bother to articulate the place because the current cognitive task does not require it. In such cases – for example, when I look out the window, see that it rains, and grab my umbrella – Dokic accepts that the place is an unarticulated constituent of the thought. For the place has some cognitive reality for the subject.

At this point, however, the question arises: which cognitive reality? The fact that the subject is able to think about the place and to conceptualise it is neither necessary nor sufficient to confer the relevant cognitive reality. A conceptual ability is not sufficient because it is a mere ability, which may or may not be exercised; and it is not necessary because it is conceptual. As Dokic rightly points out, the subject typically bears a cognitive yet *nonconceptual* relation to the unarticulated place of thinking, in virtue of which he is able to monitor changes of location so as to inhibit certain inferences that require locational constancy.

It is interesting to compare Dokic's position with Perry's. In 'Relativized Propositions' (Recanati 2007) I ascribed to Perry the view that the situation a representation concerns *must* be given in a purely external manner, rather than through some cognitive discrimination on the part of the subject. Dokic holds the exact opposite of this view. As far as I am concerned, I hold an intermediate position. Against Perry, I insist that, in many cases, the situation which an utterance or thought concerns will be determined not by external facts like the location of the speaker, but by cognitive factors such as the topic of the conversation or what the thinker is mentally focussing on. In such cases, admittedly, the situation *s* which the representation R concerns will itself have to be somehow represented or articulated – it will have to be cognitively discriminated – but that would raise a problem only if that entailed that *s* is articulated *in R*. As I point out in 'Relativized Propositions', that consequence does not follow. I therefore reject the 'No Cognitive Concerning' principle which Perry seems to accept in his discussion of unarticulated constituents and the concerning relation. But I also reject Dokic's 'Anchoring Constraint', which goes too far in the other direction.

III

There are unarticulated constituents in language and there are unarticulated constituents in thought. Dokic says that all combinations are possible: a given constituent may be articulated in language but not in thought, or in thought but not language, or in both, or in neither. I agree. The only problematic case is the case in which a constituent is articulated in language but not in thought. It is problematic because it seems that one cannot linguistically articulate something without *eo ipso* thinking about it. But in 'Relativized Propositions', I argued that an important category of thoughts, namely 'context-relative thoughts', cannot be literally expressed in language. To express such a thought sometimes the best thing we can do is to use an indexical sentence, which articulates what is left unarticulated in the corresponding context-relative thought. Thus ordinary (non-emphatic) *de se* beliefs[2] are context-relative: they 'concern' the self but are not 'about' it. As Lewis (1979) puts it, the *de se* believer 'self-ascribes' a *property*: the content of his belief, therefore, is not a complete proposition with himself as a constituent. Still the proper way of expressing a *de se* belief in English is by using a first-person sentence, in which the word 'I' articulates the unarticulated subject of the self-ascription. We cannot say 'Hungry!', we have to say 'I am hungry'. In such cases it makes sense to say that the self that is articulated in language is not articulated in the expressed thought.

Dokic sees that there is an important connection between situatedness (or unarticulatedness) and *ad hoc* concepts. He says that the simple concept RAIN that one uses when one sees rain and thinks 'it's raining' (without articulating the place) is an *ad hoc* concept 'derived from the stable concept $RAIN_2$, true of times and places, by temporarily silencing our ability to distinguish one rain event from the another (at a given time)'. But I see no reason not to proceed in the other direction. Why not start from the simple concept RAIN and enrich it into the more complex concept RAIN-AT-A-PLACE?

Finally, there is the problem of nonpersistence. Nonpersistent facts (such as the fact that it's raining, or the fact that everybody's happy) are perspectival: they hold only relative to a point of view, and may no longer hold when we change the point of view. Like Perry and many others, Dokic thinks that facts, being part of objective reality, cannot be perspectival, hence that one shouldn't accept nonpersistent facts. He may be right, but I find this metaphysical issue extraordinarily complex. Reality is, indeed, objective, but it may be construed as fragmented Fine (2005: 280–4). That is, we do not have to accept the Tractarian idea that there is a world that is the totality of facts. We can take reality to consist of... situations, without reality itself being a 'maximal' situation (Barwise 1989: 261–2). If we take this line, the issue of nonpersistent facts appears in a new light. Be that as it may, the theory of situations (including the bit about nonpersistent facts) is a tool that I find useful in theorizing about language and thought. Whether or not it makes sense as a metaphysical framework is an issue I'd like to leave open for the moment.

Notes

1. See Dokic, 'Situated Mental Representations' (ms. Institut jean Nicod).
2. The contrast between ordinary and emphatic *de se* beliefs comes from Stéphane Chauvier, *Dire 'Je': Essai sur la subjectivité*. Paris: Vrin, 2001.

References

Barwise, J. (1989) *The Situation in Logic*. Stanford: CSLI.

Chauvier, S. (2001) *Dire 'Je': Essai sur la subjectivité*. Paris: Vrin.

Fine, K. (2005) *Modality and Tense*. Oxford: Clarendon Press.

Lewis, D. (1979) 'Attitudes *de dicto* and *de se*'. *The Philosophical Review* 88: 503–43.

Perry, J. (1986) 'Thought Without Representation'. In *The Problem of the Essential Indexical and Other Essays*. Oxford: Oxford University Press, 1993, pp. 205–25.

Recanati, F. (2007) 'Relativized Propositions'. In M. O'Rourke, and C. Washington, (eds), *Situating Semantics: Essays on the Philosophy of John Perry*. Cambridge, MA: MIT Press/Bradford Books.

11
Semantic Innocence and Substitutivity[1]

Paul Égré

In 'Opacity and the Attitudes' and in his book *Oratio Recta, Oratio Obliqua*, Recanati presents a semantic theory of belief reports that rests fundamentally on the principle of *semantic innocence*. The principle of semantic innocence, first stated by Davidson and promoted in particular by Barwise and Perry, states that the semantic value of a referential expression ought to remain constant inside and outside the scope of a verb of attitude like 'believe'. On the basis of this principle, Recanati is committed to a strong version of the principle of substitutivity, stated as a general principle of intensional replacement (Recanati 2000b: 41): two genuine singular terms (proper nouns, indexicals) having the same referential content, like two predicates expressing the same concept, or two sentences expressing the same proposition, can be substituted to each other *salva veritate* in any complex sentence. As Recanati admits, this principle cannot apply unrestrictedly, due to well-known failures of substitutivity in belief contexts, but for Recanati these failures of application of the principle are to be accounted for at the level of pragmatics. A rough account of this division of labour between semantics and pragmatics would be to say that contexts of attitude are 'semantically transparent' but 'pragmatically opaque'. The picture suggested by Recanati is more subtle, however, for Recanati thinks that the analysis of attitude reports is part of a program of 'truth-conditional pragmatics', where the pragmatic components affect the truth-conditions of sentences directly, and not secondarily. The object of this chapter is to evaluate the merits and limits of this account of opacity phenomena, and to determine to what form of a division between semantics and pragmatics the principle of semantic innocence commits us. This requires a precise analysis of this notion of semantic innocence. Fundamentally, semantic innocence ought to mean *semantic constancy* (in a sense to be made precise), but under a certain conception of meaning, it means *semantic constancy + direct reference*. My claim is that the second construal is sometimes interpreted too narrowly, and that only the intuition of semantic constancy ought to be preserved. In the first section of the chapter, I review some background on opacity and contrast Recanati's pragmatic account with two other major approaches of substitutivity in belief contexts, roughly the 'fine-grained meaning' approach and a Hintikka-type analysis. I argue that both of these are compatible with semantic innocence as semantic constancy, but moreover that this interpretation of the notion of semantic innocence is probably the only one we need to preserve Recanati's intuitions about substitutivity, as discussed in the second section of the chapter.

11.1   Semantic innocence and the opacity of belief contexts

Contexts of attitude are not only intensional contexts, namely contexts in which two expressions with the same extension cannot be substituted *salva veritate*, but they are also hyperintensional, to use an expression coined by Cresswell (1973): two expressions with the same intension cannot always be substituted *salva veritate* under the scope of a verb of attitude. On standard accounts, two singular terms (proper names or indexicals) have the same intension if and only if they denote the same individual in all possible circumstances; likewise, two predicates are cointensional if and only if they express the same property, that is if they denote the same set of individuals under all possible circumstances; and two sentences are cointensional if and only if they express the same proposition, i.e. if and only if they are necessarily true together or false together, namely if they are logically equivalent.

Rather than going into the formal definition of the semantic concepts involved in these definitions, let's consider examples.[2] The proper names 'Cicero' and 'Tully' both refer to the individual Cicero, and following the analysis of Kripke, it is assumed that they refer to the same individual in all the counterfactual worlds that we can think of, and even across these worlds (by the *rigidity* thesis). Likewise, the synonymous predicates 'eye-doctor' and 'ophthalmologist' should have the same extension in all the possible worlds (although not necessarily the same extension *across* the possible worlds).[3] Finally, to use an example of Muskens,[4] the two sentences 'if door A is locked, then door B is not locked', and its contrapositive 'if door B is locked, then door A is not locked', are logically equivalent: on the assumption that the conditional is a material conditional in both cases, they are necessarily true together or false together. However we can find belief contexts in which these expressions cannot be substituted to each other *salva veritate*. It seems that we can consistently say:

(1) Peter believes that Cicero was rich, but he doesn't believe that Tully was rich.

(2) Peter believes that John is an eye-doctor, but he doesn't believe that John is an ophthalmologist.

(3) Peter believes that if door A is locked, then door B is not locked, but he doesn't believe that if door B is locked, then door A is not locked.

For (1), it suffices to imagine that Peter conceives of Cicero and Tully as two distinct individuals. For (2), we may imagine a situation where Peter takes ophthalmologists to be eye-doctors with miraculous powers, but doesn't think that all eye-doctors, including John, have this extraordinary power. Sentence (3), arguably, holds in a situation in which Peter has been told and accepts the instruction that if door A is locked, door B is open, but momentarily believes that A could be locked as he tries B first and finds it locked.

Many attempts have been made to handle these failures of substitutivity within belief contexts. Here I shall restrict myself to the consideration of three main options, in order to contrast their relation to the notion of semantic innocence and to locate precisely the conception defended by Recanati. I should point out that these options are not exclusive of each other: they do correspond to different strategies at the conceptual level, but they happen to share some representatives.

Let us start with an important preliminary. The notion of intension, as defined above, has two sides. On the one hand it is tied to the notion of *referential content* of an expression: two expressions have the same intension if and only if they have the same reference in all the possible worlds.[5] On the other hand it is intended to capture the meaning, semantic value, or *truth-conditional contribution* of an expression. What the above examples suggest is that expressions with the same intension or referential content may not have the same truth-conditional contribution within belief contexts. It seems therefore that the meaning of an expression cannot be reduced to its intension, as traditionally understood.[6]

(i) One option is therefore to refine the notion of intension, to find a level of granularity of meaning that would be sufficient to give 'Tully' and 'Cicero', or likewise 'eye-doctor' and 'ophthalmologist', or 'if door A is locked, then door B is not locked' and its contrapositive, distinct semantic values, even outside of belief contexts.

(ii) A second option is to maintain the usual notion of meaning as referential content, but to suppose that the semantic value of an expression shifts under the scope of an attitude verb like 'believe'.

(iii) A third option, finally, is to hold on to the notion of meaning as referential content, but this time to contest that the semantic value of an expression is shifted under the scope of belief operators. Instead, its introduction under the scope of a belief verb triggers specific pragmatic effects.

The first option is the most radical. On this conception, it is simply misguided to assume, for instance, that the semantic contribution of two coreferential proper names, even outside of attitude contexts, is simply their referential content. The two sentences 'Cicero was rich' and 'Tully was rich' simply don't have the same meaning, and it should come as a direct prediction that they cannot be substituted to each other *salva veritate* in belief contexts. On this view, the morphology of expressions is part and parcel of their customary meaning. Disregarding details and important theoretical differences, I would include among the main representatives of this view the advocates of syntactic meaning (Quine 1960), structured meanings (Carnap 1947; Lewis 1970; Cresswell 1985), and 'hyperfine-grained' meanings (Muskens 1991; Church 1989).

The second option differs from the first mainly on the idea that in contexts free of attitude operators, the semantic value of an expression is its objective referential content. On this view, the simple sentences 'Tully was rich' and 'Cicero was rich' do have the same meaning, and the semantic contribution of the proper nouns 'Tully' and 'Cicero' is their common reference in the actual world. But belief contexts are special; in them the semantic value of 'Tully' and 'Cicero' is not necessarily their ordinary referential content. In a Hintikka-type epistemic logic, for instance, the referential content of 'Tully' and 'Cicero' is the same in the actual world and in the counterfactual worlds that are relative to the actual world, but it may vary with respect to the epistemic worlds of the agent of the ascribed belief.

On the third option, the semantic contribution of the proper nouns 'Tully' and 'Cicero' is simply their reference in the actual world, and the sentences 'Tully was rich' and 'Cicero was rich' necessarily have the same meaning. But this time, the semantic value of 'Tully' and 'Cicero' remains their ordinary reference even when the sentences are embedded under an attitude verb. What happens in cases of substitutivity failure is a pragmatic phenomenon of the nature of a conversational implicature. This corresponds to what Recanati (1993) calls the Implicature Theory of belief reports. Recanati considers himself a representative of this conception, although with some caveats.

In his writings, Recanati tends to distinguish two options instead of three. According to him, we ought to distinguish between accounts of belief sentences that rest on a principle of 'semantic deviance', and accounts that preserve semantic innocence. Option (ii) clearly exemplifies what Recanati understands by the notion of semantic deviance. Thus Recanati writes (Recanati 2000a: 395):

> According to Hintikka (1962: 138–141), failures of substitutivity in belief contexts show that two co-referential singular terms, though they pick out the same individual in the actual world, may refer to different objects in the ascribee's belief world. That option is ruled out in the present

framework; for we want the ontology to be that of the ascriber all along: we want the singular terms to refer to the same objects, whether we are talking of the actual world, or about the ascribee's belief world. That is the price to pay for semantic innocence.

The analyses of belief sentences put forward by Frege and Quine are also mentioned by Recanati as instances of semantic deviance (Recanati 2000b: chapter 2). As an extensionalist, Quine takes the semantic value of a proper name to be its reference. But for him belief contexts behave like quotation contexts: under the scope of 'believe', the embedded sentence is mentioned rather than used, and a proper name, in particular, no longer contributes its ordinary reference. Likewise, Frege holds that proper names, in belief contexts, denote their sense, and no longer their reference. To that extent, following the typology I presented, Frege is a representative of option (ii) rather than option (i). However, what are we to say of accounts of type (i) above? Should we say that they also depart from semantic innocence?

Strictly speaking, the answer to this question should be negative. If we refer to the original quotation where Davidson introduced the notion of semantic innocence, a semantic theory departs from semantic innocence, according to Davidson (1968: 830), if in this theory:

> the words 'the earth moves', uttered after the words 'Galileo said that', mean anything different, or refer to anything else, than is their wont when they come in different environments.

Consequently, a theory that would predict that the simple sentences 'Tully is bald' and 'Cicero is bald' have distinct meanings in ordinary contexts, and that the meaning of 'believe' applies straightforwardly to these, would fully deserve the label of 'semantic innocence'. Option (i), strictly speaking, *is* compatible with semantic innocence. This conclusion, I believe, may nevertheless surprise the reader, because the principle of semantic innocence tends to be identified with a version of the theory of direct reference, according to which the meaning of singular terms, even within belief contexts, is exclusively their actual reference. The above quotation from Recanati illustrates such a view.

Before going deeper into this issue, the question I would like to address in the next section is that of the plausibility of option (iii), with respect to the view of substitutivity that Recanati defends. In the third section I will examine to what extent option (ii) is necessarily incompatible with the principle of semantic innocence.

11.2 Recanati's account of substitutivity failures

11.2.1 The principles of intensional replacement

As explained in the introduction of this chapter, Recanati defends a version of the principle of substitutivity in the form of three principles of intensional replacement (Recanati 2000b: 41):

(a) A genuine singular term t (e.g. a name or an indexical) can be replaced *salva veritate* by some other term t' provided t and t' have the same extension (hence the same content).

(b) A predicative expression F can be replaced *salva veritate* by another predicative expression G if F and G express the same concept.

(c) A sentence S can be replaced *salva veritate* by a sentence S' in any complex sentence in which S occurs if S and S' express the same proposition.

What are the predictions associated with these principles? Are these principles necessarily too strong?

Strictly speaking, only principle (a) directly makes problematic predictions. Indeed, principle (a) predicts that the inference from (4) to (5) is semantically valid:

(4) Peter believes that Cicero was rich.
(5) Peter believes that Tully was rich.

In a situation where it would be appropriate to utter (1) above, this yields an outright contradiction. As for principles (b) and (c), however, Recanati does not specify the sense in which two predicates 'express the same concept', nor the sense in which two sentences 'express the same proposition'. On a fine-grained view of the nature of concepts, propositions, and of the notion of expression, as described in option (i) above, these two principles may be perfectly acceptable. By contrast, on a classical intensional conception of referential content, as in standard possible worlds semantics, principles (b) and (c) directly conflict with the consistency of (2) and (3). Elsewhere, Recanati generally adopts a Russellian conception of the nature of propositions, in the spirit of Barwise and Perry (1983). Although this corresponds to a more fine-grained conception of the notion of referential content in general, I don't think it should make different predictions with regard to (2) and (3). To illustrate principle (b), Recanati takes precisely the pair 'eye-doctor' and 'ophthalmologist'. For full sentences, the situation is more delicate. It seems doubtful, for instance, that principle (c) should validate the substitution of any pair of mathematically true (resp. false) sentences in belief contexts. Intuitively, we wouldn't want to say that 'two plus two equals four' and 'there are infinitely many primes' express the same proposition, even in the sense in which we are ready to say that 'eye-doctor' and 'ophthalmologist' express the same concept. A Russellian theory of propositions can account for the difference, but things are less clear with example (3). I think it reasonable to assume that principle (c), on Recanati's view, would licence the substitution of two logically equivalent sentences like 'if door A is locked, door B is not', and 'if door B is locked, door A is not', if only because these two sentences can be uttered to express the same thing (more plausibly, at least, than the foregoing arithmetical sentences).

Principles (a)–(c), therefore, all make predictions that conflict with the consistency of examples (1)–(3). According to Recanati, however, these cases of substitutivity failure are to be accounted for in pragmatic terms; they do not threaten the validity of principles (a)–(c) *qua* semantic principles. The proper way to understand this division of labour between semantics and pragmatics is to go deeper into Recanati's analysis of belief reports.

11.2.2 The *what* and *how* of beliefs and belief attributions

For Recanati, belief sentences are a particular instance of what he calls metarepresentational statements. Metarepresentational statements express representations about representations. For instance, if John utters (4) in a given context, John expresses a representation about a representation of Peter's. If John is sufficiently competent, whenever he uses the noun 'Cicero' in uttering the plain sentence 'Cicero was rich', it is to refer to Cicero. Semantic innocence corresponds to the idea that the word 'Cicero', whenever used by John, ought to keep the value it has in the language of John in all contexts, including metarepresentational contexts. On this conception, the principle of substitution of cointensional expressions in contexts of attitude ascriptions is a principle of transparency *relative to the ascriber*. In particular, the substitution of cointensional, yet morphologically distinct expressions under a verb of attitude need not imply a change in the mode of presentation of the content ascribed to the agent. In *Direct Reference*, using a distinction of McGinn's, Recanati motivates this idea in the following way (Recanati 1993: 333):

> There are two aspects in a belief content: 'what is represented, and how it is represented' (McGinn 1982: 214) – the truth-conditional content of the belief and its narrow content, in the terminology of chapter 4. A belief ascription is more informative if it specifies not only the former, but also the latter. (. . .). To be sure, there are contexts in which the *how* is irrelevant – contexts in which the only thing that matters is the truth-conditional content of the belief.

Importantly, Recanati distinguishes two levels here: the level of the belief proper, and the level of the sentences used to ascribe that belief. One may call the first the psychological level, and the second the linguistic level. To each level, there corresponds further two aspects, the 'what' and the 'how'. What Recanati calls the truth-conditional content, in the case of a sentence, is what I suggested to call the referential content.[7] This notion can be extended to the level of belief proper: at the psychological level, the 'what' corresponds to the referential content of the belief, namely to what makes the belief true or false, whereas the 'how' corresponds to the subjective mode of presentation of that referential content. At the linguistic level, the 'what' corresponds to the referential content of the embedded sentence used to ascribe the belief, namely to the proposition expressed by that sentence. The specification of the 'how', however, is an optional parameter which can simply be implicated, and which would be expressed by an adverbial phrase if it were to be articulated.

An example will help to clarify those distinctions. Suppose Peter watches an individual in the distance, whom John knows under two different names, say 'A' and 'B'. Peter points to A and utters to John: 'this man must be rich'. John may then report: 'Peter believes that A is rich'. Since Peter's belief is about A, the referential content of his belief includes A. The individual A is therefore part of the 'what' of Pierre's belief. The 'how', however, is the way Peter identifies A, for instance under such and such aspect, or under such and such name or description. In the context under discussion, the 'how' of Peter's belief is irrelevant, and John might as well have said for that reason: 'Peter believes that B is rich'.

What happens in attitude contexts where substitutivity fails, according to Recanati (2000a, 2000b), is precisely the opposite. Suppose I am in the situation in which it is appropriate to utter (1):

(1) Peter believes that Cicero was rich, but he doesn't believe that Tully was rich.

In this case, according to Recanati, the 'how' of the belief is implicated by the use of two distinct proper names, and the failure to substitute can be accounted for by the presence of an unarticulated constituent in the matrix verb, of the form:

(6) Peter so-believes that Cicero was rich.

where the modified verb 'so-believes' is meant to reflect the contribution of the very form of the embedded sentence, or of some salient elements of it, to the truth-conditions of the attribution. The expressions themselves then serve as an *index* of the psychological mode of presentation underlying the ascribed belief.[8] What (6) ought to mean is something like:

(7) Peter believes that Cicero was rich, under a mode of presentation $m = f$ ('Cicero was rich').

Here f is a context-dependent speaker function, taking syntactic expressions as arguments and ranging over modes of presentations. A natural constraint on f is to suppose it one-to-one, so that in a given context it relates distinct syntactic strings to distinct modes of presentation. In this case it would be wrong to substitute 'Tully' to 'Cicero', because this would yield:

(8) Peter so-believes that Tully was rich.

namely:

(9) Peter believes that Tully was rich, under a mode of presentation $m' = f$ (Tully was rich).

Because f is one-to-one, m and m' are distinct modes of presentation, and the substitution is thereby blocked. What matters for semantic innocence, however, is that the two sentences 'Cicero was rich' and 'Tully was rich' continue to express the same proposition under the prefix 'believe that', even though they serve as indices of distinct modes of representation in the context of which (1) is appropriate.

The upshot of Recanati's theory is the following: in a belief report, the expressions of the embedded sentence keep the semantic value they have in the language of the ascriber. But the ascriber can implicate the existence of certain modes of presentation by resorting to distinct expressions in his attributions. In *Direct Reference*, Recanati conceived of the 'that'-clause of a belief report as a 'dependent expression', susceptible to name distinct propositions depending on the expressions occurring in it. In *Oratio Obliqua*, by contrast, the semantic value of the embedded sentence remains constant, and it is the prefix, 'believe that', which is conceived as a 'dependent expression'. Under the former analysis, an attitude verb like 'believe' expresses a binary relation between an agent and a variable proposition. Under the latter, 'believe' expresses a relation of variable arity, depending on the context: either a binary relation between an agent and a proposition (when the 'how' is irrelevant); or a ternary relation between an agent, a proposition, and a mode of presentation (when the 'how' becomes relevant).

11.2.3 Ascriber's meaning *vs* ascribee's meaning

An argument in favour of Recanati's analysis of substitutivity is the observation that opacity phenomena may come from an ambiguity in the embedding verb, rather than from a shift of semantic value of the embedded sentence. In a situation like that of example (3), we specified the context by saying that John hears and accepts the instruction that if door A is locked, door B is not locked. There is a strong implicature, in this case, that what John *hears, accepts*, and therefore *believes*, is a particular sentence. His belief therefore has a metalinguistic component, and it is very sensible to analyze the failure of substitution as due to a special sensitivity of the verb in this context. But there are indeed many contexts where the substitution of two logically equivalent sentences under the scope of the verb 'believe' is correct, namely situations where 'believe' does not have this metalinguistic component. Suppose it is appropriate to say (to use a classic example from Bigelow):[9]

(10) Mary believes that Robin will win.

In a context where only the 'what' of the belief is relevant, it is perfectly fine to infer and to utter:

(11) Mary believes that anyone who does not compete or loses will do something that Robin won't do.

The only restrictions on substitution that may apply in this case have to do with the ascriber's mastery of logical equivalence, and with conversational maxims: uttering (11) instead of (10) is most likely a violation of Grice's maxim of *manner* ('avoid obscurity of expression', 'be brief'), but then it is clear that limitations on the range of available substitutions are entirely ascriber- and hearer-oriented, and have nothing to do with the putative mode of presentation of the ascribee's belief. This remark casts light, incidentally, on the scope of the so-called *problem of logical omniscience*: if Recanati is right, a principle of substitution of logically equivalent sentences under the scope of a belief verb need not ascribe exorbitant logical capacities to the belief subject. It is only if belief sentences are taken to encode the 'how' of beliefs systematically that it should be so.

The intuition that the ascriber's point of view prevails on the ascribee's point of view in attitude reports is an important aspect of the principle of semantic innocence, and it can be further clarified. For each of the examples (1)–(3) given above, a common inference can be made that the ascribee misidentifies the meaning of certain expressions. For instance, on reading (1):

(1) Peter believes that Cicero was rich, but he doesn't believe that Tully was rich.

we commonly infer: 'For Peter, Tully and Cicero are two distinct individuals'.[10] From example (2), we infer that: 'For Peter, being an eye-doctor is not the same thing as being an ophthalmologist'; and similarly in (3), with the conditional sentence and its contrapositive. In all these cases, two expressions that have the same meaning in the language of the ascriber are inferred to have distinct meanings for the ascribee. But we can imagine the opposite situation, where the ascribee conflates the meaning of two expressions that have distinct meanings in the language of the ascriber. Let us imagine, following an example of Burge, that (12) and (13) both hold in a certain context:

(12) Alfred believes that a fortnight is a period of ten days.
(13) Alfred believes that Bertrand will be gone precisely ten days.

Would we infer (14) in this case?

(14) Alfred believes that Bertrand will be gone precisely a fortnight.

Burge made a more precise description of the situation, in supposing that Alfred had sincerely utterred: 'Bertrand will be gone precisely a fortnight'. He then made the following observation on this puzzle (Burge 1978: 132):

> I have found nonphilosophical native speakers on both sides. But most lean negatively. An *affirmative* answer is typically based on a desire to maintain a close relation between sincere assertion and belief.

I tend to think that, if we set aside Burge's additional specification about Bertrand's assertion, the inference from (12)–(13) to (14) is clearly invalid. This suggests that the expression 'fortnight' in (14), just like the expression 'ten days' in (13), keeps its ordinary semantic value. In other words, there is no shift to the idiosyncratic language of Alfred when an ascription like this is made. The observation that most speakers 'lean negatively' even in the situation where belief tends to be assimilated with assertion, seems just to confirm the priority of this semantic intuition. If this analysis is correct, this example provides further motivation for the idea that: *whether it is explicit or inferrable from a belief ascription that an agent misidentifies the meaning of certain expressions, these expressions nevertheless keep their ordinary semantic value in such contexts.*[11] This thesis is not in opposition with the view that some of the linguistic idiosyncracies of the ascribee can be accomodated in the language of the ascriber. For instance, Recanati reports:

(15) My daughter believes that I am a *philtosopher.*

The word 'philtosopher' is just taken from childish language and integrated into the ascriber's language. What semantic innocence does rule out corresponds to a situation of *unmarked context-shifting*, where an already existing expression is given a deviant meaning. Attitude verbs *per se* are not context-shifting operators, however: we can imagine a reading of (14) where the ascriber uses 'fortnight' in the sense of 'period of ten days', but situations of this kind have to be marked by a special intonation, as happens in cases of irony, echoic uses, or pretense.[12]

11.3 Semantic innocence in a Hintikkean framework

From what we saw above, it should appear that the notion of semantic innocence, as Recanati uses it, is not of a single block. There are two main components in this notion. The first is the intuition that an expression should retain its ordinary semantic value inside and outside belief contexts: this corresponds to what I call *semantic constancy*. The second is the identification of the ordinary semantic value of an expression with its referential content, a thesis which might be more problematic. On a fine-grained view of meaning (option (i)), opacity phenomena should be taken as primitive, and transparent readings of belief sentences may be viewed as the exception. On the view of meaning as referential content defended by Recanati (option (iii)), transparency is the default rule, and departures therefrom are of a pragmatic nature. As I argued in the first section, strictly speaking the latter option is not the only one to preserve semantic innocence, since so does the first. I shall not try to adjudicate between these two options here. Instead, I would like to examine more closely the last of the three options we considered, namely option (ii), and to argue that, *pace* Recanati, it needn't conflict with his views on semantic innocence. If you remember the quote given earlier, Recanati constrasts his approach with that of Hintikka and writes (Recanati 2000a: 395):

> we want the ontology to be that of the ascriber all along: we want the singular terms to refer to the same objects, whether we are talking of the actual world, or about the ascribee's belief world. That is the price to pay for semantic innocence.

My claim is that this commitment to the sole ontology of the ascriber is exorbitant, and is not forced upon us by the attachment to the principle of semantic innocence. In other words, a more liberal ontology, in the style of Hintikka, is permitted, but even more than that, it can very well serve the variety of truth-conditional pragmatics that Recanati calls for. To show this, it is necessary to distinguish, more clearly than Recanati does, the principle of semantic innocence from certain commitments of the thesis of the direct reference of singular terms.

Let's consider an opaque belief report like (16), in which the negation takes narrow scope over the belief verb, and which corresponds to the common strengthening of (1):

(16) Peter believes that Cicero was rich, but he believes that Tully wasn't rich.

According to Recanati, when an ascription like this is made by someone who knows that the proper names 'Cicero' and 'Tully' are coreferential, the reference of these two names ought to remain the individual Cicero. This comes from the fact that, in the ascriber's language, the proper names are supposed to be directly referential. Yet, as Recanati admits, (16) is consistent precisely because in this context the names 'Cicero' and 'Tully' become the *indices* of specific modes of presentation. As we saw earlier, the way we typically interpret the consistency of (16) is by inferring:

(17) For Peter, Cicero and Tully are distinct individuals.

By this, we commonly understand:

(18) For Peter, the proper names 'Cicero' and 'Tully' refer to distinct individuals.

This suggests that the modes of presentation are the names themselves. This, however, is not quite right: Peter may be a speaker of French, who hears of 'Cicero' as 'Cicéron', and of 'Tully' as 'Marcus Tullius'. Being a metalinguistic paraphrase of (17), (18) is therefore semantically deviant. An innocent paraphrase of (16), in the framework of Recanati, is rather:

(19) Peter believes of Cicero, under a mode of presentation $m = f$ ('Cicero'), that he was rich, and he believes of Cicero, under a mode of presentation $m' = f$ ('Tully'), that he was not rich.

Two features of this analysis should be singled out. First, this paraphrase suggests that, whatever the mode of presentation involved, each of Peter's beliefs is a relational belief *about* one and the same individual, namely the actual Cicero. A central claim of Recanati (2000a: 387, italics his) is indeed that *'even on the opaque reading of a belief sentence in which a singular term occurs, reference is made to some particular individual'.*[13] On the other hand, this analysis leaves unspecified the nature of the modes of presentation. But as the inference from (16) to (17) makes clear, we (*qua* speakers of (16)) typically infer from (16) that Peter represents to himself the same individual *as two distinct individuals*. One advantage of a Hintikka-type analysis of belief sentences is precisely to account for this intuition: the modes of presentation associated to opaque singular terms are specified as distinct individuals in the belief worlds of the ascribee. The fact that a competent speaker of (16) typically infers (17) provides a good motivation, therefore, to assume that the ontology of the ascriber is large enough to accomodate that of the ascribee. I would like to show that there is not necessarily a conflict, then, between the idea that an opaque belief is a relational belief about a certain individual from the actual world, and the fact that this individual is represented as two distinct individuals in the belief worlds of the ascribee.

A standard way to analyze (16) in a Hintikkean framework of quantified modal logic is to give it the following paraphrase (where c abbreviates 'Cicero' and t abbreviates 'Tully'):

(20) $B_{Peter}Rich(c)$ & $B_{Peter}\neg Rich(t)$

Let w be the world of utterance of (16), and assume i and j are the only two doxastic alternatives of Peter's relative to w. Suppose that in both i and j, c refers to individual d_1 and t to individual d_2, distinct from d_1. For (20) to be satisfied at w, d_1 must fall within the extension of the predicate 'Rich' at both i and j, and d_2 must fall out of this extension in both i and j. In the actual world w, however, the proper names 'Cicero' and 'Tully' refer to one and the same individual, say d_0. For Recanati, such an account goes against semantic innocence because the proper names do not select one and the same individual across all the worlds of the model. The rigidity of proper names seems to be lost, but also the relational character of belief.

To my mind, neither of these conclusions is correct. What matters for semantic innocence is indeed: (a) that the proper names 'Cicero' and 'Tully', even on their opaque reading, *retain* their common reference to the actual Cicero; and (b) that each of the ascriber's opaque beliefs can still be said to be *about* this actual individual. To satisfy condition (a), it is sufficient that 'Cicero' and 'Tully' maintain their common reference in the actual world. And condition (b) can be secured by the assumption that the individuals d_1 and d_2 imagined by Peter stand in a common counterpart relation R to d_0, the actual Cicero that the speaker has in mind.[14] We may define a belief to be *about* an actual individual d if and only if the individual represented in the belief stands in this counterpart relation R to d. Peter's belief that Cicero is rich is *about* the actual Cicero in this sense, and his belief that Tully is not rich is *about* Cicero as well. Importantly, this *aboutness* relation is primarily something the ascriber has access to, not necessarily something the ascribee is aware of. This, I believe, is moreover consistent with the view that the ascriber's perspective prevails on that of the ascribee in a belief report.

In the same way, the reason why rigidity is said to be lost in this model is that all the worlds, namely the worlds of the ascriber and the epistemic worlds of the ascribee, are put on a par. However, someone like Peter can very well misperceive the coreferentiality of the proper names 'Cicero' and 'Tully', or that of their analogues in his language, and yet interpret each of these rigidly relative to his belief worlds.[15] As Maria Aloni writes (Aloni (2001: 44–5)):

> The failure of substitutivity of co-referential terms (in particular proper names) in belief contexts does not depend on the ways in which these terms actually refer to objects (so this thesis is not in opposition with Kripke (1972)'s analysis of proper names), it is simply due to the possibility that two terms that actually refer to one and the same individual are not believed by someone to do so.

I conclude that neither the thesis of *semantic innocence*, nor the *rigidity* of proper names is jeopardized in a Hintikkean semantics. However, the idea that the belief ascribed to an agent is *directly referential*, that the belief itself necessarily bears a direct connection to the individual the ascriber is referring to, is a distinct thesis that I reject. To illustrate this point, let's examine example (21), that Recanati himself (1993: 352–3) presents as particularly problematic for his understanding of semantic innocence. Consider the case of Jean-Pierre Dupuy's son who 'has hardly heard of President François

Mitterrand', but who knows a certain ass under the name 'Mitterrand'. Dupuy then declares:

(21) My son believes that Mitterrand is an ass.

Recanati notes:

> If he (Dupuy) were to to utter 'Mitterrand is an ass', his utterrance 'Mitterrand is an ass' would express a singular proposition about François Mitterrand, but if he utters [(21)] instead, the same words 'Mitterrand is an ass' will no longer express that same proposition: rather they will express the proposition that the individual called 'Mitterrand' is a certain sort of animal, or more perspicuously, that the name 'Mitterrand' refers to a sort of animal; it is that metalinguistic proposition which is the content of the belief ascribed to Dupuy's son in [(21)].

I disagree with Recanati's interpretation of this example, but on his own grounds for semantic innocence. To say that Dupuy expresses a metalinguistic proposition is to perform semantic ascent and therefore to give up semantic innocence. My view is that (21) can perfectly mean:

(22) My son believes of François Mitterrand that he is an ass.

If (21) was purely metalinguistic, this reference to François Mitterrand would be lost. On the other hand, if (21) was indeed relational but directed toward the donkey, Dupuy would mean:

(23) My son believes of the donkey Mitterrand that it is an ass.

Then Dupuy would be ascribing a correct belief to his son, but if Dupuy meant (21) to be exclusively about the *donkey* Mitterrand, he should assume his hearer to have access to this referential value of the name 'Mitterrand', and he had better say 'know' instead of 'believe' to perform his ascription (in compliance with Grice's maxim of quantity).[16] The situation is rather the following: Dupuy's son, when people actually make statements *about* François Mitterrand using the name 'Mitterrand', thinks they are talking *about* a certain donkey. His father realizes the situation. Suppose he then utters (21) to someone whom he doesn't suppose to have heard of the donkey called 'Mitterrand'. In such a situation Dupuy is clearly referring to François Mitterrand, and saying that his son takes François Mitterrand to be an animal; in this context he is clearly ascribing an incorrect belief to his son. To that extent, semantic innocence is preserved: the name 'Mitterrand', as uttered in (21), retains its normal semantic value, namely the referential value it has for the ascriber. But although the *ascription* of belief is about François Mitterrand, the *belief* of Dupuy's son itself does not relate to

François Mitterrand *directly*, rather it involves an *epistemic counterpart* of the individual commonly called 'Mitterrand' by the speaker and hearer. As a result, I think the opposite of Recanati's conclusion is called for: semantic innocence does not rule out an ontology of epistemic worlds on top of the ontology of the ascriber. Such an ontology can consistently represent the dual contribution of referential expressions in opaque belief contexts, namely their ordinary reference relative to the speaker, and their subjective content relative to the ascribee.

11.4   Conclusion

The principle of semantic innocence is ambiguous. For Recanati, as originally for Davidson, semantic innocence means preservation of the ordinary meaning of expressions in attitude contexts, and in particular, preservation of their ordinary reference. For Recanati, however, semantic innocence is tied more specifically to the theory of direct reference. In this chapter, I have attempted to separate out the two aspects, to look at semantic innocence in the first sense, as a principle of *semantic constancy*, namely as the thesis that within contexts of attitude, *the occurring expressions retain the meaning they have more generally in the language of the ascriber*. Semantic innocence rules out, in this sense, cases of what I called unmarked context-shifting. But although semantic innocence requires that referential expressions retain their meaning and reference in all environments that do not involve context-shifting, this can't exclude the fact that in opaque contexts of attitude, referential expressions contribute more than their actual reference. As Davidson granted in the same move in which he introduced the idea of 'semantic innocence', the 'role [of words] in *oratio obliqua* is in some sense special' (1968: 830). For Recanati himself, 'semantic innocence' is compatible with 'pragmatic enrichment'. In this respect, a Hintikkean semantics for belief sentences is perfectly compatible with an integrated program of 'truth-conditional pragmatics' of the sort entertained by Recanati.[17]

Notes

1. I thank F. Recanati, P. Schlenker and B. Spector for helpful comments and criticism, and María J. Frapolli for her editorial support. Thanks also to D. Bonnay, P. Ludwig, N. Villanueva, and the participants of the seminar 'Indexicalité' in Paris, and to E. Gray for corrections on the English.
2. See Gallin (1975) for a classic exposition of intensional logic.
3. I say that two expressions have the same extension *across* all the possible worlds if their common extension at one world remains unchanged at any other world. Obviously, two predicates can be coextensional at every world, without keeping this extension fixed from one world to the other.
4. Cf. Muskens (1991), who adapts it from R.C. Moore.
5. By the *referential content* of an expression, I shall systematically mean, unless otherwise specified, the *objective* content of an expression, as opposed to the

subjective reference a speaker might mistakenly associate with it. I take it that the referential content of a proper name is its denotation, that the referential content of a predicate is the concept it expresses, and the referential content of a sentence is the proposition this sentence expresses. This is in accordance with Recanati's own use of the notion of *content* (see, for instance, Recanati 2000b: 5, 41), the content of an expression being what determines its actual reference. In possible world semantics, identity of referential content thus means identity of intension rather than identity of extension (actual reference).

6. At least, as D. Lewis (1970) writes: 'intensions are part of the way to meaning', cf. Gallin (1975: 9).

7. Indeed, the notion of proposition expressed by a sentence is what gives its truth-conditions. This notion of *truth-conditional content* must not be confused with that of *truth-conditional contribution*. As we saw earlier, two sentences can have the same truth-conditions, without making the same semantic contribution to the truth or falsity of a larger sentence in which they are embedded.

8. See Recanati (2000a: 397): the notion of *index* comes from Nunberg (1993). It is needed because the psychological mode of presentation need not coincide with the embedded sentence itself, or with the relevant part thereof: this makes it possible to bypass some classic objections against quotationalism.

9. Quoted by Heim and Kratzer (1998: 310), from Cresswell (1985).

10. This is a pragmatic inference, not a logical one. Strictly speaking, from (1) we should rather infer: 'Peter is not sure that Cicero and Tully are not two distinct individuals'. Most often, however, a sentence like (1) is uttered to mean the stronger sentence: 'Peter believes Cicero was rich, but he believes Tully was *not* rich', in which the belief verb takes wide scope over negation. In any case, Peter has to entertain at least one possible state of the world where Cicero and Tully are two distinct individuals.

11. The situation may be more complex than this specific example suggests, however. The order of words seems to matter. If (13) is changed to: 'Alfred believes that Bertrand will be gone precisely a fortnight', it seems easier to infer from (12): 'Alfred believes that Bertrand will be gone precisely ten days'. This suggests that 'fortnight' can then be read *de dicto* in the sense of Alfred, contrary to the principle of semantic innocence.

12. See Recanati (2000b), IV–V, for a detailed analysis of such context-shifting phenomena.

13. See Loar (1972), to whom Recanati makes reference. Loar writes (1972: 97): 'there are independent reasons to suppose that singular terms in belief contexts may occur non-extensionally, and yet with their normal reference'.

14. See Gerbrandy (2000) on the use of counterpart relations in epistemic semantics.

15. This means that c, at a given time, picks one and the same individual across all of Peter's belief worlds, and likewise for t, even though c and t are not coreferential in Peter's worlds. Note that if Peter comes to revise his beliefs, because he realizes that Tully and Cicero are actually one and the same individual, it is the very structure of his belief worlds that changes, not the rigidity of the names that is put into question. On the other hand, if Peter is simply *not sure* whether 'Cicero' and 'Tully' denote the same individual, there will be an epistemic world where c and t corefer, and another epistemic world where they denote distinct individuals. Then rigidity is lost relative to the epistemic worlds. But again, the names 'Cicero' and 'Tully' remain rigid relative to the worlds of the competent speaker.

16. An objection that was made to me is that Dupuy might be joking, making only *side-reference* to François Mitterrand. For instance, Dupuy's statement could be an ironical utterrance of: 'My son *is right* to believe that Mitterrand is an ass!',

in a context in which it is common knowledge between Dupuy and his hearer that Dupuy's son has only heard of the donkey called 'Mitterrand'. In this context, Dupuy's statement would be equivocal: in one sense, the son is right to believe that a certain donkey is an ass; but at the ironical level, the son is right (unbeknownst to him) because Dupuy has in mind: 'Mitterrand *the president* is a *moral* ass'. I agree but I intend my analysis of (20) to account for the more basic situation where Dupuy makes a plain report about his son's mistake.

17. An explicit account of this interpretation of Recanati's program of truth-conditional pragmatics is given in chapter 1 of my dissertation (Égré 2004), using the framework of counterpart epistemic semantics developed in particular by Gerbrandy (2000) and Aloni (2001).

References

Aloni M. (2001) *Quantification under Conceptual Covers*. Amsterdam, ILLC dissertation series.
Barwise J. and K. Perry (1983) *Situations and Attitudes*. Cambridge, MA: MIT Press, repr. CSLI, 1999.
Burge T. (1978) 'Belief and Synonymy'. *The Journal of Philosophy* 75(3): 119–38.
Carnap R. (1947) *Meaning and Necessity*. Chicago: University of Chicago Press.
Church, A. (1989), 'Intensionality and the Paradox of the Name Relation'. In J. Almog, J. Perry and H. Wettstein (eds), *Themes from Kaplan*, c. 8. Oxford: Oxford University Press, pp. 151–65.
Cresswell, M. (1973) 'Hyperintensional Logic'. *Studia Logica* 34: 25–38.
Cresswell, M. (1985) *Structured Meanings*. Cambridge, MA: MIT Press.
Davidson, D. (1968) 'On Saying That'. *Synthese* 19, quoted from P. Ludlow (ed.) (1997), *Readings in the Philosophy of Language* Cambridge, MA: MIT Press, pp. 817–31.
Égré, P. (2004) *Attitudes propositionnelles et paradoxes épistémiques*. PhD. Dissertation, Université Paris 1.
Gallin, D. (1975) *Intensional and Higher-Order Modal Logic*. Amsterdan: North-Holland.
Gerbrandy, J. (2000) 'Identity in Epistemic Semantics'. In L. Cavedon, P. Blackburn, N. Braisby and A. Shimojima (eds), *Logic, Language and Computation*, vol. 3. Stanford, CA: CSLI, pp. 147–59.
Heim, I. and Kratzer, A. (1998) *Semantics in Generative Grammar*. Blackwell.
Hintikka, J. (1962) *Knowledge and Belief: An Introduction to the Logic of the Two Notions*. Cornell UP.
Kripke, S. (1972) *Naming and Necessity*. Oxford: Blackwell 1980.
Lewis, D. (1970) 'General Semantics'. Repr. in D. Lewis, *Philosophical Papers I*, c. 12. Oxford: Oxford University Press, pp. 189–229.
Loar, B. (1972) 'Reference and Propositional Attitudes'. *Philosophical Review* 81: 43–62.
McGinn, C. (1982), 'The Structure of Content'. In A. Woodfield (ed.), *Thought and Object*. Oxford: Clarendon Press, pp. 207–58.
Muskens, R. (1991) 'Hyperfine-Grained Meanings in Classical Logic'. *Logique & Analyse* 133–4, 159–76.
Nunberg, G. (1993) 'Indexicality and Deixis'. *Linguistics & Philosophy* 16: 1–43.
Quine, W.V.O. (1960) *Word and Object*. Cambridge, MA: MIT Press.
Recanati, F. (1993) *Direct Reference: From Language to Thought*. Oxford, Blackwell.
Recanati, F. (2000a) 'Opacity and the Attitudes'. In A. Orenstein and P. Kotatko (ed.), *Knowledge, Language and Logic*. Dordrecht: Kluwer Academic Publishers, pp. 367–406.
Recanati, F. (2000b) *Oratio Obliqua, Oratio Recta: An Essay on Metarepresentations*. Cambridge, MA: The MIT Press.

Recanati's Reply to Égré

Paul Égré mentions three main strategies for dealing with substitutivity problems in epistemic contexts:

1. The *fine-grained strategy* makes the semantic values of linguistic expressions so fine-grained that the (apparent) failures of substitutivity are thereby explained. According to the fine-grained strategy, the names 'Cicero' and 'Tully' refer to the same person, but they do not have the same (fine-grained) semantic value; that is why one cannot substitute 'Cicero' for 'Tully' in belief sentences. Similarly, 'eye-doctor' and 'opthalmologist' have different (fine-grained) semantic values, even though they correspond to the same function from situations to sets of individuals. This view stands in sharp contrast to the *theory of direct reference*, according to which the semantic value of a name is its reference, and the semantic value of a general term like 'ophthalmologist' is a property coarse-grainedly construed as a function from situations to sets of objects.
2. The *deviant strategy* accounts for failures of substitutivity in epistemic contexts by treating such contexts as semantically special. In epistemic contexts (e.g. belief sentences) the semantic value of an expression is not its ordinary semantic value, but a deviant semantic value. This explains why one expression cannot substitute for another one in belief sentences even if they have the same semantic value (e.g. the same reference) in normal contexts. Within this framework, one can stick to the theory of direct reference for normal contexts, and hold that the semantic value of an expression shifts from coarse-grained to fine-grained in belief sentences.
3. The *pragmatic strategy* is like the fine-grained strategy in that it takes the semantic value of an expression to be the same in epistemic contexts and elsewhere. But the truth-conditions of utterances are said to be sensitive to pragmatic factors which, in epistemic contexts, induce failures of substitutivity. The choice of a particular name ('Cicero' or 'Tully') is such a pragmatic factor which may affect truth-conditions, in epistemic

contexts. That is so even though the two names have the same semantic value and retain that semantic value in belief sentences.

Paul Égré notes that the fine-grained strategy, no less than the pragmatic strategy, enables one to maintain 'semantic innocence', i.e. the view that the semantic value of an expression does not shift under embedding. I agree. Only the deviant strategy rejects semantic innocence. But the fine-grained strategy rejects the theory of direct reference, which can be maintained (even for epistemic contexts) if one opts for the pragmatic strategy.

Which reason do we have for accepting direct reference? I think we have strong intuitions in support of that theory. A simple utterance like 'Cicero is bald' has the property of *truth-conditional singularity*: there is an object x (namely Cicero) such that the utterance is true if and only if x is bald. In general, no one can understand a sentence of the form 'NN is F' (where 'NN' is a proper name or a referential expression) without knowing that, for any utterance of that sentence, there is (or has to be) an x such that the utterance is true iff x is F. This is accounted for by saying that names are directly referential, and that their semantic value is their bearer. From that thesis, the facts of rigidity follow.

We can weaken the fine-grained view and render it consistent with direct reference by claiming

(i) that the semantic value of a name, though more fine-grained than the reference, nevertheless involves the reference, *plus something else* (a mode of presentation);

(ii) that the modes of presentation which are an aspect of the expression's semantic value are truth-conditionally irrelevant.

This is the neo-Fregean position that I described (and endorsed) in *Direct Reference*. But this view, by itself, does not account for failures of substitution. To account for substitution failures we must either give up direct reference and stick to the (unweakened) fine-grained strategy which make modes of presentation truth-conditionally *relevant*; or, if we do not want to pay that price, we must shift to either the deviant strategy or the pragmatic strategy in order to account for substitution failures. That is, we must admit that modes of presentation *become* truth-conditionally relevant, for semantic or pragmatic reasons, when referential expressions occur within the embedded portion of a belief sentence. The advantage of the pragmatic strategy over the deviant strategy is that it enables us to save semantic innocence as well as direct reference.

II

In *Oratio Obliqua, Oratio Recta*, I categorized Hintikka's position as an instance of the deviant strategy. Hintikka equates opacity to multiple referentiality. 'Cicero' and 'Tully' refer to a certain individual in the actual world, but in Peter's belief worlds they possibly refer to distinct individuals. According to Hintikka, when the sentence 'Cicero is bald' is embedded under 'Peter believes that', the reference of the name shifts because the operator 'Peter believes that' shifts the circumstance of evaluation for the embedded sentence (much as a temporal operator does). Hintikka's view, therefore, is an instance of the deviant strategy. It violates semantic innocence since the semantic value of a name is said to shift when it occurs in the scope of an epistemic operator.

But Égré provides a novel interpretation of Hintikka's view. On that interpretation a name refers to its actual reference in *all* contexts, including epistemic contexts; but in epistemic contexts the name *also* refers to the alternative referents it has in the ascribee's belief worlds. In effect, Égré makes the semantic value of referential expressions in epistemic contexts fine-grained by enriching the ordinary reference of the term with a mode of presentation, which mode of presentation he cashes out model-theoretically in terms of the referents the name has in the believer's epistemic alternatives to the actual world. If the subject takes 'Cicero' and 'Tully' to refer to two different individuals, then, when we report his belief by saying that, according to Peter, Cicero is rich but Tully isn't, we refer to Cicero twice over – once by means of the name 'Cicero', and another time by means of the name 'Tully' – but in the same breath we refer, or pretend to refer, to two distinct epistemic counterparts of Cicero, namely the two distinct individuals a and b which, in Peter's belief worlds, are the referents of the names 'Cicero' and 'Tully'. The semantic value of a name such as 'Cicero' or 'Tully' in the embedded portion of a belief sentence can therefore be represented as an ordered pair consisting of the actual referent, Cicero, and the epistemic counterpart of that referent in the belief worlds of the ascribee. (Since proper names are modally rigid, this is the same object in all of the worlds in question.)

Égré thinks his interpretation of Hintikka's view makes it consistent with semantic innocence. But does it? The fact that the name 'Cicero' refers to (the actual) Cicero in all contexts, including epistemic contexts, is not sufficient to protect semantic innocence. For, in epistemic contexts, the actual reference of the name is only an aspect or a part of the name's semantic value. Another aspect is the mode of presentation that Egré cashes out in terms of the epistemic counterparts of the reference. The mode of presentation becomes part of the semantic value of the name in epistemic contexts; and this implies that the semantic value of the name is affected, in epistemic contexts.

There is a way to save semantic innocence consistently with the position Egré sketches, however. We may argue as follows. A name's semantic value is its actual reference and nothing more, so that 'Cicero' and 'Tully' have the same semantic value. The reason why 'Peter believes that Cicero is rich, but he does not believe that Tully is rich' is not contradictory is the fact that, by using two distinct names, the ascriber pragmatically implies that Peter mentally refers to what he takes to be two distinct individuals. Peter thinks that one of them is rich but he does not think that the other is. This means that he believes of Cicero both that he is and that he isn't rich, but holds these beliefs under different modes of presentation, i.e. by subjectively referring to (what he takes to be) distinct individuals. Thus interpreted the Hintikka–Égré view is no longer an instance of the deviant strategy. It is an instance of the pragmatic strategy – the strategy I recommend.

On the pragmatic strategy the mode of presentation (i.e., the epistemic counterpart of the reference) is introduced into the truth-conditions through pragmatic enrichment. But a different option may be available to make the Hintikka–Égré position consistent with semantic innocence. The introduction of modes of presentation can be blamed on the semantics of the epistemic verb. On this view, to say that Peter believes that Cicero is rich is to say that Peter and Cicero stand in the relation $\lambda x\ \lambda y$ *(in x's belief worlds there is a counterpart z of y, and z is rich)*. The semantic value of the name 'Cicero' (or 'Tully') is its actual reference, but the belief-relation is analysed in such a way that in order to believe something about someone there has to be a counterpart of that person in all of one's belief worlds. Of course, nothing prevents a given individual, say Cicero, from having several counterparts in the ascribee's belief worlds. In the Cicero–Tully example, there are two counterparts. Peter and Cicero stand in the relation $\lambda x\ \lambda y$ *(in x's belief worlds there is a counterpart z of y, and z is rich)*, but they also stand in the relation $\lambda x\ \lambda y$ *(in x's belief worlds there is a counterpart z of y, and z is not rich)*.

On this view the existence of a counterpart of the name's referent in the ascribee's belief worlds is entailed in virtue of the semantics of the epistemic verb. Does this mean that there cannot be transparent readings of belief ascriptions – that is, attributions where modes of presentation play no role? No – this conclusion does not follow. Transparent readings will be treated as cases in which nothing is suggested regarding the relevant epistemic counterpart, save for the fact that it exists. All other cases will be treated as cases in which more information is provided regarding the epistemic counterpart of the reference. That extra information will come from the context, not from the semantics. For example, the use of two distinct names in 'Peter believes that Cicero is rich but he believes that Tully is not rich' suggests that the relevant counterparts – the (possibly identical) counterparts whose existence is entailed in virtue of the semantics of 'believe' – are named 'Cicero' and 'Tully' respectively (hence are two distinct individuals) in Peter's belief worlds. So, even if we favour the more 'semantic' approach, we end up with something that is very close to the pragmatic strategy.

Name Index

Subject Index